STAKE OUT

Valma Muir

This book is dedicated to all those in law enforcement who choose to stand up to the corrupt and powerful.

Their bravery will be eternal.

CHAPTER ONE

They had been sitting there for hours…waiting for the scumbag, low-life perp to show.

Georgina had given up trying to shift positions to relieve the ache in her back, bemoaning the fact that unmarked police vehicles seemed to be even more uncomfortable than the standard cruisers used by uniformed officers. She glanced over at her partner Paul, a smile tugging at the corner of her mouth as she recalled his reaction when he had been informed that his new partner was Georgie Harris, only to find out that *he* was a *she*. She had been standing directly behind him as he had fired off a barrage of expletives at the hapless messenger. The resulting embarrassment when she politely tapped him on his shoulder was something she used against him whenever it suited her. Always humorously though.

Everyone called her Georgie despite her repeated requests that her full name be used. Predictably, as a team they were referred to as *Georgie Porgie* since Paul had gained a pound or two…or twenty. Too many on duty donuts and too many off duty six packs.

"What…?" he said, aware that she was watching him as he peered through his long lens camera.

"I was just wondering what dastardly thing I did in my previous life to end up now spending most of this one with you," she replied, her flecked green eyes wide in mock innocence.

He lowered the camera, turned his head slowly and gave her his best death stare.

"Make yourself useful and get us some coffee. And donuts," he said.

"Nope. Your turn." She glanced back at the apartment entrance just in time to see their perp emerge.

"There he is!" Paul's camera swung up and the shutter fired off a few shots.

"He's heading for his car," said Georgina as she reached for the ignition. However, he walked right past his battered Ford and looking left and right, swiftly crossed the road and entered the Starbucks.

They had been tagging Johnny Salome for weeks now hoping to be able to gain evidence to tie him to a series of sexual assaults on young teenage girls. He hadn't even bothered to be careful leaving enough seminal fluid for a slam dunk conviction. However, since he was not on the offender's data base, they needed something definitive by which to nail him. The judge they had approached had refused to issue a warrant for Salome's arrest to procure a DNA sample. He deemed the existing evidence as circumstantial. Georgina was furious and wondered if he would be so blasé if his own daughter had been one of his victims. They both watched the Starbucks intently.

"I think I'll go in," Georgina said.

Paul nodded and kept his camera trained on the coffee shop. She dodged through the traffic and came into view through his lens as she entered the shop. Through the reflections on the windows, he could see Salome slide onto a window stool, sipping his coffee as he watched people walking by. From inside, Georgina went through the motions of waiting in line to order whilst carefully watching Salome in case he made any move to exit the shop. Something, or more accurately someone, had caught his attention and she followed his gaze. He was watching a young teenage girl with long wavy blonde hair leaning against a bus stop sign on the opposite side of the road, fully absorbed with her mobile, oblivious to the fact that she was being watched. Her skintight hipster leggings and high-cut midriff T-shirt, displaying her smooth youthful contours with a diamanté stud in her navel did nothing to protect her from predatory male eyes.

Salome stood up, looked around and made for the door. As he stepped onto the sidewalk, a bus drew up obscuring his view of the girl. When it pulled away, she was gone and Georgina spotted her swaying down the aisle of the bus, the bra-less curve of one of her youthful breasts momentarily visible as she hastily reached up for the grab rail to steady herself as the bus lurched into the traffic. Salome saw it too and stood transfixed on the sidewalk. Georgina felt a spike of anger rise in her. How could parents allow their daughters to dress like that. He took a long slow drink of his coffee, wiped the foam from his mouth with the back of his hand and slowly sauntered down the sidewalk. Georgina followed cautiously. About three blocks down he tossed the cup into a trash bin, and slowly disappeared as he blended in the milieu of the crowds.

"Good girl," Paul murmured as he watched Georgina through his binoculars swiftly make straight for the trash bin, her hand pulling out a latex glove from her pocket as she approached the receptacle. It was an awkward stretch through the aperture of the bin to reach the cup. She rooted around carefully until she could feel it and extracted it slowly, so as not to disturb any possible DNA evidence. She carefully slipped it into the evidence bag she had pulled from her other pocket, sealing it as she turned in the direction of Paul. It was a long shot. Paper cups were not nearly as rewarding as cans or plastic cups.

Beggars can't be choosers.

CHAPTER TWO

The double doors swung open automatically as they entered the NYPD Forensic Laboratory in Queens. They both presented their badges and access clearance to the security personnel and after signing in, made their way to Room 204.

Dr. Simon Chevalier, one of the senior forensic scientists was sitting at his desk typing a case analysis report when his laboratory door opened. He looked up and immediately sighed. Georgina was not best known for her patience and was well known for getting her way. He raised his hands. "Busy, busy. No favours. Stand in line …which just happens to be three weeks long."

"I've brought goodies…" Georgina declared as she revealed from behind the evidence bag his favourite honey and caramel chocolate balls. As he reached for them, she snatched them away and swiftly placed the evidence bag in his outstretched hand.

"Not so fast sunshine!" she laughed.

"Do you want your evidence processed or not?"

Without missing a beat, he snatched the chocolates, ripped the bag open and popped four balls into his mouth. Paul sighed and rolling his eyes, leant against the wall to wait out the inevitable dance of negotiation. But he kept his counsel as he knew about the on and off love affair that had existed for years between these two totally OCD characters.

"It's CDO…" Georgina corrected him sternly when he voiced his observation once. "The letters have to be in order."

His cheeks bulging, Simon peered into the evidence bag and then sat back abruptly.

"Seriously?!!" … he said, his speech impaired. "Is this the best you can do? Do you have any idea how difficult it is to lift anything from a corrugated paper cup?"

He glared at Georgina. He looked so ridiculous trying to look fierce whilst looking like a hamster.

"I will duly speak to Starbucks and ask them to change to perfectly smooth plastic cups suitable for forensic purposes but in the interim, I need something…and fast. We must stop this guy hurting girls."

That clinched it and she knew it. Simon would fast track it for her.

"Get outta here!" Simon said. "I'll call you. And yes, it will be soon."

Georgina pirouetted like a little girl, kissing Simon squarely on his chocolate covered mouth. It always amazed Paul that she could be the toughest woman he had ever met and yet she could suddenly be so delightfully girlish. He gave Simon one of those male-to-male sympathy solidarity looks that was not missed by Georgina as she yanked him by the arm and headed for the door. She was elated. This may be the break they were looking for.

"Wanna grab a beer when we knock off?" Paul asked her as they pulled out of the laboratory parking area.
"Can't. I have a scintillating dinner date with my father and Mrs. Vacuous."
Paul laughed. "All the more reason you need a beer."
"A beer with you would only be marginally more bearable," Georgina retorted. He mock punched her on the arm.
"Thank God I have my wife to stroke my ego. You, dear partner, are painfully candid and cruel towards us poor sensitive males."
Georgina flashed him one of her gorgeous devilish smiles and said "Someone must keep you in line. You have been painfully conceited ever since you were awarded that shiny medal for bravery."
She instantly regretted her comment as she saw a shadow cross his face. The award would forever remind him of the bloodied mess of his previous partner's face, blown away as they battled to protect a group of inner-city school children who were on an outing when a gangland street shoot-out erupted. They had literally been in the right

place at the wrong time. The body count may well have been a lot higher if Paul and his partner Dave hadn't been following up on a lead in that exact street. He himself had taken three bullets, two of them entering his lower abdomen whilst the third shattered his elbow. He had been put on indefinite leave whilst he made a slow and painful recovery.

"I'm sorry," she said.

"For what? For denting my ego or that I didn't succumb to my injuries and thus preclude you the trouble of having me as your partner?"

She swallowed hard, feeling totally mortified. He burst out laughing.

"Gotcha!"

A few hours later she was pushing a salad around her plate as she listened to the usual endless inane chatter of her father's way too young new wife who was desperately trying to engage Georgina on the ins and outs of the latest Netflix soapy about some ditsy girl in Paris. Georgina mumbled something about CSI being slightly more her style as she glanced around the ostentatious gold dining room that looked like it was straight out of a Beverly Hills celebrity mansion, not a Central Park South apartment in New York. Not that the apartment wasn't exclusive as the address indicated but it was massive, way too big for two people and was a reasonably new acquisition as demanded by this high maintenance arm-candy wife. Georgina knew that her father would have preferred something more conservative and subtly stylish. But Lola gets what Lola wants. Who names their child Lola for goodness' sake! *Lola Loves Lolly*, Georgina thought. She knew that her thoughts were uncharitable since Lola did make an effort with her, so she should at least do the same.

"Can't you at least try and get on with her?" her father admonished her later as they sipped their habitual late-night scotch in his wood paneled study.

Georgina sighed and said, "Could you not at least have married someone with more than one brain cell?"

She immediately regretted her words. This was the second time today that she had spoken without thinking. He had been so lonely after her mother had died in a car wreck two years before. He had been vulnerable, and Miss Opportunity had wasted no time in filling his lonely nights. It always amazed Georgina how a highly intelligent sitting judge could have such poor judgement when it came to the affairs of the heart.

"I'm sorry Dad. That was mean and unnecessary. I apologize. I will try harder."

She drained the last few drops of her scotch, leant across the desk, and kissed her father on the cheek.

"It's okay sweetie" he said tenderly. "Your mother would have been a hard act for anyone to follow."

True. Her mother had been bright, beautiful and a force to be reckoned with and had risen through the ranks of a top property law firm to make partner. She had hoped Georgina would study law and follow in her footsteps and was clearly disappointed when she had enrolled herself in the police academy. However, Georgina had also risen through the ranks quite rapidly to make detective, an achievement that her mother truly admired. She had been secretly relieved as a uniformed officer wasn't quite prestigious enough in her eyes, snob that she was. But more than being a highly successful woman, she had been a wonderful mother and an incredible wife to Georgina's father. She simply understood him, and she had celebrated and supported his rise to become a highly respected supreme court judge. He attributed his success to her. He used to say to Georgina or anyone else who would listen…*Behind every great man...* but before he could finish the sentence, Georgina's mother would butt in and say…*is a woman rolling her eyes!* They would always laugh at this verbal duet, never tiring of repeating it.

Georgina's father watched his daughter as she gathered up her bag and coat to leave. The resemblance to her mother caused a deep pain to well up in his chest and he realized that he was still mourning the loss of the woman he had loved and adored for thirty-five years. Georgina was beautiful like her mother had been, the difference being that she wasn't aware of it whilst her mother had been patently aware of her looks and had used them to her advantage. Georgina had her mother's raven black hair, pale skin and striking green eyes. She was just simply stunning, but it was her cerebral nature that her father enjoyed most about her. Her curiosity about everything was captivating. From a young age her quick mind was one that he could engage with. Furthermore, she was a natural leader, and he had no doubt that she would attain high office in time to come.

"Night Dad. Thank you for the lovely evening," Georgina said as she kissed him on the cheek and then turned towards the elevator.

"Thanks for coming sweetie. Love you kiddo."

He stood there watching her, hands in his pockets, a mannerism so familiar to her. She turned as the elevator doors opened. He smiled at her and then lifting one hand, blew her a kiss at the same time that she blew him one. Both caught the invisible kisses mid-air and touched their fists to their hearts. It was a gesture that had endured for years; a little ritual that spoke of the unconditional love between father and daughter. As she disappeared into the elevator, he closed the apartment door, sighing deeply. He feared for his daughter. She was extraordinarily strong willed and fearless, and her job put her in harm's way. He stood quietly for a while listening to the distant hum of traffic some twenty floors down. Yep, he thought, New York; the city that never sleeps. However, Lola was long asleep, and heading back to his study, he poured himself another drink, sat down and opened the bottom draw of his mahogany desk. He drew out the silver framed photo of Georgina's mother, placed it on his desk and pretended for a while that she was there, remembering her beautiful smile as he sipped the comforting liquid.

CHAPTER THREE

It was Monday morning, and the Georgina and Paul were at their desks catching up on paperwork. She was fully absorbed with the evidence document of a drug related case when she heard her mobile ping. She glanced down and saw that there was a text message from Simon. Great she thought! He must have processed the evidence. She clicked on the message but frowned as she read his text.

Get here now. Say nothing to anyone. Come alone.

How odd she thought. So unlike Simon who never missed an opportunity to make some quip. She looked up across her desk at Paul who was absorbed with something on his computer screen, the image reflected in his pale blue eyes. She looked down and texted back.

See you in twenty. With Paul…we are partners.

"Paul…" she said.

"Yep?" he replied not looking away from his screen.

"Something odd is up with Simon. We need to go there now."

"Like right away? That kinda now?"

"Yep. That kinda now." Georgina said already getting up from her desk.

She leant down, logged off, grabbed her badge, weapon, and jacket, and swiftly headed towards the elevators. Paul caught up with her, still putting on his holster and jacket as he walked briskly.

"What's this all about Georgie?" he asked quizzically.

"I don't know," she said showing him the text message.

"What an odd message," said Paul frowning.

"Just what I thought," Georgina replied.

Within minutes they were heading to Simon's laboratory.

No smiles today from Simon as they entered his lab.

"What the hell have you done Georgina!" he exclaimed.

"What?" Georgina asked perplexed, eyes wide. "I don't understand…" She glanced at Paul who looked equally puzzled, shrugging his shoulders.

"I managed to lift the DNA from the paper cup, entered into the system and every godamned law enforcement department lit up like a Christmas tree!"

"What *are* you talking about?" Georgina exclaimed. "Our perp is hardly a risk to national security!"

"Well, I know nothing about your perp, but I do know that this is explosive. You don't seem to understand how serious this is," exclaimed Simon.

"No, I don't Simon!" Georgina replied hotly, her hands on her hips. "Perhaps you would care to explain," she added, now annoyed.

Paul had said nothing up until this point, but he looked at Simon and said quietly.

"We need to know what's going on buddy."

Simon swiftly moved around to his desk and snatched up a printout from the central data system.

"I'll tell you what this is all about!" he said brandishing the paper in their faces. "Your paper cup DNA came back as a *perfect* match to the most notorious but deceased pedophile in the country! This is insane! The guy *offed* himself in custody over four years ago! How in hell's name did you get his DNA on that cup?"

Both Georgina and Paul stared open-mouthed at him. They were battling to process what Simon had just said.

"Do you two understand what this means?" Simon yelled. "Chad Levenstein is still alive! Alive and well, swanning around Starbucks joints, undetected, right under our noses here in New York!"

Silence descended upon the room. He was right. The implications were absolutely explosive. Simon continued. "I have run the DNA test three times. It's him."

Georgina and Paul were speechless.

They all jumped when Simon's extension phone rang. He snatched up the receiver and visibly paled as he listened to the caller. He replaced it slowly, his mind racing.

"The FBI are here…with a SWAT team for God's sake!" Georgina and Paul exchanged bewildered looks, completely thrown by this turn of events. Simon suddenly became eerily calm.

"You gotta get out of here. Now. Turn right down the corridor and take the fire escape."

He marched to the door, opened it, and carefully looked up and down the corridor.

"It's clear. Go now."

Georgina and Paul were galvanized into action and as they made for the door, Georgina whirled around and snatched up the printout and stuffed it into her jacket pocket.

"Don't call me," Simon ordered as they pushed past him into the corridor. "I'll make contact with you."

"I don't understand why we have to run?" Georgina asked breathlessly turning back to him.

"No time to explain Gigi," said Simon. He was calling her by the name he had always used as an endearment when they had lived together. "I promise to explain when I can. Now go!"

Georgina and Simon's eyes locked momentarily. He gave her an imperceptible nod, a subtle communication of reassurance. He loved her. He always had and now he had a sickening feeling in his gut that this was not going to auger well for Georgina. But he would do whatever it took to protect her. Paul grabbed Georgina's arm and they headed down the corridor. Simon quickly ducked back into his laboratory, his mind racing.

As the door of the fire escape closed and Georgina and

Paul disappeared down the stairs from view, five FBI agents rounded the corner from the other end of the corridor followed by four SWAT officers. Simon had estimated that he had twenty seconds tops to prepare himself. He knew instinctively that this was going to be one big shit show. It always was with the FBI.

He swung around, feigning surprise as the door burst open. "What's going on?" he exclaimed. "Who are you?"
A very short, mean looking man with a puffy face and piggy eyes in an oversized FBI jacket moved towards Simon.
"We are shutting down your lab. Move away from your desk. Do not touch anything. Do not speak to anyone unless spoken to."
Simon opened his mouth to protest but then shut it again. He knew how these guys worked, how they abused their positions of power.

Two SWAT officers had moved out into the corridor and were flanking the door. The other two did the same but on the inside of the lab. Suddenly Simon's fear turned to white hot anger.
"Actually, I have a right to know who you are! What is your name? Why are you here?" Simon demanded. "This is a secure facility with very strict access protocols! And

where is your warrant?"

Piggy Eyes turned to look at Simon.

"I don't have to answer any of your questions, and I don't need a warrant. If you don't shut up, I will have you arrested for obstructing FBI business and you can rot in jail for two years."

He turned away and barked instructions to his minions. They started unplugging computers and searching Simon's desk. He rounded again on Simon.

"I want the key code for the sterile lab and evidence lockers. Now."

"No can do," replied Simon his temper rising. "There are multiple pending cases dependent on the evidence in those secure lockers and if you tamper with any of those, the relevant cases will be thrown out of court and high-profile criminals will not be prosecuted. You will be breaking the law if you even as much as touch one shred of evidence!"

Everyone in the room stopped what they were doing, exchanging looks between them. Piggy Eyes slowly walked back to Simon, his voice low and threatening.

"I don't care what evidence is compromised. I don't care if it means that serial killers, money launderers or drug lords are given a free get out of jail card. We are here to take everything, and I mean *everything*. And I strongly suggest you cooperate…that is if you value your career and don't want to be ordering family sized Vaseline jars from Amazon for a lengthy stay in Rikers. I want every shred of evidence linked to the DNA hit you had today. And we will be removing everything else from this lab to make sure you haven't secreted away any little mementos for your memoirs."

Simon took a step back, stunned. Slowly he turned towards the sterile lab and punched in the code. He stood there helpless as he watched every evidence locker opened, every document, every evidence bag, every piece of equipment, being packed into boxes which were then sealed. Months and months of painstaking work evaporated before his eyes. Even the underside of his desk, his chair and his personal briefcase were scrutinized. But they were not done yet. A burly agent approached him and told him to spread his arms and legs. He then proceeded to search Simon's entire person, emptying every pocket, taking his personal effects including his mobile, a small notebook and his access card with his security clearance. As they were about to take their leave Piggy Eyes walked over again to Simon and said.

"Who else knows about this? Tell me who gave the evidence to you?"

"Nobody knows except me," Simon lied. He continued. "But hey, you are the FBI remember. You tell me. Aren't you supposed to be able to work these things out all by yourselves?"

Piggy Eyes flushed and Simon savoured the fact that he towered over this little bully. They stared at each other; the room silent.

Finally, Simon said, "Now get out of my laboratory!"

Piggy Eyes held out his hand and one of his team walked over, handing him a document. He glanced at it for a moment, then looking up at Simon, smiled and slapped the document against Simon's chest.

"As of now you are on indefinite leave. You may not return to this laboratory for any reason whatsoever. You may also not leave New York City and if you violate any of the conditions listed in this directive," and he poked Simon in the chest for effect, "you will be arrested and charged accordingly."

He turned to one of his team and said.

"Instruct the boys to come up now and remove the boxes. I want a detailed inventory on my desk by the end of today."

As they all filed out of the laboratory, Simon shouted after them, "And you goons wonder why nobody trusts the FBI! You're just a bunch of schoolboy bullies!"

Piggy Eyes waved a dismissive hand.

"Like we care!" he said over his shoulder and Simon heard them laughing as they made their way down the corridor.

He was shaking with rage at the sheer audacity of what had just transpired. Within minutes uniformed police officers entered the room and started removing all the boxes. They barely acknowledged his presence. Finally, all that remained was his bare desk and worktops, his chair, a lamp, his car keys and his empty coffee cup. He slumped down onto his chair and held his head in his hands. The sheer enormity of what had just happened flooded his mind and he couldn't recall ever feeling this violated.

Georgina and Paul were back at their desks, stunned and speechless. They noticed the curious stares of their colleagues who could sense that something was up.

"Stuff this! Let's go for a coffee," Paul said.

"Good idea," Georgina agreed. They both rose and headed for the lift.

When they had placed their orders at their local coffee shop, Georgina looked at Paul with a somewhat bewildered expression and asked.

"What just happened there Paul?"

He shrugged and was silent for a while.

"I guess we have unwittingly kicked over a hornet's nest."

"What do you suggest we do?" she asked him.

"I really don't know Georgie. All kinds of shit are going to come down on us now. We must be prepared for it. And most importantly we must close ranks. Not a single chink in the armor."

"Do you think it's going to get that bad?" she asked. He stared at her for a few seconds.

"Yes, I do." His expression was both serious and pensive. "There is something else at play here Georgie otherwise Simon wouldn't have reacted the way he did. He is not the kind of character to be easily rattled. But he was clearly thrown off kilter. He knows something we don't know. Plus, there's the fact that the FBI showed up so quickly. Way too quickly."

Georgina looked through the window off into the distance but was oblivious to the long lanes of traffic, honking horns and crowds of people jostling on the New York sidewalks. She looked back a Paul.

"It just gets worse. Now we don't have the evidence we thought we had to nail our perp. He's still out there, still a threat to innocent girls. It is only a matter of time before he assaults someone again."

"I know," Paul said looking dejected. "We had better get back to the precinct. It's only a matter of time before *they* come knocking at our door."

The invisible *they*. Those with unchecked power and a penchant to use it. Long gone were the glory days when just the word FBI solicited awe and respect. Now many viewed them as a mafia with the law on their side, to be given wide berth and certainly not to be trusted.

"Well hopefully Simon will make contact sooner rather than later. I do hope the inevitable fall out doesn't extend to him too," said Georgina.

Six miles away as the crow flies, Simon was letting himself into his apartment. He headed straight to his walk-in wardrobe and pulled out his back up mobile and fired it up only to discover that his number had already been disabled. He sighed. No surprise there. Within a matter of hours his entire life had been turned upside down. He threw the phone onto the bed, kicked off his shoes and headed to the living room to pour himself a drink. He walked out onto the patio and gazed down at the sprawling city below him. It was clear to him that the reaction of the FBI and the powers behind them spoke of a very real desire to suppress this shocking situation. Not only suppress it but bury it completely.

The moment all the alarm bells started ringing when the DNA match was confirmed, that should have seen law enforcement turning over every stone to capture one of the most prolific sex offenders ever. Clearly, he had feigned his suicide (God knows how he did it!) but every effort was being made to keep regular law enforcement, the press and the public ignorant of what had just transpired. This guy must be very important to a lot of high-powered people. Certainly, there had been enough of them who had fraternized with him openly but no amount of testimony from the victims had resulted in anyone being arrested or prosecuted, except for the girlfriend of the perpetrator who took the fall for everyone. No surprise there. Powerful men seldom go to prison or face the consequences of their actions.

Suddenly Simon checked himself, realizing that his mind was spinning around totally improbable scenarios. There was no way that the guy could have faked his death and have circumvented all the checks and balances. Besides, his self-inflicted demise was in everyone's best interests, not only for the girls he preyed upon but the high-powered people who had found themselves embarrassingly associated with him. The only other alternative scenario was that he had been murdered in jail and that still resulted in a win-win situation for everyone.

No. There had to be a logical explanation, one that did not involve convoluted and outlandish conspiracies. Putting on his pathologist's hat, he applied logic to unravel the mystery. There was the possibility that Chad Levenstein had a twin. Certainly, the DNA match could not have been his brother. That would not have resulted in an exact match. But if he did have a twin, where was he? Why had the twin never been mentioned, or photographed or seen? Nothing made sense. He had a throbbing headache building behind his eyes and he squeezed the bridge of his nose. Enough. He needed to sleep. Tomorrow was another day. He drew all the curtains in his apartment, double locked the front door, threw back two Tylenols, and collapsed onto his bed, fully clothed. Within minutes he was in a deep, dreamless sleep.

CHAPTER FOUR

It hadn't taken long for Piggy Eyes to deduce from the visitors log in the reception of the NYPD Forensic Laboratory that two detectives, namely Georgina Harris and Paul Damote had signed in shortly before the FBI had arrived and had not signed out again. The CCTV footage confirmed this, revealing the detectives hot footing it to the fire escape from Dr. Chevalier's lab. Time to speak to their boss and find out exactly what case they were working on and how it tied in with the notorious, deceased sex offender Chad Levenstein. He made the call and within the hour he was en route to the Midtown North Precinct to rattle some cages.

Captain Lee Murphy replaced the receiver of his desk phone, got up and opened the door of his glass office. He yelled across the large open plan office.

"Damote! Harris! My office. Now!" and he gesticulated for emphasis.

"And so it begins," Georgina muttered to Paul.

He looked up and followed her gaze as Murphy returned to his desk, every inch of which was covered in paperwork. They often speculated whether their boss's desk indicated organized chaos or a ruse to look very busy and important. Paul pushed back his chair and said to Georgina.

"Clearly *they* are on their way."

"Sit." Murphy said, pointing to the two chairs in front of his desk, his agitation obvious and Georgina and Paul obediently sat down in what was well known in the department as the *splatter zone,* an apt description for when the shit hit the fan, which it did all the time. Murphy was the quintessential seagull boss. He would swoop in, shit on everyone and fly off again.

"Can either of you numbskulls tell me why the FBI are on their way to this precinct specifically to interview you both?" he barked, his beady eyes looking from one to the other. "Hmmm?"

He had the most irritating habit of adding *hmmm* to the end of just about every sentence and for that reason they all called him Captain Hmmm behind his back. There was no point in playing dumb so Georgina appraised Murphy of the events and timeline from the stake out to the laboratory visit.

"Jesus Christ on a bicycle!" he exclaimed. Paul winced. Being a Christian, the blasphemy jarred his nerves. Murphy continued.

"There are thousands of Starbucks cups thrown away every day in this town and yet you two wannabe sleuths have to pick up the one and only goddamn cup from a dead sex offender!"

Georgina and Paul exchanged perplexed looks but chose not to rise to the absolute absurdity of what Murphy was saying. The fact that they were regarded as a stellar team who had solved multiple high-profile crimes seemed not to impress their rotund beady-eyed boss who spent more of his time brown-nosing his superiors than paying attention to his own department. This was of course in addition to the earth-shattering fact that the dead offender was in fact not dead at all! He waggled his pudgy little fingers at them.

"Don't you dare tarnish this precinct's reputation with your antics! Best you make good with the FBI and come clean with your goings on. Clearly you have mixed up evidence. Fix it!" He glared at them. "Now get out!"

As they made their way back to their desks, Paul muttered under his breath. "If it is the last thing I do, I am going to get that prick fired!"

Georgina laughed and replied, "There're a dime a dozen to replace him."

"That is painfully true partner. God help us. Literally."

Half an hour later they found themselves sitting opposite Piggy Eyes in one of the interview rooms. What a day! Beady Eyes and now Piggy Eyes! Captain Murphy had wanted to sit in on the interview, but Piggy Eyes, who had introduced himself as Special Agent Stonehouse, had made it clear that he was not welcome.

Once Captain Murphey had left the room, Agent Stonehouse made a show of laying out his collection of pens after which he stared at Georgina and Paul for a long while before clearing his throat and commencing with the interview. He nodded to one of his wannabe tough agents who pressed the record button and who nodded back at Piggy Eyes to confirm that the recording was underway. Georgina wanted to laugh out loud. They were like two bad actors in a B-grade movie.

"Detective Harris and Detective Damote," he began. "Can you explain to me why you saw fit to leave the NYPD Forensic Laboratory via the fire escape as opposed to the front entrance and why you failed to sign out as per the strict protocol rules prescribed by the State Government? Hmmm?"

Oh God! Not another one! Was there a secret lab breeding these halfwits! But Georgina knew that this man was no idiot. She knew instinctively that this FBI agent was sly and dangerous and his evident hunger for power was not to be underestimated.

"Seriously?" said Paul. "We would have expected you to be marginally more interested in the fact that we have exposed a dead sex offender as not being dead at all. And here I thought the FBI was on top of things, but it appears that you are more concerned about petty protocols."

Georgina stared at Paul open-mouthed. This was totally out of character. Paul was a taciturn type of individual and was mostly economical with words let alone sarcasm. She saw a flash of anger in Agent Stonehouse's eyes, but he quickly regained his composure and instead of bullying them like he had bullied Dr. Chevalier, he merely smiled tightly and replied.

"You are quite right Detective Damote. We are far more interested in how our dead offender is possibly alive."

"What?" Paul exclaimed "Possibly alive? The DNA was conclusive. He is not possibly alive, or half dead or half alive! He is fully alive!"

Agent Stonehouse turned to his minion.

"Please delete Detective Damote's disrespectful comments and we will start again."

Georgina and Paul exchanged incredulous looks. His aide obliged and after the machine clicked, whirred and clicked again, Piggy Eyes turned to Paul and said with yet another tight smile.

"Shall we begin? Again."

This time Georgina took Agent Stonehouse through the events from beginning to end, whilst attempting to reassure him that Simon's actions were above reproach. Paul leaned back in his chair, his arms crossed as he closely watched Agent Stonehouse, his eyes narrowed. The interview lasted for about an hour whilst Agent Stonehouse made copious notes. He asked multiple pointed questions and Georgina answered honestly and politely. However, Agent Stonehouse's final question was where her honesty stopped. It was concerning whether she or Paul had any evidence or record of Chad Levenstein's DNA to which she replied that they did not. She was not about to tell this creep that she had snatched the printout from Simon's laboratory, and it was presently locked in her desk draw. Instinctively she knew that the whole affair of Chad Levenstein led a stinking trail all the way to the upper echelons of American power and politics and that the events of the last few days were far from over.

"Thank you for your cooperation," Agent Stonehouse concluded after indicating to his aide to stop the recording. "The FBI will take it from here. From this point on you are not to ever speak again of these events. Not between yourselves, not to your colleagues…to absolutely no one. Understand that this is a direct order from the director of the FBI. Have I made myself clear?"

He looked from Georgina to Paul and then back again. He started to get up and then Paul spoke.

"Actually no, Agent Stonehouse. Let us make something

very clear to you," he said, leaning forward. Stonehouse hesitated, frowning. Paul continued.

"This is *our* evidence and thus *our* case."

Stonehouse bristled, his skin tone reddening. He sat back down and leaned forward inches from Paul's face, finally showing his mean bullying character.

"You are not understanding me Detective Damote. This is not your choice. This is not your case. In fact, there is no case, no evidence, no record of Chad Levenstein's DNA ever being found anywhere at any time. In fact, this interview never happened and if you ever try to say anything to the contrary, the FBI will indict you for so many offences that you will still be serving consecutive terms even after you are dead. Not only will your pathetic careers be over, but your lives as you know them now, will no longer exist!"

Paul leaned even closer to Agent Stonehouse, his eyes the palest blue Georgina had ever seen. Little dust motes floated through the air between them and after what seemed an eternity, he said slowly and quietly, annunciating each word with deliberation.

"Agent Stonehouse…are you threatening two police officers, not to mention two decorated detectives of the New York State Police Department?"

The room was totally silent. Stonehouse stared at Paul for a long time and then abruptly he stood up, gathering up his pens and papers and looking down at Paul, he said.

"No, I am not threatening you Detective Damote. I am guaranteeing you."

With that he turned on his heel and marched out of the room with his minions scurrying after him.

They sat there dumbfounded. Georgina's heart was pounding in her chest. Just like what Simon had felt, the sense of violation was over whelming. Paul turned to look at her and, in a gesture totally out of character, he gently took her hand, squeezed it, and said.

"It's okay Georgie. We are going to fuck that bastard and the FBI to kingdom come and back again. We are police officers. Our job is to uphold the law and the Constitution. No one…but no one messes with that. Our lives are placed in jeopardy every day by scumbags on the streets but there is not one iota of difference between those low lifes and the likes of Agent Stonehouse. They are merely different sides of the same coin."

Georgina looked at him and felt a hot rage rise within her. He continued.

"We must go really carefully from this point on Georgie. They will be watching our every move. Something much, much bigger is at play here."

She nodded slowly. They then both stood up and went back to their desks. Out of the corner of her eye, Georgina saw Murphy talking intently on his phone, his eyes darting to her and Paul. She looked at all the teams busy working around them and with a few exceptions, she knew that these people had the metal to uphold the oath they had taken when they graduated from the Police Academy. She knew that most of the detectives were good people, who gave their best every day to keep crime in check. What would they think if they knew what Georgina and Paul had stumbled upon? No doubt they would feel much the same. Helpless on the one hand but determined on the other to address and defeat the poison that had seeped into the heart of law enforcement. The enemy may have the power, but they had the fortitude, and the battle was only beginning.

CHAPTER FIVE

Simon was wondering how Georgina and Paul were holding up. He was sitting in a diner, sipping an Americano, pondering if and when he would be able to return to work. An anger had been building inside of him. Not only because of all that he had been through but for all the victims of Levenstein who would never see justice, their lives ruined by his perverted proclivities. And then there were all the men who were as evil and sick as Levenstein, holding positions of obscene power, secure in the knowledge that they would never have to answer for their crimes either.

He picked up his new mobile deliberating whether he should call Georgina or not. Perhaps it was too soon. He knew that he had to be very careful for all their sakes. A shadow passed over the table and as he looked up, Special Agent Stonehouse slid into the seat opposite him. Slithered would probably be a more apt description.

Simon rolled his eyes but said nothing, sitting back and folding his arms waiting for Piggy Eyes to deliver some cheesy FBI monologue.

"Hello Simon," said Special Agent Stonehouse smoothly.

"Actually...it's Dr. Chevalier to you," replied Simon

sarcastically.

A waitress with a coffee jug came up to the table and as she was about to ask Stonehouse if he wanted coffee, Simon stopped her.

"He's not staying," he said to her.

Stonehouse gave his usual tight smile and tilted his head to the side.

"C'mon Dr. Chevalier…we're on the same team here."

"That we are not," Simon said coldly.

Stonehouse ignored the jibe and continued.

"However, I am just wondering why a fellow teammate would lie to me. Would you like to share with me what you and detectives Harris and Damote discussed shortly before they hastily left your laboratory via the fire escape?"

"I am sure you have asked them the same question," replied Simon. "And you know exactly what the discussion was about…your not so dead sex offender. Sorry…your highly celebrated not so dead sex offender who seems to enjoy the very best protection the United States of America can offer."

Stonehouse raised his hands, sighing loudly.

"You really do not get how vulnerable you are…how close you are to losing everything Dr. Chevalier," and he held his thumb and index finger a few millimeters apart to emphasize his point, his eyes cold and unblinking.

Simon held his gaze and then said.

"Actually, I do. But when all is said and done, you would never indict me because suddenly a lot of people would know a lot about your not so dead sex offender and a lot of very powerful people would suddenly become very nervous. My testimony would be a matter of public record and to be honest, it would be quite fun to see your house of cards come tumbling down along with all the disgusting people you are protecting. I know just what Levenstein has on all of those entitled fucks who love fiddling with underage kids and why it is so important to maintain the lie that he is dead."

Stonehouse's expression was unfathomable. He stared at Simon for a long while. Finally, he stood up abruptly and left without a word.

Across town, Georgina stood up from the trash bin that had set off the whole sorry chain of events. They had both known that it would be a long shot that the paper cup Johnny Salome had thrown away would still be there and even if it was, the fragile DNA would probably have been compromised by all the other trash that would have landed on top of it. As it turned out, it was evident that the trash had been collected as the receptable was virtually empty. She removed the latex glove from her hand and tossed it into the bin. Feeling dejected, they both looked around trying to decide their next course of action. Predictably, all the businesses within a half mile radius that had CCTV cameras, had had their video footage confiscated by the FBI. Georgina and Paul had even knocked on apartment doors to ascertain if any of the occupants by any small chance had a personal surveillance camera that showed any part of the street. Nothing.

They had been keeping a very low profile at the precinct and in fact everywhere they went. Being seasoned detectives, it was not hard for them to spot the detail watching their every move. They acted as if they were entirely focused on the various cases that they were busy with, including the Johnny Salome case and kept any reference to Chad Levenstein out of their conversations. However, the fact that Levenstein was clearly still alive was never far from their minds. They were treading water for a while until the FBI felt it safe to pull back their surveillance. They had agreed to give Simon space for a while when they found out what the FBI had done to him. In their minds, the extreme measures that the FBI was going to were clearly indicative of how badly some very powerful people wanted this all to go away. But that was not going to happen. They would bide their time and wait for the right opportunity to bring these people to book.

Special Agent Stonehouse had been summoned to the FBI headquarters in Washington. He cast his eyes around the expansive office of the director of the FBI, thinking secretly to himself that one day he would be sitting behind the high-polished desk in front of him, wielding the unmitigated power that Edgar J. Hoover and all the subsequent directors of the Federal Bureau of Investigation had done. His reverie was interrupted when the present director, Len Wyatt replaced the receiver of the phone on his desk before focusing his attention on Stonehouse. He was a handsome but arrogant man, rarely smiled and had a reputation of being vindictive. He came straight to the point.

"Do we have anything to worry about?" he asked, not even bothering to address Stonehouse by his name or rank.

Stonehouse shifted in his chair for two reasons. The chair was very hard and uncomfortable which was probably intentional to put subordinates ill at ease and to remind them that their time in the director's office was to be kept to the minimum, and because he found Wyatt's stare somewhat intimidating. He hoped that when his time came, he would be able to make those around him feel equally if not more uncomfortable. He was working on it.

"Yes and no sir," he answered. "I am confident that detectives Harris and Damote are in hand, but I'm not so sure about Dr. Chevalier. He said something odd to me."

"Go on…," said Wyatt.

"He said that he knows what Levenstein has on the powerful people for whom he trafficked young girls. He used the word *has,* not *had.*"

Wyatt rubbed his chin, deep in thought. He stared out the window for some time. The only sound in the room was the soft ticking of the ornate gold clock on Wyatt's desk, an inscribed gift from President Bush senior. Finally, he looked back at Stonehouse.

"I believe that Detective Harris's father is Supreme Judge Harris?"

"Yes, that is correct sir," Stonehouse replied.

There was another long silence.

"Is he one of us?" Wyatt asked.

Stonehouse hesitated only for a second, surprised by the question.

"No sir," he said, understanding Wyatt's meaning. "He's not."

Wyatt stared at Stonehouse, an unblinking stare that was unnerving. Abruptly he sat back in his chair.

"That will be all," he said dismissively, putting his glasses on whilst picking up a document in front of him, which he proceeded to read. Stonehouse was momentarily taken aback. He cleared his throat.

"Yes of course, thank you sir," he said as he stood up, hesitating for a moment before he headed for the door. He looked back at Director Wyatt, who for all intents and purposes was now completely unaware of Stonehouse's existence. He opened and closed the door quietly and stood momentarily outside the director's office, feeling somewhat deflated. He had been expecting a lengthy meeting with the director and perhaps even some form of recognition or praise as to how well he was handling the whole affair. After all, he had flown especially from New York for this meeting, and it was over in a few minutes. Wyatt had made him feel small and insignificant and that was something Stonehouse was not only unaccustomed to but resented deeply.

Simon stood still for a moment when he entered his laboratory after an absence of six weeks. It had taken that long to regain his security clearance. Obviously, Agent Stonehouse had stalled it for as long as possible. He was still smarting from the well-meaning comments from the security personnel downstairs who had conveyed to Simon how happy they all were that he was better now and that he had made a full recovery and was back at work. What goddamned story had Stonehouse made up? What affliction was supposed to have kept Simon from work for such an extended period of time? Shaking his head, he decided that the only way to move forward, was to bury himself in his work. It was like starting from scratch again and all the cases he had been working on before he had been suspended, were now distant memories. He had noted however that there had not been a single mention in the press about any of the cases that had been thrown out of court due to the actions of the FBI, compromising and confiscating all the evidence and files. It was as if the cases had never existed in the first place. He shook his head again as he sat down at this desk. The deals that people make with the devil he thought. And how far and wide the reach of the devil is.

There was a soft knock on the door. He looked up as Sophie, one of the forensic laboratory technicians entered. "Hello Dr. Chevalier. It is so good to have you back. You are looking well," she said smiling.

She had a somewhat reserved personality and was highly meticulous in everything she did or said. But despite her low-key demeanor, Simon always sensed that there was a great inner strength in her.

"Thank you, Sophie. It's good to be back. Are those my new case files?" he pointed to the files she was holding.

"Yes, they are Dr. Chevalier. Do you have time for me to

go through them with you and bring you up to speed?'

"Yes of course." He indicated for her to sit at the small meeting table.

"Coffee?" Simon offered her.

"Yes please. That would be lovely, thank you."

She sat down and proceeded to sort the files in order of importance. He glanced back at her as he waited for the machine to dispense the coffee and wondered if she had any inkling of how corrupted the outside world had become. By contrast, everything they did here in this building reflected an exact science, a respect of the facts and an understanding that lives could be destroyed if they were ever dishonest or sloppy at their jobs. She looked up and smiled again, her soft blonde hair framing her heart shaped face. He felt his heart squeeze. Not from any attraction at all, but from a desire to protect her from people like Levenstein…and Stonehouse.

She reminded him of his own daughter, the result of a teenage pregnancy which saw him becoming a father before he had even completed his first year of university. He hadn't seen much of his daughter over the last twenty years. Edwina's mother and her parents made sure of that. He certainly had not wanted to name her Edwina. It seemed such an old-fashioned name for his child. They had all moved away shortly after she was born and he had been devastated. As young as he was, he had wanted to raise his daughter and marry her mother. Such were the times then when fathers had virtually no rights. Were things any different now? It seemed to him that the violation of rights was now the order of the day.

They worked solidly together for the next two hours. When they had finished, he thanked her for her excellent preparation of the files. She flushed, clearly pleased to receive a compliment from one of the most respected members of the forensic fraternity.

As she was leaving, he said, "Sophie…"

She turned, looking directly at him, "Yes Dr. Chevalier?"

"What was the reason given for my absence?"

She looked away, a little disconcerted by the question.

"Not to worry Sophie. I don't mean to make you uncomfortable."

"It's alright Dr. Chevalier. The same happened to me some time ago."

Simon's eyes narrowed and he cocked his head.

"And what was that, Sophie?"

She looked down, hesitating, biting her lower lip.

"A nervous breakdown," she replied, looking back up at him.

He was stunned. There was a long silence between them. Her hand was on the door handle, but he could see that there was something more she wanted to say.

"Sophie?" he said gently.

"It's just that we all feel terrible about it. There were no warning signs, no indication to any of us of what a strain you were under. We should have been there to support you, to show you that most of us actually do care about each other. I am truly sorry Dr. Chevalier."

She smiled sweetly, turned, and closed the door softly behind her.

Simon slumped back in his chair, dumbfounded, a vice tightening around his chest. The abuse just gets worse he thought to himself. Suddenly he felt unbearably lonely. He needed to see Georgina, now. Picking up his mobile, he speed dialed her number.

Georgina felt her mobile vibrate in her pocket, but now would not be the time to take a call. She was standing next to a hospital bed looking down at the broken body of the young girl she had seen at the bus stop when she and Paul were trailing Johnny Salome. It was pitiful. Her blonde hair was matted with blood, her face bruised and beaten so badly that Georgina could hardly recognize her. Her breathing was shallow, both from her injuries and the sedation. Johnny Salome never penetrated any of his victims; he preferred to ejaculate all over them. If and when they caught him, the charge would only be assault, not rape… a crime that carried a far less harsh sentence. However, the physical and psychological damage done to the victims was commensurate with rape. Georgina felt sick inside and emotionally drained, not only by the state of this young girl but by the whole justice system that seemed so skewered in favour of the perpetrator. She couldn't bear to think of the psychological scars this poor girl would carry with her long after her physical injuries had healed.

She gently lifted the sheet, and her suspicion was confirmed. Salome always took something from his victims, something personal and the diamanté stud was missing. There was a small tear around the poor girls naval. It was possible that it had fallen out during the struggle, but it was equally possible that he had taken it. Her youthful breasts were bruised and swollen and there were further cuts and bruises down her legs. Georgina recalled that moment in the bus when the underside of one of the girl's breasts was visible as she reached up, oblivious to the fact that Johnny Salome was watching her.

That would have set him off and no doubt while she and Paul were dealing with the fall-out of the Levenstein debacle, he was stalking this young girl, lurking in the shadows waiting for the moment to shatter her life forever. A sense of hopelessness flooded Georgina. It was her job to protect this girl and she had failed.

The phone vibrated again in her pocket, and she took it out to see who was calling. It was Simon. She saw that he was calling for the second time. She quietly left the room and once she was in the corridor, she answered his call.

"Simon…I am sorry that I haven't been in touch. I thought…Paul and I thought that it was safer for you if we kept a low profile."

"Gigi…" Suddenly Simon felt all choked up. There was a long silence on the phone.

"Simon?" Georgina frowned, aware that his voice had a slight quaver to it.

"Oh God, it has been such an awful time Gigi. What the fuck is wrong with this world? Everything has been turned upside down."

"I know Simon…it's…" she searched for the right words.

"…it's utterly soul destroying."

He sighed, gaining control of his emotions.

"Things are pretty much back on track at work now, but

that fucker Stonehouse told the powers that be here that I had suffered a nervous breakdown! So now everyone here is looking at me as if I am some kind of fragile wreck to be treated with kid gloves."

"God Simon! That is vicious beyond words!"

"Yep. Tell me about it."

"Simon…I am so sorry that we caused all of this."

"You didn't Gigi. The system did. A system that seems to protect the most heinous criminals. It speaks of individuals so powerful that people like us are simply dispensable if we dare shine a light on their dark deeds." He continued. "You know, you simply can't make this stuff up. If you had told me only a few months ago that the FBI is literally there to serve the rich and powerful and to do whatever the government tells them to do, I would have pegged you as a conspiracy theory nut."

"Ditto," said Georgina. "I am still trying to process what happened with the Levenstein business. We are living in a different world now."

"I still can't get my head around the DNA match," said Simon. "It simply does not make sense. Either there is someone out there where the odds are trillions to one to have the same DNA…or…Levenstein had a lot of help faking his death. My training tells me that it couldn't the former; my logic tells me that the latter is too far-fetched.

If I mentioned this to anyone else other than you, the men in their white coats will march in to take me away and everyone at work will nod sagely, agreeing that I am a danger to myself and everyone else. Hell, at this rate I'll call the white coats myself!"

"Simon…" Georgina hesitated. "When we left your lab that day, you said that you would explain to me why Paul and I needed to get out asap. Why did you say that?" Simon was silent for a while.

"Gigi…I would prefer to tell you in person what I know, not over the phone. When can we meet?" he asked.

"Paul and I are going out of town tomorrow on a case for a week, so how about next Thursday? Say after work drinks at Columbo's?" Georgina suggested.

"Perfect," and then Simon laughed. "Only a detective would frequent a wine bar called Columbo's! See you then," he said and then he added tenderly, "Gigi…I miss you."

"I miss you too Si…a lot. See you next Thursday."

Georgina slipped her mobile back into her pocket and went back into the ward. She stood there for a while, mulling over the conversation with Simon, trying to make sense of it all. She gently touched the hand of the young girl and then left to go back to the precinct.

"How is she?" Paul asked as Georgina sat down at her desk, powering up her computer.

"Stable. She'll recover but I suspect only on the outside," Georgina replied.

Paul pushed a newspaper across to Georgina, tapping a column with his finger indicating an article on the attack of Selina Chapman, the victim lying in hospital. Georgina looked at the photo of her, smiling and carefree which intensified the anger she was feeling inside. She then read the article and started to shake her head.

"Is it my imagination Paul or is this journalist inferring that the victims are begging to be attacked?" she said looking up at Paul with an incredulous expression.

"That's why I'm showing you the article. This journalist, if one could even call him that, is clearly prejudiced against women. He is probably a founding member of the *woke* brigade, delusional bullies who are systematically marginalizing women and promoting transgenderism. Hell, apparently even men can have babies now!"

Georgina tossed the newspaper into the bin.

"Yeah right…just one minute of labour would change every one of their pathetic little pea-brain minds very, very quickly. Not a bad idea actually!"

She grinned at the thought. Paul winced.

"Noooooo! I am content with the way things are. Happy

to put the baby in there, but not to get it out!"

Georgina leant down, grabbed the newspaper, and threw it at Paul, laughing as he spilt his coffee all down the front of his shirt as he tried to duck.

"Is there any chance that you two could stop treating this precinct like a kiddie's playground, hmmm?" a voice boomed. Georgina groaned. Captain Murphey was glaring at them from the door of his office. She lifted her hands to indicate surrender and turned to concentrate on her screen, trying her best not to laugh while Paul was doing what he could to mitigate the stains on his shirt.

"Damn it, Georgie. I have an interview with a witness in twenty minutes!"

CHAPTER SIX

On the top floor of the Sheldon Wagstaff building in New York, was a very exclusive club that only a handful of people knew about. The members were men only but there were women there too. However, they served a different purpose. The club was run by a woman called Lela Hinton, probably one of the most discreet connectors and influencers in New York. As for the other women, she ruled them with an iron fist. They were there to attend to every need of the members, and they all knew only too well what the consequences would be if they were to ever divulge what went on in those plush corridors.

The women were called *Nymphs* and the job benefits were substantial. They were accommodated in the very best designer apartments with accounts at expensive stores and boutiques. Their gym fees, healthcare and salon visits were paid for in full. No expense was spared in making these women as close to perfection as possible. After perhaps doing this job for two or three years, these women would be in very good financial positions to take a few years off, or to pursue other interests. Often those interests included becoming mistresses to wealthy businessmen who knew nothing about the club and never would know. Either way, their affluent lifestyles could continue.

Their side of the deal was to be single, beautiful…and naked. The moment they arrived at work they had to strip. The only things they were allowed to wear were thongs (so minuscule that dental floss would have covered more), very high heels and designer jewelry. Lela Hinton would inspect each girl at the beginning of their shift. If there was a hint of cellulite or a blemish on their skin, they would be sent home. She even had an in-house beautician who ensured that their make-up and hair were perfect. They were all tall, slim but curvaceous with perfectly upturned pert breasts and firm, shapely buttocks and narrow waists. The quintessential woman. They always wore diamanté masks so that they could never be recognizable in the street. These women were so perfect that they looked as though they had been airbrushed. And they came from all over the world. Lela Hinton had her scouts who would find them and her contact at immigration, who received a healthy sum of money per girl, ensured that papers were never a problem.

Len Wyatt glanced up briefly from the text message he was reading from his wife as one of the *Nymphs* leant down and placed the drink he had ordered on a gold filigree coaster on the marble coffee table. He reached out and absently mindedly ran a finger along the profile of her shapely breast, trailing it down towards the curve of her hip and moving it around to briefly run his hand down the inside of her thigh. The girls were never allowed to object to such liberties taken by the men and if they did, their positions were immediately terminated. He gave her bottom the lightest dismissal tap and focused again on his mobile. He replied to his wife saying that his meetings in New York would continue late into the evening and that he would be flying home to Washington in the morning. They were hosting a lavish dinner party at their home over the weekend with very important guests in attendance. He assured her that he would be home by midday and would give her a hand if there were any last minor things to attend to. For the moment though, he had the whole night to himself. He had been waiting for this evening for some time now. He closed his mobile and looked around. Lela Hinton glided between the tables, smiling, and engaging in small talk with the club members. She knew the proclivities of each and every man and ensured that their desires were met with ease and comfort. The annual fees for the club were prohibitive, but then again what went on there, was too. Smiling to himself, Wyatt contemplated the plethora of excuses the members present would have given to their wives for not being home on a Friday night. The art of lying was to present a story that was totally believable and in keeping with normal daily life. He never used any outlandish excuses.

Ten minutes later, Lela Hinton bent down smiling and whispered into Wyatt's ear that his order was ready in Room 14. He thanked her, drained his glass, stood up and headed down the west corridor, his footfall silent on the plush deep red carpeting.

Edward Baker was just coming out of Room 12 as he was passing. The police commissioner and Wyatt chatted amiably in the corridor for a short while. It was never a point of embarrassment to bump into anyone he knew. They were all there for the same thing. They all kept the same secret, and they all understood the rules of the game. "I'd like to meet with you privately Ed. There's something I need to discuss with you," said Wyatt. "I'll call you, is that okay?"
"Of course, no problem. Look forward to it Len," Baker replied.
They shook hands and Wyatt continued on to Room 14.

He entered the room and glanced towards the massive four poster bed with ivory silk drapes. Quietly he closed the door and locked it. Not that it was necessary. One's privacy was never invaded in this club. There were no time restraints and no rules as to what transpired in these rooms. Men were free to do whatever they desired to the woman or women who would be there, waiting for them. But this was not the usual liaison with one, two or more of the *Nymphs*. This was a special occasion…not his first and certainly not his last. But the exquisite pleasure he derived from it never diminished.

He walked over to the drinks table and poured himself a scotch. He glanced back again at the bed, observing the young naked girl sitting quietly hugging her knees. He had paid a lot for this order. Ordinarily, he would not have been able to afford such luxuries on his paycheck, but his close friend Joey Levenstein from Wall Street had always provided him with highly profitable insider information, with the result that Wyatt was a very wealthy man. He chuckled inwardly…guys named Levenstein seemed to be able to offer all manner of great services. Thus, he could indulge his base need for very young girls. He walked over to the bed. She could not have been a day older than twelve. He had been guaranteed that she would certainly be under fourteen and a verified virgin. Lela Hinton had assured him that the girl had been examined by a physician who confirmed that the hymen was intact. This one had cost him a fortune, $80,000 to be exact. And he had been waiting a good three months for this order to materialize. He had been told that she was from France. He didn't speak French, but no matter…she wasn't here for the conversation. Nor was he.

He put down his drink and sat down on the side of the bed. She shifted nervously away from him not making eye contact and he could see that she was trembling. He liked that. It made it all the more exciting. She was very slight in build and there was just the hint of her breasts developing. Her skin was so perfect that it looked translucent, and her fine features, deep blue eyes and soft tendrils of blonde hair made his chest tighten. The young virgins from Mexico or South America were far less expensive, but he had a penchant for the pale skinned waifs who looked as though they hailed from Nordic aristocracy. He ran his eyes over every part of her, seeking out the hidden folds of her girlhood. Finally, he stood up and headed for the bathroom, taking the key with him. He was going to take this very slowly and savour every moment, but first, he wanted a long hot shower.

Whilst he showered, his thoughts swiveled to his son who was turning fourteen next month. Soon it would be time to introduce him to the delights of female flesh. All the men who belonged to the club arranged a sexual rite of passage for their sons. They taught them that marriage was for convenience and alliances. Unfettered access to women was their birthright and the *Nymphs* were perfect for their introduction into the world of sensuality. Lela Hinton was more than willing to accommodate this ritual on her premises, as it ultimately translated into more members and more money. One could not buy one's way into the club; if that were the case she would be inundated with applicants. No, this was a closed shop for the privileged few vetted for entry by the other members. So, when a young man was introduced to the all-important sexual aspect of his existence, the men would supervise and guide the young teenagers in the art of love making…not that there was much love in it since they taught their sons that taking whatever they wanted when it came to sex was acceptable and persuading women that it was in their interests to be compliant and submissive, was laudable. If their future wives lost interest in sex, which usually was the case, this was not an issue. They could have sex when they wanted it and how they wanted it. There were no limits except for what it cost. He himself had not come from a privileged background and over the years, a deep resentment had festered in him due to his wife's neglect of his own sexual needs. However, as he accumulated more and more wealth, he could buy sex that was far more pleasurable than what his wife could and had ever given him. So, she had her high society friends and clubs…but so did he. She just didn't know it.

It never occurred to him that what he was about to do to this young, frightened girl was beyond criminal. He never equated his sick desires with the fact that he had a daughter at home, who was more or less the same age as this girl and no doubt was as innocent, the difference being that this poor girl was far from home with no one to protect her. Men like Len Wyatt continued their lives and their perversions with impunity, safe in the knowledge that the desired merchandise would always be available, no matter the price tag. His needs had to be satisfied and that was all there was to it. And Chad Levenstein not only enjoyed the same needs but ensured that he profited handsomely from the same desires in other men.

Perversion was good business. It had been for centuries.

The next morning Lela Hinton herself removed the stained sheets from the bed where Wyatt had violated every inch of the girl's body, and after carefully folding them, she slid them into a vacuum sealed bag. She then downloaded the videos from the four hidden cameras in Room 14. She only managed to watch a few minutes of the hulking Wyatt holding down the small girl, pushing her slim pale legs apart. She could see his hand over the girl's mouth, her eyes wide with terror, her thin little arms flailing helplessly. Lela hastily locked the memory card in her safe. Later that day she took the sheets to her private lock-up which was located on the other side of town, far from prying eyes.

She was no fool. Whilst initially she hadn't been entirely comfortable with being the go-between for underaged flesh, she soon overcame that discomfort. She had her retirement to think of and she intended to enjoy it in the luxury she considered herself worthy of. If everything were to go pear-shaped, she was not going to find herself holding the short straw like Chad Levenstein's girlfriend. Only a few of the club members had a taste for this type of sick indulgence. If the other members found out, she knew they would be horrified. It's one thing enjoying the sexual attentions of willing beautiful adult women. It was an entirely different matter having intercourse with girls so young that they were probably still playing with dolls. So, to this end, she was very careful that other members never knew that underaged sex transpired on the club's premises. Privately, she detested these entitled men, but she put on an entirely convincing front that she understood them and even held them in awe, and that anything they desired was totally acceptable.

Early that morning a limousine had pulled up in the basement garage and the young girl had been bundled in and whisked away. No doubt the poor mite would be trafficked again to some pervert who couldn't afford a virgin but would be none the less satisfied with her age, whilst the girl's parents somewhere in rural Provence would continue to feign devastation at their daughter's disappearance for a respectable time, secure in the knowledge that the untraceable payment would remain hidden from the authorities, or anyone savvy enough to work out what had happened. They had another daughter who was nine years old, but they doubted that they would be able to pull the same stunt again.

Helen Wyatt glittered in the flickering candlelight of the solid silver candelabras adorning the sumptuous dinner table, wearing a very expensive diamond necklace that Wyatt had bought her for their anniversary. She was still a very attractive woman, her breasts presenting titillating curves against the deep burgundy velvet of her dress. Matt Portman, the CEO of TFC was clearly enjoying the view, Wyatt observed wryly from the opposite end of the table. He cast his eye over the thirty guests, the quintessential who's who of corporate America with a couple of senators thrown in. Five of the guests were club members, two of them shared his taste in underaged female flesh.

After the Michelin standard seven course dinner which had been prepared by a highly celebrated local chef, everyone retired to the drawing room for cigars, cognacs, and more conversation. The women eyed each other competitively, sizing up who had the most expensive dress or jewelry. It was a perpetual dance of shifting alliances depending on the financial status and power of their respective husbands. Only one of the women present was on the same level as the men. Sabrina Newton, the CEO of a massive retail company called SASSY, with stores right across America, Europe, and the UK, was beautiful, unmarried, intellectually engaging and deliciously mysterious. Her semi-transparent bronze organza dress followed the contours of her shapely figure, pulled tightly in at her waist, showing every curve and detail of her body. The women fumed at her attire. The men were enthralled. Her breasts were nothing short of exquisite, emphasized by a large topaz stone setting on a gold chain nestling in her cleavage and all male eyes were drawn to the slight hint of her rosy nipples below the gathered folds of fabric. The slits on either side of her dress went all the way up to the top of her thighs, showcasing her shapely legs and strong calves and it was fairly evident that she was not wearing underwear. Every man present wanted to bed her. None had succeeded. Every woman wanted to exile her. None could afford to.

Wyatt subtly gestured to Alan Turner and Roy Sedgefield, both big tech and social media CEOs to accompany him to his private study. He closed the door softly and the three men moved to the sofas on either side of the fireplace. Wyatt wasted no time in bringing his friends up to speed. "We have a problem gentleman. A freak series of events has revealed to certain parties that not only is our man Levenstein alive but is in New York too."
There was a stunned silence. This had been the best kept secret amongst all of them and the possibility that it may

come out publicly was catastrophic.

"I have contained it for the moment," continued Wyatt "but there are still a few loose ends."

"Christ!" said Roy. "Chad has been very careful. We only chatted a couple of days ago. How in the hell did this happen?"

Wyatt went through the entire sequence of events ending with Special Agent Stonehouse's heavy handedness with the detectives and the forensic scientist.

"Idiot. His actions have clearly alienated the three people involved," said Wyatt.

"Can they be bought?" asked Alan.

"No," replied Wyatt. "No chance. And to makes matters worse, Detective Harris's father is Supreme Judge Harris, an incorruptible bastard."

"Does Chad know?" asked Roy, clearly worried.

"Not yet," said Wyatt. "It may not be necessary to tell him. We don't want our source to disappear on us."

Both Roy and Alan nodded but neither of them looked reassured.

"Where is the evidence now?" asked Alan.

"I have everything under lock and key with the rest of the evidence. It's totally secure. No one has knowledge of or access to the facility, not even my second in command."

"And your agent? Is he a loose end too?" asked Roy.

"He could be…but I have arranged to transfer him to Washington…a promotion, so he thinks. I'll be able to keep an eye on him, so he doesn't fuck up again."

"What about the forensic chap?" asked Alan.

"He may be a problem. He has the bit between his teeth. We have tried hard to intimidate him, but he knows that we can never indict him. Everything would then be public knowledge and obviously we can't have that," said Wyatt.

"So, what do you suggest we do to bury this before it can get out?" asked Roy.

"I have a couple of ghosts who are watching his every move. And they are watching the detectives too. I am reasonably confident that we have all the evidence in hand which means that none of them can expose anything. However, if the forensic guy did retain anything, he will play his hand sooner or later. Then we will move swiftly."

"Should we not eliminate this guy now?" suggested Alan.

Wyatt was silent for a while and then he said.

"No, I think that would be too risky and it would raise the suspicions of the two detectives. We should not do anything like that…yet."

"Do you think we should cut Levenstein loose?" Roy asked.

"We can't even consider that!" said Wyatt looking at Roy incredulously. "Our trafficking will grind to a standstill, and we need him on the Pomona operation. Besides, that's not what we do. We stand together or fall together. That loyalty is what binds us together."

"You are right," agreed Roy looking away, somewhat embarrassed. Alan was nodding. Wyatt looked from one to the other and thought to himself that this was not something he should have to remind them about. He would keep that in the back of his mind. Wyatt stood up. "We had better get back to the others. I will keep you posted. Let's not worry until we have something to worry about. I have the resources to take care of it any which way. I simply wanted to let you know what has happened because we are all in this together."

"Yes, Len. Thank you, we appreciate it," said Alan.

"I agree…thank you Len," Roy echoed. "Aside from that, how was the little French girl?"

"The best I have had thus far. A little fighter," replied Wyatt.

"Levenstein has one in the pipeline for me," said Roy.

"He always delivers. We must keep him sweet. It will be hard to build a relationship with another supplier," observed Wyatt.

"Yes," agreed Alan. "And it's hard to enjoy a fully open rose after one has tasted a tight little bud," he added grinning.

They all laughed and made their way back to the party. Just the conversation had caused Wyatt to have stirrings in his loins. Pity none of the *Nymphs* were present here tonight he thought to himself. The release would have been pleasurable. But they were in New York, and this was Washington. It was better to keep a healthy separation.

He recalled a moment when he had been banging a dinner guest in one of the guest bedrooms of his home, when his wife and one of her friends had walked into the room. Very fortunately, moments before, his vigorous thrusting had caused them to roll off the bed onto the floor. They both lay dead still, out of sight, whilst his wife rummaged in a cupboard to retrieve a Gucci bag she wanted to show her friend. She had then noticed the rumpled bed and throwing up her hands, had complained how useless the help was, while she straightened the counterpane. They both left the room, bemoaning the stresses of managing domestic staff. Wyatt noted with pride that the close call hadn't even affected his erection and he continued the business at hand with even greater vigor. In fact, it was quite stimulating almost getting caught.

Georgina tapped her pen against her teeth while she read a lengthy document about a high-profile businessman's fraudulent activities. Paul cleared his throat and Georgina glanced at him. She ignored him and continued to read. And tap. Paul shook his head, smiling to himself.

The businessman in question had always presented himself as a pillar of society but no matter how well connected one was, insurance companies were particularly averse to insurance fraud, and his so-called friends from the District Attorney's office were no longer returning his calls. He was caught in the grey zone. If you were wealthy but not mega-wealthy and you did not breathe the rarified air of the elite, you were still subject to the law. However, if you were one of the elites who enjoyed obscene wealth and privilege, then you were an untouchable. The mega wealthy of the world were the new aristocracy, not much different from the French aristocracy before the French Revolution. And like those hapless individuals who lost their heads, the present aristocracy were also inclined to think that their world was impenetrable and perhaps for the moment it was. But a chain of events was starting to unfold and no matter how much money the powerful elite have, ordinary folk will only be fooled up to a point. The sad thing about the world thought Georgina, as she put the document back into its folder, is that most people are good people. They just want reasonable lives and to be able to provide well for their children. They don't have a need to change the world to enrich the few and disenfranchise the many. However, a miniscule percentage of the global population, right at the very top were extremely powerful people, many of whom were either sociopaths or psychopaths, or both. They had decided that the world should be remolded and reset to their version of how things should be, where they had total control over everyone and ownership of everything. And with this obscene ambition, came unacceptable behavior. Had Georgina and Paul unwittingly stumbled across a collusion so huge that it was totally unbelievable?

Her thoughts turned to Simon. She felt both curious and uneasy regarding what he was going to tell her about this evening after work. She knew him very well, probably better than anyone else on the planet. He was one of the most measured and logical people she had ever met. He was presently very unsettled and that spoke volumes. Well, she would have to wait and see. She had asked Paul to join her, but he demurred; one of his kids had a concert and if he missed that, he would be in for the high jump with his wife and both daughters. They were all thick as thieves. He was indeed outnumbered in his household, so he would have to get the low down from Georgina in the morning.

Simon looked up at the entrance of the FBI building and read their motto, *Fidelity, Bravery, Integrity.* Yeah right, he thought. What should be inscribed is *Quis custodiet ipsos custodes...* who guards the guards? Who was there to keep the power of the FBI in check was the question foremost in his mind. He was waiting to meet a friend from university days who he hadn't seen for years and who worked at the FBI. For good reason he did not want to set foot in any FBI building. He sauntered over to a nearby bench and sat down. He spent most of his life in a laboratory, and so he was reveling sitting in the warm sun, gazing up at the azure blue sky. Next thing a figure blotted out the sun and squinting, he looked up at his friend standing over him.

"Brad! How are you?" Simon jumped up and man-hugged his friend.

"Good to see you, Simon. It's been a while. How are you doing mate?"

"Been better. Long story…won't bore you…yet!"

They both laughed and set off in the direction of the Grey Goose coffee shop. Once they had ordered, Brad said to Simon.

"So, what gives? How is work? Any fabulous women in your life or are you still hankering after that gorgeous force of nature?"

Simon sighed. "I guess I will only ever have eyes for Gigi, but we just don't seem to be able to live together. She is a handful. So driven," he added.

"And you're not?" Brad exclaimed. "Two peas in a pod I would say!"

"I suppose you're right. But something has happened with Georgina, and I am worried about her. I need your help with some information."

"Really?" said Brad, his face looking serious now. "Shoot."

So, Simon told Brad the whole story from beginning to end, sparing no detail. He could see that Brad was shocked not only by the turn of events but how Simon had been treated by the FBI.

"Wow…" he said. "If I didn't know you better, I would say that all of this is the figment of some conspiracy theorist's imagination."

"I wish it were my friend. I ran the DNA three times. It's him."

Brad sat back, uncertain of what he should say. He deliberated for some time and then looking intently at Simon he said.

"My advice is to leave it alone." There was a long silence.

"I can't," said Simon, shrugging his shoulders.

"I thought you would say that," said Brad sighing.

Simon leant forward, looking around briefly.

"Not one son of a bitch associated with Levenstein who clearly participated in his perverted goings on has been prosecuted. As you know the only person who took the fall was his girlfriend and she's not saying much…for good reason. I know for a fact that there was plenty of evidence in Levenstein's residences that could put a lot of people away for a long time. He had cameras everywhere and all the evidence was taken by the FBI. I want to know why they have buried it."

Brad was silent and he looked down at his coffee. Simon continued.

"I was told that they all knew they were being filmed, that it was some kind of a brotherhood guarantee that they would all remain silent and protect each other, a show of loyalty. I also know that Levenstein had more than just video evidence…" He let the sentence hang in the air.

Brad looked up at Simon.

"Why would you say that? How would you know?"

"Forensics is a small world, Brad."

"So what further evidence are you referring to Simon?" asked Brad leaning back in his chair briefly scanning the coffee shop, checking if anyone he knew was there.

Simon hesitated, deliberating if this was the right time to tell Brad or if he should wait and see what Brad would volunteer. Eventually he decided to go for broke.

"Levenstein had DNA evidence on all the people for whom he trafficked underaged girls and the FBI took that too. I want to know where it is."

"Hell Simon!" exclaimed Brad rocking forward. "Do you have any idea how powerful these people are?"

Simon noted that Brad had not commented on the information about the DNA. He did not appear surprised. Perhaps he knew about it.

"Yes...I do know only too well how easily they can smear anyone, anytime. Their reach is to infinity and beyond."

"So why in the world would you want to shake this tree Simon if you know what you are dealing with?" Brad asked incredulously.

Simon was silent for a few seconds, his expression somewhat hard.

"Brad...we are both in law enforcement albeit in different

disciplines. We go back a long way, and we have both taken vows to uphold the law and the Constitution. I am not about to let *anyone* trash that, especially entitled and perverted fucks who hurt children. Because that is what those girls are…they are underaged. They are children."

Simon was silent for a few moments and then he continued "Brad, I know by telling you all of this I have compromised your position, but I wouldn't do it if I didn't know that your moral compass is above reproach, as is mine."

Brad looked out of the window, his jaw line muscles working. Simon could see that he was conflicted. Eventually he looked back at Simon.

"Give me time to think about this. It's a big ask Simon but like you, I abhor anyone who hurts children…or women. I'll be in touch next week. I just need time to gather my thoughts. This is the most explosive information I have ever encountered."

"Exactly the words I used when I told Georgina," said Simon.

"Do you still have any proof that Levenstein is in fact alive?" Brad asked.

The question hung in the air. Simon hesitated, eventually answering him.

"Yes Brad, I do. The FBI didn't get everything."

Brad looked away clearly disconcerted. He stared out of the window for some time, deep in thought. Then looking back at Simon, he abruptly stood up.

"I'll be in touch Simon," he said.

And with that he left the coffee shop. Simon stared after him and watched him walk briskly back towards the FBI building. He wondered if his judgement had been right to trust Brad. People change and they hadn't seen each other in years. Had he opened up to the wrong person? He was feeling uneasy and unsure now. Well, he would bounce it off Georgina this evening. See what she thought. Sighing, Simon stood up, paid the bill and left for the laboratory.

That evening, he was already waiting for Georgina at the bar when she walked in. She looked around, saw him and smiling, made her way to him. He noticed how many male heads turned and watched her and although he was accustomed to the effect she had on men, he none the less had that familiar surge of jealously in the pit of his stomach.

"You're looking lovely Gigi…as usual," Simon said as they embraced.

"And what do you want Si?" she teased. He squeezed her hand and turning to the barman ordered a glass of her favourite wine. He didn't need to ask her what she wanted, and she didn't need to tell him.

"How is Paul?" he asked, as he helped Georgina onto her barstool, "or should I say how is Paul coping with you?"

She laughed. "Well, we've been partners for a year now and no blood has been spilt…yet! Besides, if there's going to be blood, it's not going to be mine."

"Obviously," Simon gave her a knowing look. "I know only too well."

She laughed and then asked.

"How is it going at the lab? Good to be back?"

"Well, the work is keeping me sane, but I simply can't let go of this Chad Levenstein issue. I can't sleep well at night knowing that he's out there…and no doubt continuing with his predatory crimes."

The barman smiled at Georgina as he placed the glass of wine in front of her. This bar was a favourite haunt of the NYPD detectives, and the staff served them well.

"I know. Paul and I can't let it go either," said Georgina tilting her wine towards him, their glasses clinking. She took a sip and then narrowing her eyes said. "So, what were you going to tell me Si?"

Simon shifted in his seat to face her directly. He looked around briefly to check that no one could overhear their conversation and then lowering his voice he said.

"When Levenstein's residences were raided, the FBI

found way more than just photos, videos etcetera. Wait for it Gigi…Levenstein had DNA evidence on all of them!” Georgina looked visibly shocked. He continued.

“He must have had someone from a lab processing everything for him. And I think the DNA served two possible purposes; one…as a loyalty test for the rest of the pedos, that is if they knew about it…and two…if they didn’t know about it, it would have been his insurance policy. He would have used the DNA records as leverage when he was arrested and incarcerated. I think everyone involved would have been highly incentivized to hatch a plan to get him out. Alive.”

Georgina stared at Simon and asked incredulously.

“And the FBI buried all this evidence? Why in the world did they not haul everyone into court, put them all on trial, parade them in front of the whole world? It’s their godamned job to do that!”

“Well, I imagine that the cover up goes all the way to the top. Just look at the company Levenstein kept…all top guys in corporate industry, big tech, government…even royalty,” Simon added.

“But if the FBI was in possession of the DNA evidence, then surely they would have felt secure in the knowledge that Levenstein couldn’t use it. In fact, it would be in their interests to knock him off,” said Georgina.

"Yes…but only if he didn't have duplicates of the DNA hidden somewhere else," Simon countered. "I have no doubt that he did, and he would have made sure that the FBI knew about it. So, they couldn't afford to mess with him. Levenstein was…is…a very clever guy. Those kinds of people always have insurance."

Georgina looked away, lost in thought. Simon continued.

"I met with a mate this morning who works at the FBI here in New York." Georgina looked back at him. "I asked him to help me get information and evidence. We go way back to university days. He's a good guy but he looked very edgy about it. Understandably."

"That's a long shot Simon," said Georgina frowning. "Do you trust this guy?"

Simon was silent for a moment and then he said.

"Intuitively I do. Perhaps if you can meet him at some point in time you can give me your opinion."

"And the evidence?" asked Georgina.

"Well, I have asked him to see if he can find it," replied Simon.

Georgina shook her head.

"Not likely Simon. The FBI will have all that evidence in such a secure location that I doubt anyone will be able to get near it. Besides, they may well have destroyed everything anyhow."

"Yes, I agree. But even if that is the case, they still don't have *all* the evidence," said Simon with a hint of a smile. Georgina raised her eyebrows. He continued.

"You have the printout Gigi…I gathered that you had grabbed it off my desk when you and Paul made your getaway down the fire escape, and I know you would have secreted it in a secure location."

"Yes, in fact it's in my father's safe although he doesn't know that. But why do I get the feeling that you have more to tell me Si?" asked Georgina her eyes narrowing. Simon's smile turned into a grin.

"Gigi…I swopped out my Starbucks coffee cup with the Levenstein cup!" he exclaimed looking triumphant.

Georgina opened her mouth and then shut it again. Simon continued.

"It was on my desk all the time while they were trashing my lab. I had brought a Starbucks coffee in with me that morning. I simply fished it out of the trash bin in my office and then swopped it out with the Levenstein cup. When you and Paul exited my lab. I knew that I had twenty seconds tops to do it. Remember, the FBI had no idea at that point in time that the DNA had come from a Starbucks coffee cup. While they were packing up everything in my lab, the cup just sat there on top of my desk in full view."

"Wow!" exclaimed Georgina. "You do think on your feet

Dr. Chevalier!"

"It's my job to do that Gigi. Besides, this is not my first rodeo with the FBI."

"My oh my…you never cease to amaze me!"

She shook her head, admiration showing on her face. Simon grinned, that boyish grin she loved so much.

"Well in that case Detective Harris…how about I amaze you all over again with a delicious creamy salmon pasta at my place?" he said, getting off his bar stool and gesturing towards the door.

She laughed as he helped her down.

"Somehow I suspect that I may be on the menu too…"

"Indeed, you are my darling Gigi," said Simon, his eyes twinkling.

He peeled off a few notes and left them on the counter, and with his hand gently placed in the small of her back, he guided her to the exit.

Ryder Mullens, one of Wyatt's ghosts watched them go and sat back deep in thought. From where he was sitting, he had not been able to hear their conversation, but he had been in this game long enough to glean from Detective Harris's expressions that some important information had been shared. He flipped open his mobile and dialed Wyatt.

"Our man has been busy," he said when Wyatt answered.

He then told him about Dr. Chevalier meeting Agent Brad Townsend that morning for coffee and then meeting Detective Harris for drinks.

"Thanks for the update," said Wyatt. "Keep a close eye on him. If he is going to make a move it will be soon, the tenacious little bastard. Too good at his job for our own good. And find out asap what was discussed with that FBI agent Townsend."

"Yes sir. Will do."

"In the meantime, I am going to see if I can get those two detectives transferred out of New York. It looks like they are starting to nose around again, and we don't need that."

"Quite so sir," agreed Mullens.

"Keep me posted," said Wyatt and he rang off.

Mullens snapped his mobile shut and headed to Simon's apartment building to watch for any further developments.

There were indeed further developments going on inside the apartment. After dinner, Simon took Georgina by the hand and led her to his bedroom. How many times had they done this and yet it never ceased to enthrall them. They were not able to live together but they loved each other and somehow that was a compromise they could both agree on. They knew each other's bodies so well and the intimacy they shared was as powerful as the cerebral similarities of their personalities. Tonight, their love making was slow and languid, both feeling a tenderness towards each other. Perhaps it was a sense of their vulnerable situations. They both knew how evil the world could be and that they had been pulled into a web of deceit and intrigue not of their own doing. When or how it would end was a question that neither of them could answer.

Simon listened to Georgina's steady breathing as she slept cradled against his shoulder. Sleep evaded him; his mind was too busy seeking a solution to expose these utterly evil people. It should never be this hard to do the right thing he thought angrily. Criminality was festering right in the very heart of law enforcement, an enemy within, corrupting all that they were supposed to represent. History was littered with such conspiracies, perfectly summed up by the well-known quote…*evil flourishes when good men do nothing.* That was too kind thought Simon. *Evil flourishes when weak men do nothing.* After a while, his mind quietened, and he eventually fell asleep.

Georgina woke early and after showering in the guest bathroom so as not to waken Simon, she looked down at him sleeping, a lock of hair across his forehead. Smiling to herself, she dressed quietly and with her shoes in her hand, tip-toed out of his apartment. Down in the street as she waited for her Uber, she suddenly felt that prickle that she was being watched; call it the seasoned instinct of a detective. She casually freshened up her lipstick using her small compact mirror, carefully observing the street behind her. Bingo. She spotted him, pretending to look in a shop window whilst surreptitiously looking her way. She must warn Simon that he was also now being watched. She took out her mobile and pretended to be reading a text message. Pressing the camera icon, she expanded the zoom and quickly snapped off a photo as he looked her way, confident that he would not have known what she had just done. She then made as if she was typing a message. At that moment her Uber arrived. Perfect timing.

CHAPTER NINE

Stonehouse preened with pleasure. He was being transferred to Washington, the Headquarters of the FBI, apparently at the behest of the director himself. He thought about the previous somewhat disappointing meeting with the director but now he felt elated. Wyatt obviously had noticed his good work after all and clearly, he wanted him at headquarters because of his evident abilities as a special agent. He swiveled back and forth in his chair, savouring and reliving the moment when his boss had told him the news, barely concealing his jealousy. Well, Stonehouse thought to himself; when you're good, you're good! In fact, he considered himself to be brilliant. He was one step closer to his final ambition. The sense of power was intoxicating, and he was anticipating with glee how Washington would offer him a whole lot more of it than New York had done. He couldn't wait to get home and tell his wife Molly. She would be thrilled. She may even concede to some celebratory sex. His smile broadened.

He had three weeks to hand over his files in New York and leave for Washington. He would leave the move and all the details of kids' schools etcetera for her to sort out. He was too busy and important to get involved in all those minutiae. He usually ate the sandwiches Molly prepared for him in his office, but today he would go to the canteen and enjoy the looks of envy and awe from his colleagues.

He was not disappointed. He could feel everyone looking at him as he walked in with just the hint of a swagger, taking his time slowly deliberating whether to have a pastrami sandwich or a cheese bagel. For the first time in his life, his height of five foot two didn't worry him. He was walking on the clouds. He was right about everyone staring at him but not for the reasons his conceited little mind had determined. They were all absolutely delighted with the news that this little tyrant would soon be gone and that they could get on with their careers without constantly having to remove knives from their backs.

Stonehouse turned and smiled at everyone, enjoying the audience he was getting. As soon as he turned back, someone made a wanking gesture, and everyone burst out laughing. Stonehouse fumed. He has seen the gesture reflected in the stainless steel of the coffee machine. They could laugh all they wanted. He was the one going to Washington. He was the one that the director of the FBI had singled out.

Two floors down, Brad Townsend was sitting at his desk, shaking his head wondering what had just happened. Some goon, who refused to introduce himself had just walked into his office, without knocking, wanting to know about his meeting with Dr. Chevalier the previous day. Brad had looked up at him and asked.

"Is there any chance you have a name, or did you leave your manners in the corridor?"

"I don't have a name. Just answer the question," Wyatt's ghost barked.

"It wasn't a meeting," said Brad sarcastically. "It was coffee…or have you been reading too many spy novels?"

"What did you talk about?" asked the man, his eyes unblinking.

"Oh…let's see now," drawled Brad. "Screwing women, baseball, beating up wannabe sleuths…like you…you know, that kinda thing."

Mullens leaned forward and said quietly to Brad.

"Please don't misunderstand your position here which is not nearly as secure as you like to think it is. Whether you are FBI or not, you are always subject to scrutiny, so just answer the fucking question."

There was a long silence.

"University. We spoke about our days at university. That's what old friends do. They reminisce," said Brad coldly.

"Nothing else?" asked Mullens.

Brad looked at him for a long time and then said.

"Until you show me your badge and credentials, get the hell out of my office and go back to the hole you crawled out of."

Who the hell never blinks thought Brad as Mullens continued to stare at him. After some time, Mullens quietly pushed the chair back, stood up and walked silently from the room, like a cat, not making a single sound. Brad sat back in his chair, perplexed. What in the hell was that all about? How had they known about his coffee with Simon? They must be tailing him. Clearly Simon had hit a nerve… with a sledgehammer.

Police Commissioner Edward Baker's personal assistant popped her head around the door and advised him that the director of the FBI was here to see him.

"Yes, Hillary, I have been expecting him. Please show him in."

Edward Baker stood up as Len Wyatt walked into his office, both reaching out to shake hands.

"So good to see you in New York again Len," said Baker with a smile.

"Good to see you too Ed," replied Wyatt. "How is Lynn? And the boys?"

"Everyone is well, and I presume your family are all fine too?"

"Oh yes…Helen is busy as usual with her fundraising and the kids are of an age where having parents is no longer fashionable!"

They both chuckled and Baker indicated for Wyatt to take a seat on the leather sofa as he came around from behind his desk. Hillary came in and placed the coffee tray on the table and then left, closing the door quietly.

Handing Wyatt a coffee Baker asked, "So, what brings you to New York Len? The last time we met some time back, you indicated that you wanted to see me. How can I be of assistance?"

"Well, it's a bit of a delicate matter," said Wyatt stirring his coffee.

"Yes?" said Baker. Wyatt continued.

"You have two NYPD detectives in the Midtown North Precinct and it appears that they have been hampering an FBI investigation. I know it's a big ask Ed, but I wondered if there's any possibility of them being transferred out of New York…perhaps upstate, or to an entirely different division?"

"Well, it would help if I knew who they were Len," said Baker, his eyebrows raised.

"Detective Harris and Detective Damote," said Wyatt.

Baker nodded and was silent for a moment. Then he said.

"And what is it all about? How are they involved in an FBI matter?"

"Well, that's the thing. I am not at liberty to discuss any details as it's a very sensitive matter. It would just be in everyone's interests if they could be…well…moved sideways as it were," Wyatt ventured.

Baker looked at Wyatt quizzically.

"Everyone's interest or just the FBI's?' he asked pointedly.

Wyatt shifted on the sofa, the leather creaking under him.

"I wish I could elaborate more Ed," said Wyatt spreading his hands. "But…as I said, it is highly sensitive but important enough for me to have travelled from Washington to discuss this with you."

Baker was silent as he looked out the window and thought to himself…*well you're not discussing it with me, are you.*

He looked back at Wyatt and then said.

"Detective Harris…that's Judge Harris's daughter, right?"

"Yes, I believe she is," Wyatt conceded.

He was starting to feel uncomfortable. He had anticipated that his request would have been granted with ease. After all they were both club members even though they did not share similar tastes when it came to their age preferences of the female sex. Of course, Baker would know nothing of his preferences, of that Wyatt was confident.

"Detective Damote was awarded a medal for bravery quite recently. And so was Detective Harris, about a year ago," Baker said.

"Yes, I heard that too," replied Wyatt.

A silence descended upon the room. This was not going well Wyatt thought to himself, feeling uneasy.

"Len…" Baker hesitated. "These two detectives are viewed as one of the best teams we have, held in high regard by those who matter. If I am going to help you, I will need more details."

He sat back and waited to see what card Wyatt would play.

"Ed…" Len began. Yep, thought Baker, he is going to play the *we go a long way back* card.

"We go a long way back Ed and that must count for something. We also share similar tastes…" he let the insinuation hang in the air.

Inwardly, Baker groaned. Surely, he wasn't going to play the blackmail card regarding the club! Wyatt continued.

"We need to take care of our friendship," he said, his tone sounding a little too plaintive.

"That we do Len," said Edward Baker "*but*…not at the expense of the NYPD. These are two detectives I respect, and this department needs them. So, with the greatest of respect, I would ask you to find a way to work around whatever issue you are dealing with."

There was a long pause. Wyatt realized that he had overplayed his hand. Baker wasn't quite the walk over he thought he would be. Now for damage control.

"You know Ed, you are absolutely right and on reflection, I think I may well have over reacted. Let's say that this conversation never took place. I apologize if I have offended you in any way," ventured Wyatt forcing a smile.

"No offence taken whatsoever Len. And yes, let's move on." said Baker.

They both stood up and shook hands.

"Thank you for your time, Ed. It's been good to see you. Please send my best to Lynn," said Wyatt.

"I will do that Len. And my best to Helen too," said Baker smiling, but Wyatt noted that his smile never reached his eyes. He turned to go, hesitated, and then said to Baker.

"No need to discuss this with the detectives or their captain. It's a closed chapter as far as I am concerned."

"Yes of course. A closed chapter. Understood." agreed Baker as he opened the door for Wyatt.

Once Wyatt had gone, Edward Baker stood for some time contemplating the conversation that had just transpired. He then moved behind his desk and buzzed his assistant.

"Hillary?"

"Yes sir?"

"Please set up an appointment with detectives Harris and Damote from the Midtown North Precinct. Liaise with them directly, not through Captain Murphey."

"Yes sir, will do."

Baker sat down at his desk. His years of experience told him that Len Wyatt was someone to be very careful of. Not that he felt intimidated, far from it. However, his instincts told him that this was not something that was a momentary lapse of Wyatt's judgement. Something was afoot and he intended to find out what it was.

CHAPTER TEN

Johnny Salome was in the wind. Since the attack on Selina Chapman, he had literally disappeared into thin air. He had not been back to his apartment and his Ford had been towed away by the authorities.

Georgina and Paul had shown a photo of him to multiple residents in the area, but no one had seen him. Police work was ninety percent hard slog and frustration, five percent exhilaration and five percent full on depression. They both knew that there were two possible scenarios. Either he was deceased or… he had chosen a new hunting territory. The former was not likely, and there was not a chance that he had suddenly developed a conscience and had decided that he wouldn't hurt a fly ever again in his life, let alone young women. Men like Salome could never satisfy their appetite. It was a nagging hunger that drove them to commit crimes over and over again.

Selina Chapman was no longer under sedation and Georgina had been to the hospital to interview her twice. It was pitiful to see how empty her gaze was. All the brightness of her complexion, her hair and eyes were gone.

It was as though nobody inhabited her body anymore. She answered Georgina's questions, but her voice was monotone and there was no spark of life in her. Her mother was there and the pain in her eyes was unbearable. As a parent, you will take any pain or hurt so that your child doesn't have to, no matter what their age. As Georgina turned to leave, Selina's mother touched her arm saying.

"Please find him. Please destroy him like he has destroyed my baby."

Georgina took the woman's hand.

"We won't stop until he has been stopped," she said, looking directly into her eyes. "We will keep trying to find him. You have my word."

Paul wasn't at the precinct when she got back. Often, they split up work that had to be done so as to be able to accomplish more. She settled down in front of her computer, logged in and checked her emails. For a moment she thought she was seeing things but there it was, an email from the Police Commissioners office. She clicked on it, and it opened. Well, that was odd. It was a direct request to attend a private meeting with Police Commissioner Edward Baker at headquarters at 11h00 on Wednesday…which was tomorrow. Georgina sat back perplexed. Either they were in big doodoo or something significant had happened. They had both only met the commissioner once when they had received their medals respectively a year apart. Georgina looked up at Captain Murphey's office; he was on his phone as usual and thankfully, Georgina was not on his radar. For now.

Her interest was indeed piqued because normally such a request would be routed through the precinct's captain. Clearly this had not been the case. She picked up her mobile and texted Paul.

Where are you?

A few minutes later he replied.

At the National Archives.

What? Didn't know that's where our suspects hang out.

You would be surprised. See you in an hour.

Make it thirty. Gotta big surprise for you.

Ah…you wanna propose to me?

If you were the last man on earth, I would date outside my species. Georgina grinned to herself. That would shut him up. There was another ping and she looked down.

Too cruel. See u in twenty. U'r dead meat.

Twenty minutes later Paul slumped down into his chair and glared across at Georgina.

"You are an ego assassin. I wonder how many men in your

life are now resident in looney bins, dribbling in straight jackets. You are cruel beyond words!" he said, feigning a broken heart with his hand on his chest.

Georgina laughed. "You will forgive me instantly when I tell you who we are seeing at 11h00 tomorrow…"

"You have ten seconds to spill the beans, or I will reach across this desk and strangle your scrawny little neck."

She wrote something on a sticky note and slid it across the desk to him. She wasn't about to announce anything with flappy ears Monica within earshot who was Murphey's private informer…and lover. Paul glanced at the note and his head shot up. He mouthed.

Are we in doodoo?

Georgina and Paul had a private vocabulary which annoyed their colleagues, but which delighted the two of them no end.

She grabbed another note and wrote…*If we are, best we elope. Now.*

He wrote back…*Sorry, you lost your chance. I'm taken.*

"Do we pay you two to pass childish notes or solve cases!" boomed Murphey. Both Georgina and Paul jumped in their seats. Good God Georgina thought, I wish he wouldn't sneak around like that! Monica at the next-door desk smirked whilst pretending to be fully absorbed with a document. Paul discreetly placed his hand over the note about the Police Commissioner and Georgina busied herself with the nearest file. Murphey glared at them both, growled and then went back to his office. Paul caught Georgina's eye and whispered.

"See you in the interview room in five." She nodded.

He got up, grabbed a file, slipping the Commissioner's appointment note inside whilst pretending to head to the copier machine. Georgina discreetly scribbled a few words on another sticky note and slid it over to Paul's desk, knowing full well that the moment she left her desk, Monica would sidle over and take a peek at the note to find out who they were seeing tomorrow. A few minutes later, Georgina made a show of picking up her coffee cup and headed for the interview room. Not ten seconds later, Monica looked around, saw that everyone else was fully absorbed in their work and moved towards Paul's desk. She surreptitiously leaned in sideways and turned over the note which read… *Monica and Murphey…who would have guessed!*

Monica straightened up abruptly and blushed a bright red, hastily beating a retreat, scrunching up the note and throwing it in the wastepaper bin. Had it been that obvious she asked herself, now totally panicked. She had better let Captain Murphey know.

Georgina slipped into the interview room and told Paul what she had done. He burst out laughing shaking his head at Georgina's antics.

"You are incorrigible Georgie! I would love to have seen her face!" he added still chuckling.

Georgina grinned. It was good to see Paul like this; he was normally such a serious introverted character. Eventually they got down to business and they both discussed why they thought the Police Commissioner wanted to see them. Georgina said.

"Well, it couldn't be for any more medals. We've done that."

"It may well be about the Levenstein business," Paul ventured.

"Really? You think so?" asked Georgina. "How is that possible? I can't see how he could even know about it. Every shred of the DNA evidence was swiftly deleted off every system, probably by the FBI."

"Well perhaps he doesn't but we have been slap bang in the middle of a major shit show and perhaps he has gotten wind of it. It's possible he just wants to find out what is going on," said Paul.

Georgina nodded, lost in thought as she clicked her pen on and off. Paul gently removed the pen from her hand and placed it on the table. She smiled.

"It's so easy to annoy you." Ignoring her comment, Paul continued.

"So…I think we should be prepared for any eventuality tomorrow. If he has heard about Simon, the lab, the FBI etcetera, what are we going to tell him?"

Georgina shrugged. "The truth I guess."

Paul nodded slowly but then he sat back and said, "Perhaps not all of it. Not yet."

"Why not?" asked Georgina.

"Well, let's be real," suggested Paul. "It took both of us a long time to get our heads around the fact that Levenstein is alive given the confirmation of his DNA. And yet, I still find myself doubting the possibility and plausibility. Hence my visit to the archives today."

"Well, what did you discover?" asked Georgina, her interest piqued.

"It's not a matter of what I discovered. It was a matter of looking at things with fresh eyes, seeing past what was presented to the world when Levenstein committed suicide in prison."

"Go on…," said Georgina.

"It would be better if I showed you, but we need time for that. And we don't have the time needed before we see the Commissioner. Don't forget we are both testifying in court this afternoon."

"Yes, I hadn't forgotten. We'll be drawn and quartered if we don't show," Georgina added. "And we have that insurance witness coming in tomorrow at nine," she reminded him.

"Okay…so we go to headquarters tomorrow, listen to the Commissioner and take it from there," suggested Paul.

"Agreed," said Georgina. "Coffee?"

"Yes please. And this time don't make me spill it all over myself!"

They both got up, Paul headed back to his desk and Georgina went via the coffee station. When she got back to her desk, Monica had turned her chair away from them to avoid any eye contact. Georgina and Paul exchanged looks as she handed him his coffee and sat down, both grinning, doing their best not to laugh. Georgina glanced towards Captain Hmmm's office. He was glaring at them, then quickly looked away. Yes, you idiot she thought to herself. You know that we know.

Paul mouthed to her…*how did you know?*

Georgina shook her head and sighed.

Women know everything.

CHAPTER ELEVEN

Brad Townsend sent an encrypted and untraceable email to Simon telling him that he would be in contact soon, but they were onto him which meant that someone would be following Simon too. *Be careful. I will be in touch… lie low for a while. Looking for info…*was the last sentence. The email had no salutation or sign off.

Simon sat back in his chair.

"WTF!" he exclaimed. Georgina had said the same thing to him. Bastards he thought to himself. It was now two and a half months since Georgina had brought the paper cup to him for analysis. *Enough!* he thought to himself. Time to start rattling some cages, time to let the lions out.

He swiveled in his chair, racking his brains as to who could still be called a journalist in this town. Since Covid, it had become patently obvious that the press, TV stations etcetera took their orders from government and big pharma, who in turn were obedient to their elite masters. To find a journalist with a set of balls was like looking for a saint in the Vatican. They were all just reporters now…reporting whatever narrative was dictated to them. What happened to the days when newspapers kept governments in check, questioning everything and were not intimidated by anyone? So, he crossed off the newspapers. TV stations were just as bad. They were off the list too. Well, it would have to be social media on one of the independent platforms since it appeared that all the main social media platforms were in the government's pockets too. Vile bunch of colluding pricks. Simon made a list of potential independent commentators with one at the top of his list; a fearless presenter who took no prisoners. The fact that this man was under constant attack was a clear indication of how close he was to the truth. How he would contact him would be very difficult since it appeared that the FBI were watching his every move. However, he had never been intimidated by anyone in his life; he was not about to start now, no matter how formidable the enemy was. And that was what the FBI had become, the enemy. They had allowed themselves to be become servants to the rich and powerful, and whilst there were still many good, dedicated agents, rot has a way of permeating into every nook and cranny. Hopefully sooner or later, this would dawn on the American people.

"You can go in now detectives," said Edward Baker's personal assistant Hillary. She added smiling.
"Coffee for both of you?"

"That would be lovely. Thank you." said Georgina. As they headed towards the Commissioner's office, Georgina and Paul exchanged looks which spoke volumes… *well if we are being offered coffee then that is a good sign. Perhaps we're not in doodoo after all.*

Police Commissioner Edward Baker looked up from his desk as Georgina and Paul stood to attention.

"As you were detectives," said Baker. "Please take a seat," and he indicated the two chairs in front of his desk.

"Thank you, sir," they both said in unison, sitting down. Once they were settled, Baker asked looking from one to the other.

"Do you know why you are here?"

"We have an idea sir," ventured Paul.

"Okay," said Baker leaning back in his chair. "Let's see if we are on the same page."

"Well sir…" began Paul. "Could this have something to do with the FBI?"

"Indeed, it does detective," said Baker. "I have heard via the grapevine that you two have been hampering an FBI investigation."

Georgina and Paul exchanged perplexed looks.

"With all due respect sir, it is in fact the other way around."

Hillary knocked softly on the door and brought in the

coffee. They were all silent as she placed the tray on the Commissioner's desk. Baker thanked her and she quietly left the room.

"Go on..." he said as he gestured for them to help themselves to coffee. Paul continued.

"The FBI shut down an investigation before we could even initiate it. In fact, they confiscated all relevant evidence. Our evidence sir."

Paul then looked at Georgina and she took the cue.

"We came across some evidence quite by accident, whilst working on a totally unrelated case. We lodged what we thought was evidence for our case with the forensic laboratory and were indeed shocked by the result. The result was automatically red flagged on the system which immediately caught the attention of the FBI, no doubt because it could have far reaching consequences. As Detective Damote mentioned sir, the evidence was confiscated by the FBI and from that point on, we were told to forget about it, as if nothing had ever happened. In fact sir, we were told that it was a direct order from the director of the FBI."

"But you didn't forget about it, did you?" ventured Baker.

"No sir. We didn't. It's not our job to forget," said Georgina politely.

Baker looked at them for a long time.

"Do you still have any proof in your possession pertaining to this evidence that you say potentially has far reaching consequences?" he asked. Georgina and Paul looked at each other.

"Yes sir, we do," she replied. Paul added hastily.

"We are however still piecing the puzzle together sir,"

"So, to all intents and purposes, you both decided to ignore a supreme order from the director of the FBI and are still involved in the matter albeit in your own capacities?" Baker looked at them quizzically.

"With all due respect sir, our supreme orders come from you, not the director of the FBI," said Paul steadily, not breaking eye contact with Baker.

There was just a hint of a smile from the commissioner as he held Paul's gaze.

"That is correct," said Baker "And when do you think you will have completed this puzzle?"

"Difficult to say sir," replied Paul.

"And in your estimation, how many people know about this?" Baker asked.

"Within the FBI sir, we have no idea. Outside of the FBI…both of us, the forensic scientist, Dr. Chevalier at the laboratory…and Captain Murphey," Paul answered.

Baker sat back in his chair placing his fingers together like a steeple. After a lengthy silence he said.

"Conjecture is dangerous, but facts can be even more dangerous, depending on which side of the truth one is on." He continued "You are both exemplary police officers and detectives and I trust in your judgement and integrity. I ask that you gather as many facts together as possible, and when you have semi completed the puzzle, with enough of the pieces in place so that a picture is emerging, you are to come back to me. As an exception to the rule, I ask that you contact my personal assistant directly to make an appointment to see me. Furthermore, you are not to discuss this with any of your colleagues, your boss, friends, or family. Have I made myself clear?" asked Baker looking from one to the other.

"Yes sir" replied Georgina and Paul together.

"Thank you. You may go," said Baker.

They both stood up and stood to attention.

"Thank you, sir," said Paul.

Baker nodded. As they turned to leave the room, Baker added.

"Be careful out there detectives."

"Will do sir." replied Paul and with that they left the commissioner's office.

As they entered the lift, they both exhaled deeply looking at each other wide-eyed. Well, that was one for the books!

Only once they were well clear of the building did Paul turn to Georgina saying.

"Well let's get 'em partner!" and they both high-fived each other and laughed. Then Georgina sobered.

"We're going to have to be very careful Paul. We are dealing with people who have no compunction in sweeping troublesome chess pieces off the board. Strange that he didn't ask for specifics," she added frowning.

"Not necessarily…I think he's the type of man who approaches everything in a very measured way. And besides, he may know more than he is letting on. So, regarding our way forward, no discussions ever at the precinct. Nothing on our emails or mobiles," said Paul making the scouts honour sign.

"Agreed," said Georgina, smiling to herself as she remembered as a child how she had refused point blank to join the Girls Guides organization since she considered herself far more suitable as a Boys Scout. She had voiced her opinion very clearly to her parents. She laughed inwardly at the memory, recalling how her mother had admonished her whilst her father had given her the thumbs up from behind her mother's back.

When they got back to their desks, there was a note from Murphey advising them that he wanted a full appraisal of all their cases on his desk first thing on Monday morning ahead of their performance review which was coming up the following week. Sighing Georgina said.

"You would swear Captain Hmmm has it in for us."

"No! You think?" said Paul wide eyed. He continued "Make us some coffee woman and make it snappy. Know your place."

Georgina smiled and asked him sweetly.

"My dear partner, would you like to drink your coffee…or wear it?"

CHAPTER TWELVE

Simon came out of the sterile lab, removed his latex gloves and disposable goggles, threw them in the trash and sat down at his desk. His personal laptop pinged, indicating a new email. This one was from a friend called Julian Leyton confirming their weekend hiking getaway in Simon's favourite hiking area, the Catskill Mountains, which was about two hours' drive from New York City. He said that he would send a location pin where the cabin was located. He ended his email with…*it will be great to catch up buddy!*

Simon laughed out loud. Firstly, he had never heard of anyone by the name of Julian Leyton, secondly, he hated hiking and thirdly, he had never been near the Catskill Mountains! Good on your Brad! The FBI goons would have a hard time following them there. Still chuckling, he replied to the email thanking Julian for arranging everything adding that he was really looking forward to seeing him again. He ended the email with a question… *any females coming?* If his emails were being monitored which he was pretty sure that they were, *they* would view this hopefully as merely a get together of two single buddies getting back to nature, in more ways than one.

He would have to let Georgina know about this arrangement as they had planned to meet for lunch on the Saturday. He texted her advising that he was going away for the weekend, asking her if he could take a rain check. *No problem, have fun!* she replied. He didn't mention anything about hiking as he knew that if he did, she would be rolling about laughing clutching her sides at such a notion. That would give the game away.

Director Len Wyatt drummed his fingers on his desk, lost in thought. Ryder Mullens and Seb Collins waited patiently for him to speak.

"So, you are absolutely sure that both detectives visited the NYPD headquarters?" asked Wyatt looking at Collins.

"Yes, absolutely sure sir. However, I couldn't determine who they saw there or what their purpose was. I managed to look at the visitor's log and they went to the 7th floor," answered Collins.

"The commissioner is on the 15th floor," mused Wyatt, rubbing his chin.

"Could be to do with the insurance case they are working on sir. I know that most of the white-collar fraud records are kept on the 7th floor," added Collins.

Wyatt swiveled his attention to Mullens. "And our nosy scientist? What has he been up to?"

"Not much sir. He hasn't been in contact again with Agent Townsend and he seems to be snowed under with work. He's going hiking this weekend. I checked out the email source of the guy he is meeting there. All seems legit," said Mullens.

"Seems or is?" asked Wyatt and then he went on coldly. "I don't want to hear about possibilities, only certainties, and that applies to both of you."

"Well then sir…I am certain that it is just a weekend away in the mountains," said Mullens feeling somewhat annoyed by the director's sarcasm.

"And what about the NYPD?" he looked squarely at Collins.

"I will go back to headquarters sir and see if I can find out who Harris and Damote met with," said Collins.

"Why didn't you do that in the first place?" snapped Wyatt. Both ghosts knew better than to answer.

"That is all," said Wyatt shaking his head and the two men got up to leave. As they neared the door Wyatt barked.

"You, Mullens, get your hiking boots on and watch Chevalier's every move this weekend. We can't assume anything. And you Collins, I want to know who the detectives met with at headquarters, who that person's grandma is and what she had for breakfast! You are both getting slack! Now get out!"

They both scuttled out and after they had gone, his secretary knocked softly on his door and popped her head around.

"Sir, I have Special Agent Stonehouse here to see you…he doesn't have an appointment but said that he was sure you would…"

"No, I don't!" roared Wyatt cutting her off. His secretary jumped. "Tell him to make an appointment like everyone else!"

"Yes sir," she said meekly, softly closing the door.

"God in hell!" muttered Wyatt to himself. "It's like Grand Central here!"

Wyatt sat back and glared out of the window, then suddenly leaning forward again, he pressed the buzzer.

"Yes sir?" his secretary said timidly.

"Get me coffee!" He barked.

"Yes sir. Right away," she answered.

Wyatt's secretary apologized profusely to Stonehouse making an excuse that the director was very busy, but Stonehouse had heard Wyatt yelling and was furious at the rejection. His fragile little ego had built up the scenario that Wyatt held him in high regard. Well, he would just have to prove himself further. His ultimate goal was to be sitting in that very office. Absolutely no one was going to stand in his way.

As Wyatt sipped his coffee, he was contemplating everything that had happened up until now. Something did not feel right. Everything was too calm. Originally it seemed like the two detectives and the forensic guy had acquiesced to Stonehouse's clumsy threats. But now he was not so sure. And the commissioner's coolness worried him too. He hadn't seemed worried at all about the veiled threat regarding the club. No, he thought to himself…he had honed his instincts over the years, and he knew this was the calm before the storm. Now he just had to make damn sure that he had weather insurance firmly in place.

Well, that seems odd thought Mullens. For a guy who supposedly loves hiking, why was Chevalier buying hiking boots and hiking gear? Perhaps Wyatt was right. Better not to assume anything. At the same time, Collins was back at the NYPD posing as a messenger from the Midtown North Precinct. When he got to the 7th floor, he made an excuse that he had lost the paper with the information regarding who he was supposed to deliver a file to, thus having an excuse to enquire as to who detectives Harris and Damote had seen the previous day. No problem said one of the secretaries…she looked up the sign-in register and confirmed that they had been there lodging documents but had not in fact had an appointment with anyone. She offered him her desk phone to call the detectives to find out who he should give the file to. He said not to worry, apologizing for any inconvenience, and thereafter making a hasty retreat. She smiled sweetly at him, and he could have sworn she was flirting with him. Idiotic woman he thought.

As soon as he was out of the building, he texted Wyatt to reassure him that the detectives' visit to the NYPD headquarters checked out as purely work related. What he didn't fully appreciate was that he was trailing seasoned detectives and they had coordinated a work-related visit to the seventh floor with the express purpose that it would act as a smokescreen for the real reason that they were there. After lodging the documents, they headed back to the elevator, but instead of returning to the ground floor they had continued up to the fifteenth floor for their meeting with the commissioner. On exiting the building Paul had spotted Collins and he hoped that their ruse had worked. It had.

On Friday morning, Paul suggested to Georgina that they go to the National Archives and then onto the New York Library. He wanted to show her what he had ascertained from all the recorded press clipping, photos, and footage of Levenstein's suicide in the Metropolitan Correctional Centre. Ahead of getting there, he told Georgina that they would split up about a block away and that he would meet her inside. She looked at him quizzically but didn't argue. She knew that whatever Paul did, it was for a good reason.

So, a block away they split up. This left Collins in a quandary. Who should he follow? Predictably he followed Detective Harris, considering her to be the prime target. Perfect. This offered Paul the opportunity he wanted to double back and come up behind Collins. He kept a safe distance so that he wouldn't be spotted. Once he had seen Collins go into the archive building, he stopped off and bought three coffees. He found Georgina easily enough and winked at her when she looked pointedly at the three coffees in his hands, eyebrows raised. He put down two of the them. Collins had positioned himself just out of sight but within earshot and was pretending to study a document when Paul came up behind him, leant across him and placed the coffee in front of him saying.
"We are going to be here for a while mate. Insurance cases are very long winded and boring. Thought you might enjoy a coffee…on us."
Collins looked up, his face darkening with anger. He said nothing. Paul then said.

"Why don't you just fuck off? You are an absolute amateur. I am sure the Police Commissioner would love to hear that the FBI is tailing two of his detectives. Tell your boss to back off, or we will make his life a misery."

"You've no idea who you are dealing with!" spat Collins.

"Oh, but we do. The question is, does your director know who he is dealing with?" said Paul, his expression hard. Collins glared at him, got up and left, leaving the coffee untouched. Paul chuckled and returned to Georgina telling her what had just transpired. She laughed, promising to give him a gold star on their return to the precinct. She even promised with a mischievous smile that he could choose where he wanted it. Paul rolled his eyes…this woman was incorrigible. Down to business.

Paul took Georgina through at least thirty photos of the Levenstein suicide. He focused mainly on the exterior photos of Levenstein being wheeled out of the detention center on a gurney. His running commentary included the fact that usually a body would be brought out either in a body bag or covered with a sheet. Levenstein was in full view on the gurney. It appeared that the powers that be were trying too hard to show the world that it was Levenstein himself on that gurney and not a stand-in body under a sheet. Then there was a fleeting moment when a paramedic placed an oxygen mask over Levenstein's face; not exactly normal practice with a corpse one would say. Furthermore, Levenstein's skin colour clearly did not have the pallor of a dead person and lastly and most importantly, he showed no evidence of the injuries caused by hanging, self-inflicted or inflicted. To emphasize the point, Paul showed Georgian photos of people who had suffered hanging both by suicide and homicide. This was not new to her. The photos were grotesque; some of them had their tongues swollen, extending out of their mouths. Some of victims' eyes were bulging and all of them had a purple hue to their skin. Levenstein had none of these critical signs. He looked like he was simply asleep. They also looked at some of the police photos showing redness on the back of his neck, a poor attempt at supporting the notion of self-inflicted strangulation. The whole scenario simply did not add up.

Georgina sat back in her chair shaking her head.
"God Paul, you are right!" she said. "I have attended enough suicides and homicides involving hanging to know what a hanged person looks like post-mortem."
She shook her head and then continued.
"You know what…I watched a four-part docuseries on Levenstein, and I remember towards the end of the last

episode, watching his body being brought out on the gurney and I distinctly remember that something worried me about that moment captured by the news media, but at the time, I couldn't work out what was bothering me. Now it is clear. He simply looked like he was asleep."

Paul nodded his head slowly and then asked Georgina. "Do you want to hear my theory?"

"Most definitely," she replied.

Paul looked around. Satisfied that no one was within earshot he began.

"Firstly, we know that the guards admitted that they hadn't done their rounds and check-ups on the inmates as per the required protocol. Secondly, the cameras in that section of the detention centre where Levenstein was being held were inoperable at that time. Neither were coincidences. Three days before his arrest Levenstein transferred vast sums of money and assets to nobody knows where, although I am pretty sure the FBI knows only too well. My theory is that the pedo cabal never wanted Levenstein to go to prison *or* to fall off his perch. They wanted him alive and free to continue business as usual. It was part of their honour code since he was the spider in the centre of the vast web of human trafficking and it is even possible that the arrest was a ruse."

Georgina was looking at Paul intently, concentrating on

his every word. Paul continued.

"My theory is that he was put into an induced coma which would not have been difficult to do with all the security cameras not recording anything… hence the reason why the paramedic topped up his oxygen momentarily on the gurney outside the prison. That is how they got him out of there. They ensured that the whole world saw Levenstein on that gurney. And even if people didn't believe the suicide story, they were none the less satisfied that he was dead, even if it was murder. He was gone, finito, popped his clogs, pushing up daisies."

Paul made a slicing gesture across his throat. Georgina was nodding, deep in thought.

"Job done and dusted. That was until we came along," she said leaning forward, examining the photos again. She continued.

"Yep, I think you're right partner. This was a faked suicide and the whole world was suckered in," she murmured. Paul then said.

"Let's go to the library and I will show you the footage that clearly underpins my theory."

They closed the file and returned it to the librarian. They left the Archives and headed to the New York library, both casting their eyes around, looking to see if they were being followed. The coast looked clear. When they got to the library, Paul went through the scenario again, this time with video footage shot by the various news stations. Same story; Levenstein simply did not look like a corpse.

"They really slipped up in the make-up department. They should have had a professional make-up artist make him look like the real thing," said Paul.

"Do you think this theory is enough to go back to the commissioner? Plus, the printout and the paper cup with the DNA that Simon has?" asked Georgina. "We have in fact got a substantial amount of evidence if you think about it."

Paul was silent for a while.

"No…I don't think so." He was processing something in his mind, so Georgina waited. Then he looked at her.

"Georgina, we *must* find Levenstein. We have to identify him definitively, how he looks now. He would most definitely have had facial altering surgery."

"How in the hell are we going to do that?" asked Georgina throwing up her hands. "All the surveillance footage from the Starbucks and a five-block radius was confiscated by the FBI. We have no way of identifying him."

"I know. But if this whole thing is blown wide open now, he will simply vanish and the chances of finding him and bringing the whole cabal down will be zero," said Paul.

"What if we were able to get hold of the CCTV footage

that the FBI confiscated from the street where we had seen Johnny Salome?" asked Georgina. Paul shook his head.

"We will never get our hands on any of it. It may even have been destroyed already. No…I say we work out a way to identify Levenstein and then we can go to the commissioner," said Paul.

"Okay…" conceded Georgina. She thought for a while and then said "The printout is secure in my father's safe but what about the cup? I think we should ask Simon if we can rather take care of it. I am concerned about him becoming a target, that is of course if they find out that the evidence they confiscated was bogus. We can't assume they won't find out at some point in time."

"Yes, I agree. Perhaps we should do that as soon as possible," Paul said.

"He has gone away for the weekend. I'll get hold of him first thing on Monday," said Georgina.

"Okay good. Do you think the cup can go into your father's freezer? Paul asked.

"No problem with him. He probably doesn't even know where his freezer is. His ditsy wife may be an issue. Let me think on it. It would be the best place as I doubt anyone would think about the evidence being there. Besides, imagine trying to get a search warrant for Supreme Judge Harris's home!"

They both laughed and headed back to the precinct.

Collins was too embarrassed to tell Wyatt about his screw up in the archives, so he texted him saying that the detectives were working on their various cases and gave no indication of interest in the issue at hand. Wyatt ordered him to continue his surveillance 24/7. Collins sighed. What a prick he thought. Well, he was being paid a shit load of money, so if that was what Wyatt wanted, then he would oblige. He would just be a bit economical with the truth when it suited him.

CHAPTER THIRTEEN

Special Agent Stonehouse was hard at work trying to determine where all the original evidence on Levenstein had been secreted away. Certainly, the evidence was not where it should have been, that being in the NYPD Evidence Storage facility in Brooklyn which he knew for a fact was where it had been lodged over four years ago. In terms of who had subsequently collected it and where it had been taken to, the trail was cold, and all information had been deleted. He was not only looking for the evidence from when Levenstein had originally been arrested but also for the more recent evidence that he himself had confiscated from Chevalier's laboratory. All the boxes had been delivered to the evidence storage by himself personally but appeared to have been quickly relocated. Too quickly for comfort. Probably for the same reason the original evidence was moved. To protect very powerful people. So, if he could find where it had been moved to, then that would demonstrate to Director Wyatt how valuable he was to seek out any small cracks in the armor. He was confident that Wyatt would be impressed beyond words.

One of Stonehouse's special talents was hacking. Beyond that he was a pretty useless agent due to his need to have his ego constantly boosted. Discretion, lateral thinking, efficiency and no desire for accolades or recognition are the best qualities in an FBI agent. Stonehouse had none of these. As he navigated the classified FBI sites, the most important thing he thought to himself was to cover his tracks so that no one would even know that he was looking. He was not concerned. He considered himself to be a highly talented hacker, probably the best the FBI had. Modesty did not come naturally to Stonehouse.

However, when it came to hacking, Agent Brad Townsend was way ahead of Stonehouse, and he sat back in his chair wondering what Stonehouse was up to. He had been looking for the same thing and suddenly he became aware that someone was running a parallel enquiry. After *hacking the hacker,* he managed to identify Stonehouse. Well, he would keep an eye on him and see if his efforts led anywhere. Prior to joining the FBI, Brad had been one of the most elusive and competent hackers in the world but had finally been caught in a sting operation. He never forgave himself for the mistake that had led to his arrest. He knew that it was unlikely that any defense lawyer could help him, especially since he had hacked into multiple classified sites. He had tried to escape to the UK but had been stopped at Kennedy airport. The choice was obvious…prison for a very long time or working for the FBI. Naturally he chose the latter. This was not common knowledge and in fact, his entire previous criminal history had been expunged. If anyone ever investigated Brad Townsend, they would find an exemplary individual who had not so much as a parking violation to his name. He knew that Simon had no idea of what he had been up to after university when they had lost contact and he had inwardly winced when Simon had attributed a strong moral compass to him. He certainly did not qualify for that, but he did share Simon's abhorrence of pedophiles. That they most certainly did have in common. And the truth be known he was glad to be in touch again with Simon. They had been good mates at university.

He entered multiple codes and created an invisible tag on Stonehouse and then doubled up on his own anonymity. This would be interesting he thought to himself to see who found the prize first. He shut down his computer system and packed the last few things for the weekend away with Simon. He was looking forward to it. It would be like old times with a bit of intrigue in the mix.

Mullens homed in on the log cabin with his military grade binoculars and watched Simon and his mate Julian carry their backpacks and supplies from the pick-up truck into the cabin. Both were wearing peak caps so at first, he wasn't sure who was who. However, when Julian removed his cap to swot a fly, he suddenly realized that he was looking at none other than Agent Brad Townsend. He whistled to himself…the sneaky bastard!

Mullens had intercepted the text message with the location pin sent to Simon's mobile and was in place shortly before the guys arrived. There were only four cabins in this part of the secluded woods, and he felt secure in the knowledge that they had no idea he was there, safely ensconced in the next-door cabin about two hundred feet away. When Brad and Simon had driven past the first three cabins, they all looked unoccupied with the drapes drawn and unswept leaves on the front porches. There were no vehicle tyre tracks anywhere either. Their cabin, the fourth one, had been cleaned and prepared and was the last one in the row, so they were pretty sure that no one else was around. Mullens would make sure they would never see or hear him. It wasn't too long before Simon and Brad set off towards the lake down a narrow path through the forest with a cooler box no doubt containing beers and snacks.

Mullens watched them go and waited a full ten minutes before he made his move. He exited his cabin from the back door, took a wide circuitous route to their cabin and quietly slipped in unnoticed. Within fifteen minutes he had rigged the microphones; one in the kitchen and one in the front living room. He tested them both and once he was satisfied that they were not only well hidden but were functioning perfectly, he slipped out the back door and returned to his cabin. It was going to be long cold weekend for him. No warmth from a fire or even a lamp for when it was dark. Such was the work he did. Discomfort went with the territory.

Even though it was spring, there was still a chill in the air and when Brad and Simon returned, they lit the fire and started cooking. Their chatter was fairly inane about their university days but later after they had eaten, they settled into the large armchairs on either side of the fireplace and their focus turned to the Levenstein affair.

"All the evidence that the FBI took from the various Levenstein residences has vanished. No records, no trace. This must go all the way to the top Simon," said Brad.

"Yep. No surprise there. To be honest, I am still finding it hard to comprehend that the bastard is alive and kicking, but the DNA was absolutely conclusive," replied Simon.

"And all those captains of industry and big tech, not to mention presidents and politicians, and God…I almost forget royalty…they all deny having anything more than a casual acquaintance with him. Lying bastards. They all visited his illicit island and flew on his mile-high fuck wagon," said Brad with contempt in his voice.

"So, the question is, how are we going to take them all down?" asked Simon.

"Very carefully. We're not just playing with fire mate. We're playing with military grade thermite. It makes TNT look like kiddies' playdough." cautioned Brad.

"Yeah…" mused Simon. "I remember where else that was used. That was also a case of literally burying the evidence under mountains of rubble. Another beer buddy?"

Brad nodded. Simon continued as he fetched a beer from the fridge.

"So…let's go through what we have. Firstly, Georgina has the printout confirming the DNA match and secondly, I have the actual DNA evidence," he said counting off his fingers. "And thirdly, the FBI have no idea that they have bogus evidence. What do you have Brad?"

Mullens sat bolt upright his eyes widening. My God! Did he hear that right? He pressed the headphones tighter on his head so that he wouldn't miss one syllable.

Brad cracked open the can and Mullens winced. It sounded like a gunshot in his headphones. He heard Brad taking a gulp. He must very close to the microphone.

"All of the original Levenstein evidence and the DNA records that Levenstein kept on his buddies, plus the stuff they took from your lab have been removed from the original secure evidence location in Brooklyn, and all records of who collected the evidence have been deleted. I am still looking for where everything was moved to. When I find it, that in itself would precipitate an enquiry. And I *will* find it Simon. It's only a matter of time."

"But should we wait until then?" asked Simon. "We have enough to blow this whole thing wide open, don't you think?"

"Not one single newspaper or TV station will touch this. They are all totally controlled by their paymasters," said Brad.

"Yes, I know, which is why I have identified a top social media personality who cannot be bought or silenced."

"Yes…?" said Brad his eyebrows raised. "Who?"

"Matt Logan," replied Simon.

"Hmmm…he's a good option but he's up to his eyeballs in lawsuits. Can he afford another? These entitled pricks have all the money in the world to bury him in a legal landslide," countered Brad.

"Not if he has the support of the only two senators who seem to have any balls," suggested Simon. "Congress will not be able to ignore this."

"You do realize that we're going up against the likes of Wyatt who not only takes no prisoners, but he can also make people spontaneously combust!" exclaimed Brad.

"But Brad…," said Simon. "This is the classic David and Goliath scenario…and guess who won that battle."

"Yes, but there are no guarantees," replied Brad. "First off, I think we need to brainstorm with your detective buddies. Four heads are better than two and from what I know about them, they're a pretty powerful team."

"That they are," agreed Simon imagining in his head Georgina and Wyatt in the boxing ring; it would not be a happy ending for Wyatt. He continued.

"So, let's set up a meeting asap. We must be very careful though. We are all being watched by the FBI goons… present company excluded."

"Not necessarily. Internal espionage is rife in the FBI, believe me," said Brad.

"I was referring to you not being a goon!" said Simon laughing and Brad rolled his eyes.

Simon stood up and yawned. "Okay buddy, I'm turning in. I want to be fresh to humiliate you on the trail tomorrow. It's gonna be a slaughter."

"Not a chance, not with those girlie booties you brought with you!" laughed Brad. "Real cheerleader stuff."

Simon clipped Brad on the back of his head as he made his way to his room.

"See ya in the morning bud. Night night."

Brad waved his hand dismissively.

"Try not to be afraid of the dark now. Black as ink here at night," he laughed.

A few minutes later, the cabin was silent. Mullens sat dumbfounded in the darkness. This couldn't wait. He had all the info he needed. He quietly packed up his gear, not concerned about leaving the microphones behind in the other cabin. Silently, he slipped out of the back door and headed towards where he had left his car about two miles away. He had excellent night vision, but it was so dark that he had no choice but to don his night vision goggles. The last thing he needed was to trip or fall. When he was back in mobile range, he texted Wyatt telling him that he had some critical information and needed to see him asap. It couldn't wait until morning. Wyatt texted back saying that he would wait up for him. *Message me when you're close by. I'll meet you in the pool house.*

Mullens fired up the engine and sped towards the local airstrip where he had left the Cessna. He would be in

Washington in three hours. He carried out a quick pre-flight, strapped in and turned the engine. He then keyed in the frequency to control the runway lights. It was a J type ARCAL system, so he clicked the mike five times and the runway lit up. Within minutes he was airborne.

Wyatt paced up and down his study, his anxiety levels rising as he wondered what was so urgent that Mullens had to see him tonight. Eventually he poured himself a double and settled in one of the sofas flanking the fireplace. Helen popped her head around the door.

"Are you not coming to bed darling? It's late."

He shook his head as she came over to him.

"I'll be up a bit later. I must attend to some matters. You go on ahead," and he tilted his head upwards as she leant down and kissed him.

It was two in the morning when Wyatt received a text from Mullens. He quietly let himself out of one of the porch doors and headed to the pool house. Mullens was waiting there for him.

"So, what's up?" asked Wyatt discarding any niceties or salutations.

"Detective Harris has the printout of Chad Levenstein's DNA," replied Mullens.

Wyatt groaned, shaking his head. Mullens continued.

"There's more, it gets worse sir. Dr. Chevalier has the actual DNA evidence. The evidence that Stonehouse thought he had confiscated was bogus."

"What?" exclaimed Wyatt. "That little prick Stonehouse! I am going to kick his ass so hard he's going to taste my shoe polish!"

"Also…" Mullens continued, "it turns out that the hiking friend was none other than Agent Townsend."

Wyatt stared at Mullens, his eyes wide.

"This is a quintessential shit show!" he exclaimed.

There was a long silence, filled by the gentle lapping of the water and the soft hum of the pool pump.

"So now what sir?" asked Mullens.

"We have to get our hands on the evidence," replied Wyatt. "I will formulate a plan of action but I'll need to consult with some people first. Then we'll have to move fast, very fast indeed."

"Okay. I will wait to hear from you sir." said Mullens turning to go.

"Mullens…," said Wyatt.

"Yes sir?" Mullens said looking back at him.

"Good work."

"Thank you, sir." And with that Mullens vanished into the darkness.

Wyatt returned to his study and fired off an email to Roy Sedgefield and Alan Turner.

We need to meet as a matter of urgency.

That was all he said. He finally went upstairs to bed, but sleep evaded him and by daybreak he had a thumping headache. He showered and dressed, telling Helen that he was going to have an important meeting at home and that he did not want to be disturbed under any circumstances.

At nine thirty, Sedgefield and Turner arrived at Wyatt's home, and they went straight to his study. Wyatt's expression was grim, and he wasted no time in bringing them up to speed with the latest developments.

"They have the proof that Levenstein is alive. They have the actual print out plus it transpires that our forensic scientist still has the original DNA. It appears that my agent confiscated bogus evidence which must have been the work of the forensic guy. No need to tell you that this is catastrophic. We are damned lucky they haven't exposed the whole thing yet. We must act fast and as soon as possible."

Both Sedgefield and Turner looked at each other shocked.

"How in the hell did that happen?" demanded Turner.

"What the hell does it matter!" barked Wyatt. "What matters now is how we contain the situation!"

"Okay…" said Sedgefield slowly. "So, what do you want us to do?"

"We have to silence Chevalier, the forensic scientist. We can't touch the detectives. That will bring a ton of shit down on us," said Wyatt. He continued. "I can't use anyone from my team…too close to home. I need one of you to arrange it."

The truth be known, Wyatt was in the position to do anything he wanted, but by getting one of these idiots to do the dirty work he was putting some distance between himself and a criminal act. Sedgefield and Turner looked at each other. Then Turner said to Sedgefield.

"Do you think you can use the same guy who did the oil deal hit?"

Sedgefield was thinking along the same lines of Wyatt and wanted to keep himself out of the firing line.

"No…he's gone to ground," he lied. "What about your guy who offed that stupid estate agent?" he said to Turner.

"It's going to cost us chaps," replied Turner.

"And what do you think it is going to cost us if we're all arrested?" demanded Wyatt. "Stop deliberating. Get everything lined up!"

"Okay!" exclaimed Turner. "Consider it done."

"No…" interjected Wyatt. "Wait for me to give you the go ahead. My team will first look for the DNA evidence in

Chevalier's apartment. I am pretty sure he has it there and we may have to coerce him into giving it to us before we eliminate him. We have someone in the lab who has been informing us of any goings on there and has checked Chevalier's lab. Nothing there. I will let you know when we have it in hand so your guy *must not* make a move until I tell you," said Wyatt looking at Turner. He continued. "And it would be best if this hit looks self-inflicted. Agent Stonehouse put it about that the guy had a nervous breakdown, so suicide is not out of the ballpark."

"Right, got it," said Turner nodding.

"That makes it less messy," said Sedgefield. "Good idea."

"What about the printout that the detective has?" asked Turner.

"Once the DNA is gone, it isn't even worth the paper it's printed on," said Wyatt. "Could be put down to a systems error."

"Good to know," said Turner.

Wyatt had decided that once the evidence had been found he would keep it safe in his sticky paws since it appeared that no one else could be trusted.

"Right, I must be off," said Sedgefield.

They all stood up, looked at each other momentarily, shook hands and then Sedgefield and Turner left Wyatt's house.

Wyatt sat down again after they had gone, sighing, and rubbing his temples. He felt very uneasy, not because they were planning to murder a top forensic scientist but because he felt things were spiraling out of control. At the end of the day, he could always finger Turner and Sedgefield. They didn't deserve the unspoken loyalty of the cabal and he had the power to massage the facts any which way he wanted to. However, an alternative plan was formulating in his mind and that was to blame Stonehouse, peg him as an overzealous agent who had gone rogue. In fact, that would please him no end. And then there was the issue of Brad Townsend. He had decided not to tell Turner and Sedgefield about him. They would start thinking that he had no control over the FBI. He sat back and commenced mapping out a strategy as to how he would direct events. Within minutes he had definitive direction. Suddenly feeling energized and with Helen and the kids out the way visiting her sister, he settled in front of his laptop, keyed in an access key and opened a secret site on the dark web. He sat back, enjoying the erotic rush wash over him as he watched videos of explicit sex with minors. He thought back to the little French girl and felt an immediate arousal and loosening his belt, he unzipped his fly so that he could massage his genitals whilst he thought about that night and watched the screen. It had been the best he had experienced to date. The way she had struggled had been unbelievably stimulating. She had been so small that he had to really force his way into her, and he remembered her warm virginal blood. He had also sodomized her and in fact, that had been even more arousing. There would be more like her. Levenstein could provide whatever Wyatt needed and in exchange, he would ensure that the world would never know that he personally had orchestrated Levenstein's fake suicide.

Wyatt never contemplated for one moment that he could be caught and disgraced for being a pedophile. In fact, he didn't even see himself like that. With the media being manipulated and controlled, pedophilia, transgenderism and all manner of deviancy was slowly being normalized. None of it evoked the same public outrage as it had in days gone by. It was all part of the woke agenda and those who dared to question any of it were cancelled, shadow banned, disgraced, and isolated. Deviancy was now seen as diversity, and even worse, sexual deviancy was becoming the new normal. The word pedophile was now frowned upon and regarded as unacceptable. Pedophiles were now known as MAPS. *Minor attracted persons.*

The world had gone mad. Literally.

CHAPTER FOURTEEN

When Simon got back to New York on Sunday evening, he texted Georgina to arrange for them to meet for lunch. It was after all her birthday on Tuesday he reminded her.

Would love to! And hey, I am out of perfume! she texted. Simon laughed. Such a vixen. *Consider it done!* he texted. Georgina sent a smiley face, adding…*And I want a new coffee cup!*

Simon sat back in his chair somewhat perplexed. *What?* he murmured to himself. Why in the world would she want a coffee cup? He texted *???…* and waited.

I want one like the one you have…the one that says Gotcha! It's my all-time fav.

Suddenly he clicked. She was referring to the Levenstein DNA cup. Simon considered what Georgina had just asked of him. It made sense; it was more likely that she could keep the Levenstein evidence safer than he could mainly because it was only a matter of time before they would work out that they had bogus evidence and would come looking for the original. No doubt she had a good plan as to where she would hide it. Probably in her father's freezer. He texted back.

Whatever the birthday girl wants, the birthday girl gets!

See you Tuesday 12h30 sharp at La Boheme. Don't be late! xxx.

Oooh! Georgina texted. *I am being spoilt! See you then. Mwah!*

On Tuesday morning he went down to the basement in his apartment building to his lock up garage. He took the Levenstein evidence out from its hiding place in the small countertop freezer. The Starbucks cup was in a sterile bag, with a further two bags for extra security. Inside another small, sealed plastic bag were the sterile glass slides with two samples of the DNA. Back in his apartment, he wrapped everything in bubble wrap, placed it carefully in a small cooler box with ice bricks, and then gift wrapped the box. He walked over to his briefcase and lifted out a bag containing an identical Starbucks cup. Sometimes his job was fun he thought to himself. It was in a sealed forensic bag, with some new bogus slides that he had put together in his lab plus everything necessary to make it look like the original Levenstein evidence. However, he had left a little surprise in the evidence bag, something to really annoy whichever arrogant FBI prick scrutinized everything. He then placed it in his freezer. If they did work out that the evidence they had was bogus, and if anyone who knew what they were doing did come looking for it, they would make a bee line for the freezer. What they wouldn't know is that they had been outwitted. Again.

On his way to work, he passed by Georgina's favourite perfumery and bought her something she would love. Hell, she was an expensive date! But then again, she was worth it. He loved spoiling her and her delight always thrilled him. A few hours later, he left to meet her at La Boheme. The restaurant was buzzing, and Simon looked around as he waited for Georgina. He assumed that he had been followed but to date he had never been able to spot the detail. He felt a soft kiss on the back of his neck and turned to see Georgina's sparkling eyes. He stood up and as they embraced, Simon buried his face in her neck.
"Why have I bought you perfume when you already smell so delicious my darling Gigi?" he murmured.
"A girl can never have too much perfume," she countered, laughing as she sat down. Simon shook his head, smiling. Lamb to slaughter.
"Well, I have ordered your favourite champers and while we wait, I shall present you with your gifts!"
With that he leant down and took out from a bag the beautifully wrapped perfume accompanied by handmade chocolates and presented them to her.

"Wow Simon! Did you rob a bank?" her eyes lit up as she unwrapped the Joy perfume from Jean Patou. "This is such an indulgence!"

"Only the very best for my girl," said Simon, delighted that she was happy.

"And these choccies! Briefly on the lips, forever on the hips!" Georgina exclaimed.

"Well, perhaps I can do a personal inspection later to see if that in fact is true…" he ventured.

"Whoa cowboy! I must get back to work after this!"

"I can wait…" said Simon winking at her. "Oh, and before I forget, I have the coffee cup you wanted so dearly!" He handed her the box.

"Thank you, my darling Simon. I shall leave it in the wrapping as no doubt it is fragile."

Their eyes met and a thousand words passed between them. The waiter poured the champagne and lifting their glasses, Simon said.

"A very happy birthday to my gorgeous Gigi!"

After they had both sipped their champagne, Simon leant in close and whispered in her ear that there was also a burner phone in the package loaded with the number of his burner phone. She nodded, fully understanding his reasons and squeezed his hand under the table.

Their food arrived and they both sat back to enjoy the sheer culinary delights that La Boheme was famous for.

"Wow, this is sublime," said Georgina, closing her eyes in ecstasy.

"Mine too," said Simon. "Oh…before I forget, can you and Paul make dinner tomorrow evening at my place? I want you to meet Brad my FBI mate. He suggested that the four of us have a brainstorming session."

"Yes…of course," replied Georgina. "I will check with Paul, but I am pretty sure he can make it. I'll confirm in the morning,"

"Great. Now even more people get to experience my brilliant cooking skills," laughed Simon.

"But clearly not your modesty," retorted Georgina.

Mullens slipped on a pair of latex gloves and paper booties after the superintendent had let him into Simon's apartment. It is amazing how the mere words *gas leak* open a myriad of doors. The concierge had tried to reach Simon, but he was not answering his mobile. Not surprising with the noise and clamor of the restaurant. Mullens set about looking for the evidence. Of course, there was no guarantee that it was there, but he was going to give it a good shot. He knew that he had about a twenty-minute window before suspicions would be aroused with the super. He made straight for Simon's freezer as that would be the ideal and obvious place to store the evidence. Within a few minutes he had found it, hiding in plain sight in a fast-food box. He rolled his eyes…for a forensic scientist, Dr. Chevalier was indeed quite the amateur. He immediately texted Wyatt. *Got it*! He looked around the apartment to be sure that he hadn't disturbed anything. All looked fine. Had he looked a little harder though, he may have noticed one or two of the hidden cameras. The thing about arrogance, is that it makes people overconfident and then they start making mistakes; errors that sooner or later could cost them dearly.

Wyatt felt a sense of relief wash over him. He wasted no time in letting Sedgefield and Turner know that all was in hand. Mullens was on his way from New York to Washington and would deliver the evidence personally to him that evening. This time, he himself would keep it safe. Or perhaps he should destroy it.

Is it still necessary to take care of the forensic guy? texted Turner. Wyatt weighed up the options for a moment. Chevalier no longer had the evidence so no matter what he said, he would not be able to back anything up with proof. In fact, he would probably look like a conspiracy theory nut. After some deliberation, he texted Turner.

No need. The guy is not stupid. With the evidence gone, he'll know the game is up and it would be better to keep his mouth shut.

Four hours later Mullens arrived in Washington with the evidence. Later that evening, Wyatt locked his study door and carefully opened the forensic box and placed each piece of evidence on his desk. There was a small envelope which he carefully opened. Ah…another printout of the DNA. This was good. As he folded it again something caught his eye. The identifying name wasn't Levenstein. It was Chevalier. That's odd. Perhaps it was stating who had processed the forensic material. He peered closer, then felt himself go cold. It stated clearly that the DNA belonged to Dr. Simon Chevalier. Wyatt sat there frozen, feeling his mouth go dry. He tipped the envelope and out fell a photo of Mullens outside Chevalier's apartment building, but the final humiliation was still to come. A torn piece of paper fell to the floor with one word written on it. GOTCHA!

Wyatt roared with anger, violently sweeping everything off his desk onto the floor. He sat there stunned, absolutely fuming, breathing heavily. This was now war! Dr. Chevalier had gone too far. Nobody, but nobody humiliates the director of the FBI. He grabbed his mobile and punched in the code name for Mullens.

"Get back to Washington asap!" he yelled. Then he threw the mobile across the room, unable to contain his rage.

CHAPTER FIFTEEN

Back in New York, Georgina arrived at her father's apartment to have dinner with him and Lola. Not ideal celebrating her birthday with Lola from La La Land, but what could be done.

"Hi Dad!" said Georgina, hugging her father when he opened the door.

"Happy birthday my darling girl!" he said, embracing her warmly.

"Thank you. I hope you and Lola haven't made a five-course dinner. Simon spoilt me rotten at La Boheme today."

"Hmmm…lucky girl. Nope, I am afraid it's takeout tonight," her father said shrugging.

Well, that was a surprise. Georgina looked at him and could immediately sense that something was different. She put down her bag and asked.

"What's up Dad? Are you okay? Where's Lola?"

Her father sighed and then said "Well that's just it. There is no Lola."

"What *are* you talking about Dad?" asked Georgina, her eyes wide.

"Looks like you were right. Lola loves lolly! She left me

for a much richer man. About two weeks ago."

"What? Oh Dad! I am so sorry!" exclaimed Georgina moving towards him.

"No, you're not," he waggled his finger at her and then he smiled. "But…you were right all along. Believe it or not, it is somewhat of a relief for me. She was tiring me out with all her endless spending and one upmanship with her equally shallow friends."

Georgina reached up and hugged her father.

"I am truly sorry Dad. Even if it's ultimately a good thing, it is still awful for you to go through this. What's going to happen with the apartment?" she asked.

"Nothing. The divorce will be uncomplicated. She wants it to go through as quickly as possible so that she can strike while the iron is hot and nail the next poor bastard. Besides, she had wheedled a lot out of me already. And I doubt she will part with all the jewelry and the flashy Mercedes Benz I bought her."

"Good riddance!" exclaimed Georgina shaking her head.

"C'mon kiddo. Let's have a fabulous bottle of wine with some delicious beef Teriyaki, courtesy of the takeout around the corner."

"Sounds perfect," Georgina smiled and linking arms, they headed to the kitchen.

When Simon got home that evening, the concierge handed him a note from the superintendent advising him that a gas technician had checked a suspected gas leak in his apartment. Hmmm…is that so, thought Simon. He immediately checked the cameras. Wow! So, they had come looking. That was a close shave getting the evidence to Georgina, although he doubted they would have found the real evidence where he had previously hidden it. His car was parked in the open area of the underground garage of his apartment building, and it probably wouldn't have occurred to them to check if he had a lock up. However, it was never sensible to underestimate the enemy.

He poured himself some wine and settled comfortably on his sofa so that he could enjoy the show. At one point, he laughed out loud watching the guy Georgina had snapped a photo of, creeping around his apartment. What a jerk! He downloaded the footage and sent it to Georgina's burner phone with a covering comment, *Comedy Hour!* He then sent it to Brad via the encrypted email address that Brad had first contacted him on. However, Simon doubted that Brad would find it so amusing given that he was FBI himself. He probably would find it very embarrassing because there was no doubt that this guy had to be associated with the FBI, one way or another.

After dinner, while her father was rummaging around for something sweet to have for dessert, Georgina checked her mobile and the burner phone. She saw the message and gasped at the video of guy who had been tailing Simon, creeping around his apartment. She had been wanting to broach the subject with her father to keep the DNA evidence in his freezer, but given his position as a supreme judge, that made it complicated and she would be skirting around the edges of ethical conduct.

"Dad…" she said when he walked back into the room.

"Ah…that tone of voice always makes me nervous," he said with a twinkle in his eye. "Okay…what does my darling girl want?"

"I'm not going to burden you with too many details or compromise you in any way…suffice to say that I need a place to keep something safe for a short while and here would be the perfect place. In your freezer."

Her father raised his eyebrows. "Not a body I hope?"

Georgina laughed and then continued.

"No…not a body! Not this time. But it is very sensitive, and if you don't know what it is, then there can't be any real harm in it, right?" she said tentatively.

"Well, I could be cited for aiding and abetting a criminal, hiding state evidence…" replied her father feigning consternation.

"Hmmm…," said Georgina. "But that would only be if you *knew* that it was evidence. It could be for example, an important piece of venison steak…" her voice trailed off.

Her father shook his head and placed his hands on her shoulders.

"Sweetheart, I trust your judgement implicitly and if you must keep something safe in an unconventional manner, then I have no doubt that you know what you are doing. Mind you, as you said, I cannot know what it is," he added.

"Thank you, Dad. I appreciate you trusting me on this. If I may, I would like to pop by tomorrow on my way to Simon's. Paul and I are having dinner with him and a friend of his. A brainstorming session."

"No problem my darling. Always good to see my most favourite daughter," he replied.

"You only have one daughter," said Georgina dryly. "In fact, only one child."

"Yes…but there is no harm in ingratiating myself with my one and only offspring," he chuckled. "Besides, other than you late mother, you're the only female I can trust."

"Well, that's true! However, there is one more thing…"

"Oh, yes…and what is that?" he said rolling his eyes.

"There just happens to be an important document amongst my papers in your safe too," ventured Georgina.

Her father laughed and shook his head.

"You are incorrigible young lady! But no problem. I won't peak. It will be safe there. C'mon, let's go to my study. There's no dessert and I need a scotch. My daughter is driving me to drink!"

Wyatt met Mullens in the pool house just after midnight. He was not going to risk Helen over hearing any of the conversation he was about to have. He told him about the bogus evidence created by Dr. Chevalier for the second time and he registered the look of shock on Mullen's face. "I am so sorry sir," began Mullens but Wyatt stopped him. "You couldn't have known. It's done. Let's move on."

With that he outlined his plan to Mullens. Chevalier had to be eliminated and he was going to pin it on Stonehouse. Simple as that. Mullens would have to look again for the evidence but if he didn't find it, it wasn't too serious. If Chevalier had hidden it so well, that meant that it was not likely to be found by anyone else, any time soon. So, the plan was that Mullens had to get to New York asap and gain access to Chevalier's apartment again. Wyatt would ensure that Agent Stonehouse would visit Chevalier the following evening with instructions to intimidate him into silence. A complete ruse, but Stonehouse wasn't to know that. He would also be instructed to tell the concierge that he was Detective Damote. He was to flash his badge but not close enough for inspection. The concierge would then call Simon asking permission to send Damote up.

"How can we be sure that Chevalier will be at home tomorrow evening?" asked Mullens.

"'Our lab spy overhead him say that he was going to leave the lab a little earlier tomorrow since detectives Harris, Damote and another mate would be coming over for dinner at six thirty," replied Wyatt. He continued.

"So, Chevalier will be expecting Detective Damote. It is very important that the concierge can testify if it comes to it, that it was without a doubt Simon's voice on the intercom giving permission for Damote to go up to his apartment. Of course it will become clear later that it was in fact Stonehouse masquerading as Damote."

Mullens nodded, analyzing and absorbing every detail. Wyatt continued to lay out the plan. It was in that small window of opportunity that Mullens had to kill Chevalier *and* preferably make it look like a suicide. If time didn't allow for the latter, then no big deal. Ultimately, Stonehouse would be fingered anyhow. Mullens was to leave the front door of Chevalier's apartment ajar after he had killed him, so that Stonehouse would walk into the apartment thinking that Chevalier had left it open for

Damote when in fact, Stonehouse would be walking straight into a trap. It was up to Mullens how he got out of the building, but he was to make sure that no one saw him. If at some point in time there was an enquiry…for example if the coroner did not agree on the cause of death as suicide, then the only person who could possibly have done it, would be Stonehouse. All the evidence would point to him.

A rogue agent. A perfect plan.

CHAPTER SIXTEEN

The next morning, although Wyatt's anger still raged inside of him, he did feel somewhat calmer. He knew though that he still had to do some damage control with Agent Townsend. He was not sure how to contain that particular situation but first things first; he had to silence Chevalier. He couldn't even think of contacting Sedgefield and Turner again. He would look like a complete idiot. Time to put his plan into action. He buzzed his secretary to summons Stonehouse.

Simon heard his mobile ping and he glanced at the text message from the concierge advising him that the gas company would be carrying out their monthly monoxide detectors inspection and please could he confirm if he would be home at six fifteen that evening. Odd, thought Simon…the gas company usually carried out their work during office hours unless it was an emergency. No matter, he would be home preparing dinner for Georgina, Paul and Brad. He thanked the concierge and refocused on the report he was reading. But then he had a thought. He texted the concierge and asked if it was the same gas company that had inspected his apartment the previous day. The concierge replied.

No sir. It is the regular company that always carries out the monthly monoxide inspections. They just asked if they could do your floor a bit later in the day due to workload.

Simon thought about it and then texted back.

No problem. Thank you for letting me know. Just a heads up... Georgina and her work partner Detective Damote will be arriving around about six thirty. Another friend called Brad Townsend will be arriving at seven.

So...thought Simon. If the monoxide inspector did turn out to be the same goon who had been recorded on camera in his apartment, then that meant that he had seen that the evidence he took was bogus. But then again, the inspection date was more or less consistent. Well, either way, having two armed detectives arrive around about the same time was advantageous, so he wasn't particularly concerned.

Wyatt's mobile buzzed. It was a message from Mullens. *Good to go.* Wyatt sat back in his chair, going through the plan in his mind. He needed to be absolutely sure that there were no holes or eventualities that he had not thought about. It was critical that nothing at any time could lead back to him. Now for Stonehouse, the idiot thought Wyatt. Just thinking of him made his blood pressure rise.

Stonehouse was feeling on top of the world again. He got up from his desk and made sure that as many people as possible heard him tell the guy next to him that the director had just asked to see him personally. Much like his former New York colleagues, everyone had worked out very quickly that Stonehouse was a little tyrant, *little* being the operative word regarding his height or lack thereof. He also exhibited illusions of grandeur and absolutely no one was impressed. They dubbed him SASS, which stood for *Special Agent Short Shit*. However, all his swagger instantly vaporized as soon as he entered the director's office. Wyatt's fierce and accusatory glare, his knuckles white as he leant forward on his desk, made Stonehouse shrink visibly. Wyatt immediately launched into a tirade.

"Your monumental incompetence has caused an absolute shit show!" he bellowed. "The FBI has been made to look like an amateur detective board game because of you! The DNA evidence was supposed to have been confiscated by you personally, yet one of my operatives has learnt that Dr. Chevalier still has it in his personal possession!" Stonehouse was totally blindsided by this revelation. He opened his mouth and shut it again. What could he possibly say? He was having difficulty even processing this information. Wyatt continued unabated, not done with humiliating Stonehouse.

"You are nothing short of an incompetent idiot! You were entrusted to do one simple job and you screwed up totally! One simple job!" he roared.

Stonehouse winced and the ensuing silence was deafening. He wondered how many people would have heard Wyatt's yelling. This was humiliating beyond words. How in hell's name had Dr. Chevalier managed it!

Wyatt sighed and eventually sat down, shaking his head. He then continued; his tone much quieter to ensure that no one could overhear this part of the conversation.

"This forensic scientist must be brought to heel, and I am going to give you *one* more opportunity to do so, only one more chance and if you fail again, you're out. A dishonorable discharge from the FBI will ensue, do you understand?"

Stonehouse just stared at Wyatt.

Do-you-understand?" Wyatt annunciated each word as if he were talking to a child.

Stonehouse snapped back to attention.

"Yes sir!" he stammered in a somewhat bewildered voice.

"Of course, sir." His mind was racing. "What is it that you want me to do?"

Wyatt looked at him long and hard and then said.

"This evening at *exactly* 18h20 sharp you are to enter Dr. Chevalier's apartment building and tell the concierge that you are Detective Damote. Flash your badge but not close enough for him to see your name. Once you are in, you are to ensure that Chevalier hands over the evidence and that he undertakes to *never* mention the issue again. *Ever.* So, you had better get on the next plane to New York chop chop. Have I made myself clear?" asked Wyatt.

Stonehouse could not decide which was preferable. Wyatt yelling or the quiet threatening tone of his voice now.

"Yes sir…but how will I know if he is home?" asked Stonehouse.

"He will be home. Stop asking idiotic questions and do as I say!" Wyatt barked. "Do not screw up! 18h20 exactly!" And he stabbed at his watch to emphasize the point.

"Yes of course sir. And um…thank you sir." He hesitated for a moment as he turned to leave, and then said. "Sir, I would like to take this opportunity to..." but Wyatt abruptly cut him off.

"Oh, just get out of here you imbecile!" Wyatt waved his hand as though he were swotting a fly.

Stonehouse flushed bright red but retained his composure. He turned on his heel and left the office, feeling like a frightened schoolboy who had been severely scolded by the headmaster. Once he was out in the corridor, he stood there shaking with rage. Chevalier had hoodwinked him and had made a complete fool of him. For that there would be a reckoning. Furthermore, Wyatt had humiliated him for all to hear. He held the title of *special agent* and as far as he was concerned, that should automatically translate into some measure of respect. It never occurred to him however as to how utterly disrespectful he was towards just about everyone else. His narcissistic take of the world was of one viewpoint only. Everything was about him.

He noticed that Wyatt's secretary was avoiding eye contact, and he was sure that word would have spread like wildfire of the berating he had received from the director. So instead of returning to his desk, he decided to go straight to the airport and buy his ticket from one of the counters. He would text Molly and say that the director himself had sent him to New York on an urgent case and that he would be back either very late tonight or tomorrow. At least she would be impressed. Sooner or later however he would have to face the smirks of his fellow agents. Well, he would wipe the contempt off their pathetic little faces. He would redeem himself and Chevalier would pay for dearly for the humiliation he had suffered. Five minutes later he was in a taxi heading to the airport.

Brad Townsend was slowly but surely peeling away the cyber layers as he continued to search for the location of the Levenstein evidence, or any indication as to who had moved it and where they had move it to. He knew that Stonehouse had lodged it there after he had raided Simon's lab. But someone else had collected everything from the evidence storage in Brooklyn, and that meant that there had to be some sort of paper trail and cyber trail. He knew that the checks and balances of moving evidence were not simple for good reason, but it did appear as though every paper record had been destroyed and every computer record had been deleted. However, every hacker knows that nothing is ever really erased. The deletion of files just makes it a bit harder to find what one is looking for. He would find something, somewhere, somehow. He just didn't have the luxury of time on his side since Stonehouse was looking for it too. Simon was tracking Stonehouse's every move though his mobile. He glanced at the latest location and was surprised to see that Stonehouse was presently at Washington's Reagan National airport. He screened his credit card activity and saw that a purchase for a return ticket to New York had just gone through. Well, well, well. Stonehouse was coming into town. What was his little agent up to? Normally, for FBI business, tickets were bought through the correct channels to ensure good record keeping. He would have to keep a close eye on Stonehouse. He was up to something. Again.

Mullens left the hardware store with all the materials he needed to set up Chevalier's suicide. He had paid with cash and had ensured that his peak cap was pulled down low over his face so that there would be no possibility of facial recognition. Killing was just a job to him. He had done it enough times. One thing he did however relish, was the thought of what people in the street would say or do if they knew that they had just brushed past a killer. The thought empowered him. It was intoxicating.

The important thing was to subdue Chevalier as quickly as possible. He had a small syringe that he had used many times to incapacitate his victims so as to preclude any possibility of resistance. The issue he was dealing with was the restricted time frame. From the moment that the concierge would hear Simon's voice giving permission for Damote (who would actually be Stonehouse), to go up to his apartment, Mullens probably had two minutes tops to incapacitate Chevalier and make it look as though he had hanged himself. It would be very tight but he could do it. After all, he was an experienced killer.

His escape would be easy. He would wait in the hiding place he had identified on the 10th floor until Chevalier's apartment building was crawling with police and forensic personnel. He would then simply blend in wearing full white forensic gear and make his exit at the right time. Hiding in plain sight had worked many times for him. No surveillance camera would be able to distinguish him from any of the other forensic technicians.

Georgina logged off her computer and gathered up her things. Paul was fully absorbed reading a document and didn't even seem to notice. She threw a pen at him. He looked up startled.

"I'm going to drop off something at my father's apartment so I will meet you at Simon's at six thirty."

"That is if I don't first arrest you for assault," said Paul as he retrieved the pen from the floor. "Were you this bad as a kid?"

Georgina laughed and said "Just as well my aim is lousy. You still have two eyes. Be grateful for small mercies."

Paul shook his head. "See you there Georgie. I'll bring some wine."

"The Scarecrow Cabernet Sauvignon will do."

"Yeah right! Straight after I have robbed a bank." Paul retorted. "It's going to have to be the local shop's special."

"Cheapskate," said Georgina and she flipped his hair as she walked past him. "Don't be late! Brad will be there at seven." As she passed Monica's desk she added.

"Mons, don't forget to tell Captain Hmmm who his stellar detectives are having dinner with tonight. Makes great pillow talk."

Paul rolled his eyes. He knew that Monica hated being called Mons. She blushed and turned away. Things had cooled off considerably between her and Murphey after she told him what she had read on the note. Clearly, she was dispensable if he felt compromised and she resented the rejection deeply.

CHAPTER SEVENTEEN

Stonehouse's anxiety levels were rising as the taxi from Kennedy airport was moving at a snail's pace. For the fourth time he asked the taxi driver what time he would get to his destination and finally the driver turned in his seat in exasperation.

"If you ask me one more time fella you can get the hell out of my taxi and find yourself another ride. This is New York. Not Disneyland!"

Stonehouse whipped out his FBI badge and shoved it in the taxi drivers face.

"Don't think you can fuck with me! Now do your miserable job and drive!"

The shocked expression on the taxi driver's face gave Stonehouse immense satisfaction. He always enjoyed pulling rank on ordinary folk. The driver turned away, his face dark with anger and the taxi lurched forward, the gears grating.

"For God's sake!" said Stonehouse throwing up his hands. "A taxi driver who can't even drive!"

Georgina's father said nothing as he watched her place a package carefully in the bottom drawer of his freezer. He did however feel conflicted; whatever she was doing, it meant that the official means of evidence storage couldn't be trusted, and this worried him enormously. He wanted to protect her, but he knew to pry would not only be to no avail but would be totally inappropriate given his position in the judiciary. Georgina was headstrong…yes…but she was also very measured in everything she did. She had a way of seeing things as they really were, not how the world would like them to be. She was one of the most dependable and objective people he knew and the fact that she was his daughter was a great privilege in his mind.

"Thanks Dad," said Georgina closing the freezer door. "The moment I am certain that the evidence will be safe in the Brooklyn facility, I will collect it. For now, I must protect it with my life."

"I hope you don't mean that literally my darling. Your life is worth far more than any evidence," said her father.

Georgina smiled. "Of course, Dad. Don't worry. I am being very careful."

"I will always worry sweetheart. You're my daughter. The moment one becomes a parent, one lives with anxiety from that day onwards. When you were little, protecting you was far easier to manage. I only had to prevent you from launching yourself out of trees…or setting the house on fire! Now I have to worry about a whole lot more."

Georgina looked at her dad closely and noticed how tired he looked. He was in his late sixties and yet he still had a grueling schedule on the bench. He was up late most nights reading through reams of evidence and documents. She reached up and cupped his face in her hands.

"Dad…we are cut from the same cloth. We simply never stop until we have done what we set out to do. However, we both must remind each other of our human fragility. You are looking tired. Get some rest Dad. You have been through a lot with Lola."

"Thank you, sweetheart. And yes…you are right. I am feeling tired."

Georgina hugged him and said "Why don't we get out into the country this weekend? It will be good for both of us."

"Good idea! Yes…let's do that. We can chat on Friday. Plan on where we are going."

Georgina turned to go and then stopped.

"Dad…if anything happens to me, the evidence I have hidden here will point the way."

Her father opened his mouth, but she stopped him.

"I am not in danger. I would tell you if I were. I just don't know which direction this case is going to go. So please just keep that in the back of your mind."

Her father looked at her for a few seconds.

"Okay Georgina. As I have said many times, I trust your judgement. Just know that I will do anything for you. Including not asking questions when you don't want me to. However, always remember how much I love you kiddo. I have your back. Always will."

Simon looked at the kitchen clock. Six fifteen. The monoxide testing guy should be here any minute. There were only three apartments on his floor, and he imagined that the guy would start with his first. It never took long, five minutes max so he would be gone by the time Georgina and Paul arrived. He continued to slice the onions and sticking his finger in the sauce simmering on the cooker, he tasted it. Hmmmm…delicious.

The doorbell rang. He wiped his hands and flicked the tea towel over his shoulder. On opening the door, he immediately recognized that this was the same guy who had been in his apartment the day before. He was instantly alarmed but quickly concealed it. Mullens then said.

"I am here to test the monoxide detectors sir."

Simon cocked his head and said, "Yeah right. And I'm the captain of the Titanic."

Mullens was momentarily thrown off balance.

"Seriously mate? You think I am just going to let you in

and hand over the evidence?" exclaimed Simon.

Mullens suddenly surged forward, grabbed Simon by the collar and pushed him towards the lounge area, throwing him down onto the sofa. Simon tried to grab Mullens, but he twisted away.

"Sit down and shut up! We have unfinished business," barked Mullens.

"You don't say! You think I'm afraid of you?" said Simon.

"Shut the fuck up!" He put down his toolbox and opened it, keeping an eye on Simon.

"What…now for the torture tools? This is not going to work you idiot. Two armed detectives *and* an FBI agent will be here any minute and they are more than pissed at you!"

Mullens looked up frowning. FBI? How could Chevalier know about Stonehouse? He was about to say something when the doorbell rang.

"Told you," said Simon getting up. "Showtime sunshine! Don't say I didn't warn you."

He walked over to the intercom, pressed the button and glanced back at Mullens.

"Sir, there is a visitor by the name of Detective Damote to see you," came the tinny voice through the intercom.

Simon glanced back at Mullens and then turning back to the intercom, he said to the concierge, "Send him up!"

Simon started to turn again but Mullens had moved with the speed of a panther and was now positioned directly behind him. All Simon felt was a sharp prick in the base of his skull. Within seconds the room started to spin, and he felt his legs give in. He clutched at Mullens, gasping, trying to scream but no sound came out. Slowly, he slumped to the floor, a darkness closing in on him.

And then there was nothing.

Well, that was easy thought Stonehouse as he waited for the elevator. The concierge had only glanced at his badge, not even checking his name. The doors opened and on entering he pressed floor fourteen. His mind turned to the task at hand. He was going to play both good cop and bad cop. He was confident that Dr. Chevalier would eventually see things his way. He had memorized a long list of codes pertaining to felony charges that he would threaten him with if he didn't cooperate. Those would do the trick.

Georgina paid the cab driver and entered Simon's building trying to decide whether she should wait for Paul or go up. "Good evening, Ma'am," said the concierge politely. She smiled at him. "Hello John. How are you?" "All good Ma'am thank you."

"I'm just going to wait here for a friend," she said sitting down on the reception sofa.

"Of course, Ma'am," said the concierge. Her mobile pinged and holding up her hand apologetically, she fished it out of her bag. It was Paul.

Running five minutes late.

She replied to him.

No problem. Will ask the concierge to send you up.

Paul texted back.

Great. See you shortly. Got the wine.

And then she saw him go offline. She stood up.

"John…a detective by the name of Paul Damote will be arriving in about five minutes. Could you please send him up to Dr. Chevalier's apartment. No need to buzz. I'm going up in the interim."

For a moment the concierge looked puzzled and then said.

"Ma'am, he's already here. He arrived only a few minutes before you, and Dr. Chevalier said I should send him up."

"What? I don't understand." Georgina looked perplexed. She looked at her mobile and checked Paul's messages.

"Are you sure?" she asked frowning.

"Yes Ma'am. Absolutely. He showed me his badge."

Now Georgina was really confused but this was quickly replaced by suspicion and then fear. She stood up and walked towards the reception counter.

" John…what did he look like?"

The concierge cocked his head.

"Um…. short, very short and dumpy. Not someone who should audition for the Chippendales!" he added, laughing at his own wit. His smile faded rapidly when he saw Georgina's expression. She opened her mobile and stabbed at Paul's number as she said.

"That was not Detective Damote!"

The concierge looked totally confused. Georgina started to run towards the elevators and shouted over her shoulder.

"Tell Detective Damote the moment he arrives to get up there as quickly as possible!"

She stabbed at the button repeatedly. God, where is an elevator when you need one! As she watched the floor numbers light up on the panel whilst the elevator descended, Paul's mobile was just ringing. No answer. Damn! She glanced up again. She noted that the other elevator was on floor fourteen. Finally, the doors opened and out spilt five laughing teenagers. She pushed past them and pressed the floor fourteen button repeatedly. "C'mon! Close dammit!!" she yelled.

Stonehouse had found the front door to Dr. Chevalier's apartment slightly ajar. He entered slowly and tentatively, feeling uncomfortable but not really knowing why. The apartment was eerily silent. He could smell food cooking, but something felt really odd. Beyond the lounge was the kitchen and he could see what looked like a dining room off to the side. He moved forward slowly.

"Dr. Chevalier?" he called. Nothing. He walked towards the kitchen. "Dr Chevalier! I am not sure what you are playing at but…"

Suddenly he heard a scream that sounded very far away and then he realized that it was his own. His feet were skidding as he fell backwards, and he felt a jarring pain in his hip as he landed on the hard flooring. Hanging from a hook in the ceiling was Dr. Chevalier, his body swinging slowly from side to side, his neck at an awkward angle, his eyes bulging, his mouth open. Stonehouse was scrabbling to get away from the horror, aware of the acidic bile rising up in his throat.

"Christ no!" he yelled. This had not been part of the plan! He skidded backwards on his buttocks trying to put a distance between himself and the grotesque scene. He finally reached the front door and rolling over he scrambled to his feet, slipping as he tried to gain purchase. He ran into the corridor and frantically stabbed at the elevator buttons. He glanced up and saw that the right elevator was still on the floor fourteen and the other elevator was ascending. He stabbed at the button again.

His eyes darted to the panel above the other elevator and he saw floor thirteen light up. He then heard the motor slow as the elevator neared floor fourteen. It seemed an absolute eternity before the right elevator doors finally opened and he pushed through the gap, his shoulder bruising against the rubber edges of the doors, his hands shaking uncontrollably as he aimed for the ground floor button. The doors closed as he slumped down into the corner. He heard the ping of the other elevator arriving on floor fourteen just as he started to descend. Perspiration was pouring down his face. His mind was racing but it was just a jumble of horrific images. He could hear his own heavy breathing and his heart was pounding in his chest. As the elevator neared the ground floor, he pulled himself up, his legs still feeling like jelly. He saw his reflection in the mirrored interior and gasped at how grey his face was. The doors opened and he stumbled out of the lift and ran for the exit.

"Detective Damote!" called the concierge as he scooted around the counter, but Stonehouse was out of the doors. He stumbled and fell down the steps but scrambled up again and within seconds was out of sight. The concierge had no idea what to do. Something was very wrong! He dashed back behind the counter and dialed Dr. Chevalier's apartment. No response. He reached under the counter and pressed the panic button. Then he grabbed the phone and punched in 911. Oh God he thought. What has happened!

CHAPTER EIGHTEEN

Paul found Georgina slumped on the floor, her arms outstretched and there was a strange keening sound emanating from her. She was crawling towards something. He looked up and an enormous shock coursed through his body when he saw Simon. He rushed past Georgina into the kitchen, seized the knife off the cutting board and dragging one of the dining chairs, scrambled up to cut the rope. As the knife sliced through the fibers, he grabbed Simon and they both tumbled to the floor with an almighty crash. He rolled Simon over, shaking him, trying to get a response, trying to ascertain if he was still alive.

"Simon!" he screamed. "Simon!" He felt for a pulse, but his hand was shaking so much that he couldn't steady it enough to feel anything. What he did feel was something tugging at his jacket and turning he saw Georgina, her mouth open, her eyes imploring. She was trying to say something, but no sound would come out.

In one movement, he picked her up and strode to the lounge, depositing her on one of the lounge chairs, pushing her down, telling her not to move. She had seemed so floppy in his arms, and he realized that she was in extreme shock. He rushed back to Simon and started CPR. Time seemed to condense and expand simultaneously and his own cries seemed to come from another distant place. "Simon! C'mon buddy! Come back to us!" he implored. He continued to pump Simon's chest and breathe into his mouth. Over and over again, not letting up. It seemed like an eternity that he had been doing this. He glanced back at Georgina; she was white as a sheet. He turned back to Simon, tears streaming down his face, his voice hoarse. "C'mon Simon! Stay with us! Simon…"

A police vehicle screamed past Brad as he was walking the last block to Simon's apartment building. As he rounded the corner, he stopped dead in his tracks. Multiple police vehicles were parked at the entrance, their blue lights flashing, and he saw an officer set up a perimeter with striped crime tape. What in the hell was going on? He looked up and could see lights blazing on the 14th floor and an officer was peering over the patio railing. His first instinct was to show his badge and go in, but he was unsure if that would be a good move. He had a sickening feeling that something had happened to Simon, and he wondered if detectives Harris and Damote were there too. He approached an officer and asked what was happening. "Can't tell you I'm afraid," said the officer.

Brad showed him his badge. The officer immediately straightened up.

"There has been a suicide on the 14th floor sir. One of our own. A forensic scientist from the Queens lab."

Brad felt the blood drain from his face. Oh God no! His heart was racing. He turned to the officer and asked.

"Who is up there at the moment?"

"Just the responding officers, I think. The coroner and forensics are on their way sir," replied the officer.

Brad stared up at the 14th floor, doing everything he could do to hold onto his composure. He was undecided what he should do. If he went up it may well get back to the FBI that he had been there. At the same time, he wanted to assist in any way that he could. Eventually common sense prevailed, and he turned away and walked back the way he had come. He knew that he would have to keep a low profile. Nobody must know that he had been there, not if he was going to try and find out who did this. There was not a chance that Simon had killed himself. That he knew. He crossed over the street and went into a diner from where he could watch the goings on.

Paul felt a hand on his shoulder, and he looked up to find himself staring into the eyes of a police officer. Everything was a blur. Next thing there were arms lifting him up and he heard a kind voice say.

"He's gone. So sorry buddy. He's gone."

"No!" screamed Paul and he lunged back to where Simon was. Strong arms pulled him back and he heard another voice say.

"Keep him back. The medics are on their way up."

Next thing he was slumped down on the sofa, and he looked across at Georgina. She was just staring into space, her expression blank, her red dress a stark contrast to her deathly pale skin. He looked back at where Simon was lying and between the police officers who were kneeling around him, he saw that Simon's eyes were open, unblinking, a lock of hair across his forehead, his skin a pale mauve colour. In that moment, Paul felt as though he had lost a limb. Some intrinsic part of him was gone forever. He recalled the bloodied mess of his previous partner. Nothing made sense anymore. Nothing would ever be the same again.

Some time must have passed when Paul became aware that a medic was leaning over Georgina, a syringe in his hand. He looked back to where Simon lay and saw a sheet covering his body. The police officers were in a huddle, and he heard them discussing the cause of death. They were divided in their opinions; one was adamant that it was suicide, another was shaking his head saying that it was a homicide for sure. Through the open front door, he saw the stricken face of the concierge, his eyes wide and uncertain. A police officer took him gently by the arm and he disappeared from view.

The coroner and a team of forensic technicians arrived and quietly dispersed to do their respective jobs. Until suicide was fully confirmed they had to treat the scene as a potential crime scene. They looked like ghosts in their white suits, gliding around, ethereal, and unreal. Captain Murphey arrived on the scene and immediately walked over to Paul.

"Hey Paul…" he said gently. "We need to get you and Georgina outta here. The investigators can talk to you tomorrow. Can I take you both to Georgina's apartment? Can you stay there with her for a while?"

Paul nodded, and slowly stood up. Captain Murphey said something quietly to one of the police officers and they helped Paul get Georgina onto her feet.

In the back of one of the cruisers, Paul held Georgina in his arms. He stared out of the window, watching the city pass by and continue as if nothing had happened. People in the streets, bright lights and honking horns. He saw his own hollowed out eyes in the reflection of the window and he felt as though he was dreaming and that he would wake up and the four of them would be around Simon's table, laughing and eating. His mind swiveled to Agent Brad Townsend, and he wondered if he had arrived at the apartment building and had seen the commotion. Was he still there? Did he know what had happened?

When they got to Georgina's apartment building, he found her keys in her bag and Murphey helped him get her up to the apartment. Paul thanked Murphey for his help and quietly closed the door. He walked over to the sofa and looked down at Georgina. Her eyes were half open, but she was too drugged to really comprehend anything. Lifting her gently, he carried her to the bedroom, laying her carefully onto her bed, pulling the comforter over her. He closed the door quietly and went into the living room to call his wife. He told her what had happened. She was utterly shocked.

"I'm going to stay here with Georgina. I hope you understand," he said quietly.

"Of course, I do," said his wife. "What can I do? I am worried about you Paul. You shouldn't shoulder this on your own given…" and her voice trailed off.

"It's okay darling. I'll be fine. We will get through this.

I'll call you in the morning. Don't say anything to the girls please."

"Of course not. Call me if you need me. Paul…I love you." his wife whispered into the phone.

"I love you too…" he said gently after which he closed his mobile.

The door of the cleaning utility room on the tenth floor of Simon's apartment building cracked open slowly. Mullens cautiously looked around before he emerged fully, closing the door quietly behind him. Silently he headed up the fire escape stairs to the fourteenth floor, kitted out head to toe in a white forensic suit. He carefully looked through the window of the fire escape door and observed the goings on. He needed to time it perfectly to blend in with all the other forensic technicians. Two police officers flanked Chevalier's front door ensuring that nobody entered who did not have the relevant clearance to be there. He glanced up at the corridor camera and noted that it was still angled away from Simon's front door. This he had done the previous day to ensure that at no time was he on camera. The important thing was that the camera still covered the elevators which he had never used. He only used the fire escape stairs where there was no surveillance. So, the camera would have recorded Stonehouse getting out of the lift and walking towards Chevalier's apartment. It would have also recorded his frantic exit which Mullens had observed through the window of the fire escape's door. It had looked quite comical in fact.

There was a momentary fuss as Simon's body was wheeled out of the apartment and whilst the officers assisted the paramedics to maneuver the gurney into the elevator, Mullens slipped behind them into the apartment. Nobody noticed him and after five minutes or so, he headed to the elevator with his toolbox looking the perfect part of a forensic technician who had completed his work. He kept up the ruse until he was well clear of the building and of all the law enforcement officers who were positioned at the entrance. Slipping down a side alley where he was sure he would not be observed, he stripped off the forensic gear, stuffed it in the toolbox and set off for the airport. Job done. No need to text Wyatt. He would be glued to the news sooner or later anyhow.

Special Agent Stonehouse sat in the airport lounge, nursing his third whiskey. He was in a state of shock and his skin prickled with apprehension. There was a nagging voice in the back of his mind that told him that it was no coincidence that Director Wyatt had sent him to Dr.

Chevalier's apartment at that exact time. It was slowly dawning on him that he may well be a patsy, that possibly he had been set up to take the rap for a murder he didn't commit. Despite the likelihood that the news media would claim that it was suicide, he knew that it would only be a matter of time before the word *homicide* would start creeping into the narrative. A guy doesn't prepare a meal for his guests and then simply hang himself.

He felt like a trapped animal. It was like the holes in slices of cheese; they were all lining up perfectly…his flight to New York, the taxi, the concierge, the cameras, him running from the building. He had heard Dr. Chevalier's voice on the intercom when the concierge had buzzed him, so it must have been in that small window of opportunity whilst he was in the elevator that the killer had struck. Whoever had killed Chevalier was already in the apartment, waiting for that exact moment to murder him and then to make it look like suicide. Suddenly he was overwhelmed with guilt, an emotion mostly foreign to him. *He* had been the one who created the narrative that Dr. Chevalier had suffered a nervous breakdown. He had unwittingly laid down the fertile ground for his alleged suicide. The lies that had slipped so easily off his tongue were now coming back to haunt him. Then the reptilian part of his brain kicked in. He had to survive this. He simply could not be framed for a crime he didn't commit. He weighed up his options. If he ran, he would look guilty. If he didn't run, he would be a sitting duck to be arrested and charged with murder, since the evidence would be overwhelming. It would be a slam dunk conviction. The third option was to go to the authorities and put forward his theory that it was a hit, and that he was the patsy. But which authority? In a case like this, the FBI *was* the authority. Slowly it dawned on him that this had been planned to the last very detail and that it may well translate into the perfect crime.

His reverie was interrupted with his flight being called. He could only hope that there wasn't anyone waiting for him at the other end to arrest him. He had absolutely no one that he could talk to. Molly, his wife was not the sharpest tool in the box. He had no friends to speak of, and all his colleagues couldn't stand him. Suddenly he felt like the loneliest guy in the world. He shuffled in the queue towards the boarding gate and a horrible image of himself shuffling in leg irons crept into his mind. He felt a sense of panic rising up inside of him and he had to fight to maintain his composure. He knew that he had to keep control of his emotions in order to prove his innocence.

Paul poured himself a double scotch and went back to Georgina's bedroom. He dragged her dressing table chair closer to the bed and sat down, watching her breathe steadily. A soft warm glow from the city lights washed over the room and the tranquility of the light brought sharply into focus the contrast of the unmitigated violence of Simon's murder. And murder it was. There was no doubt. The slow realization of how vicious these people were when they were threatened crystalized in his mind. He had underestimated them, and he knew that it was unlikely that he could ever forgive himself for doing that. He continued to watch Georgina. It was the first time he had ever seen her vulnerable. She just always seemed so invincible, so in control. He also had never realized how deeply she loved Simon. They were both such powerful personalities and so committed in everything they did. Why had Simon not seen the real danger Paul asked himself. Perhaps he had. Perhaps it was down to the fact that Simon is simply fearless. *Was*...thought Paul. The realization that everything about Simon was now in the past tense made his throat constrict with a deep sadness.

He looked at the time. It was eleven pm. He sipped the scotch slowly and felt the burn of the liquid slide down and mix with the fire of rage that was building and rising up in his belly. This rage would in turn become revenge and he knew that this was a monster he simply had to control for his survival. And Georgina's survival too.

CHAPTER NINETEEN

Early the next morning, Brad Townsend sat dumbfounded in his kitchen as he watched the news about Simon's alleged suicide. He had been awake the entire night and felt exhausted. The newspapers and news stations extolled Dr. Chevalier's virtues as a forensic scientist but also mentioned his recent nervous breakdown which they speculated was due to critical mistakes he had made recently. *A great scientist who had lost his way* they said. There was even speculation that the FBI had been investigating whether Dr. Chevalier had been bought off by organized crime and had fudged evidence purposefully to preclude the possibility of certain convictions. This would explain why some recent pending high-profile cases had been struck off the roll.

Brad felt utterly sickened. These people didn't only destroy your life and reputation whilst you were still alive; they kicked it all the way down for generations to come, forcing your offspring and loved ones to endure the shame of what you had done…what they, the invisible *they* had deemed the appropriate narrative of what you had done, manufactured to distract and hide from the anyone any inconvenient truth that could threaten them. And here he was in the midst of it all. He was part of a tainted organization which was in fact the one that had lost its way. The lines of law enforcement and crime were so thoroughly intertwined now that it was no longer possible to distinguish between the two. Simon had been murdered, that he knew and around the edges of his mind skirted the Levenstein files. He knew that the two were inextricably connected. If Simon could be so easily eliminated, who else did they have in their crosshairs? Were they going to come after him too? And Harris and Damote? He would have to be one step ahead of them because now it was clear that all bets were off.

Georgina had woken up and she walked unsteadily into the lounge. The morning sun was streaming in, and little dust motes floated through the air. She felt dazed and groggy, her mind trying to grasp the events of the night before. She switched on the news. The news reader's voice woke up Paul who had fallen asleep on the sofa. A loud sob escaped from Georgina as she listened to the newscaster and Paul jumped up, grabbing the remote, muting the newsreader's vitriol, her red mouth reduced to working furiously and silently as she regurgitated the contaminated lies about Simon. He pressed the remote again and the image disappeared from view. Georgina turned on Paul, sobbing uncontrollably, her fists pounding his chest.

"The bastards! The evil bastards! They murdered him, Paul! They murdered my Simon!" she wailed. "And now they're trashing him!"

He caught both of her wrists in one of his hands and pulled her towards him, rocking her gently. He cradled her head against his chest, holding her tightly against him while she sobbed. After a while, he felt her go limp in his arms from exhaustion. He laid her down gently onto the sofa and went to her bathroom, rummaging through the cabinet until he found what he was looking for. Tilting her head back, he put a glass of water to her lips after slipping a sleeping pill into her mouth. She dribbled slightly but swallowed it and he wiped her mouth gently with his thumb. He then picked her up and took her back to the bedroom. Sleep was the very best thing for her right now. She had her whole life ahead of her to grapple with the reality of losing Simon. For now, she simply needed deep healing sleep.

He knew now with absolute certainty that Chad Levenstein had not died in that detention centre. Any nagging doubts he had harboured over the last few months, evaporated. He understood now that everyone would think that Levenstein's suicide or even murder would suit the pedos who associated with him. But now it was clear that this wasn't the case. He was one of them and they stick together no matter what, like proverbial shit to a blanket. They were all nothing other than a stinking pile of vile faeces and Levenstein was the spider at the centre of the foul web. He could give them what they wanted with all bases covered; no chance of being caught or convicted. Yes, he was alive and well, and yes, he would have had face altering surgery, that was a certainty. To this end he would look just like any another insignificant person on the street. But wherever he lived, it would be luxurious, opulent, and secure with a revolving door of underage girls satisfying his and his clientele's needs. How they'd fooled the whole world was astounding, but they had done so. Seamlessly.

They would now feel safe with Simon being out of the way but sooner or later they would come after Georgina and him and anyone else who possibly stood in their way. Well, they had shown what they were capable of. And now he had to stop them. He heard a soft knock on the front door. He walked over and opened it. There stood Georgina's father. He looked ashen as he shook Paul's hand, asking how Georgina was. Paul cupped his elbow and guided him into the apartment.

"She is in deep shock Judge Harris," said Paul.

"Please…call me William," interjected Georgina's father. He continued. "Has a doctor seen her, treated her?"

"Yes, she was sedated last night, and I have just given her a sleeping pill. Sleep is the best thing for her right now." Georgina's father nodded in agreement.

"I am sure there is much for you to attend to," he said. "Perhaps later you can help me get her to my apartment?"

"Of course, William. That would be best for her. She needs you now more than ever," said Paul.

"Where is she?" her father asked.

"In her bedroom, sleeping," replied Paul.

They both walked through to the bedroom and Paul watched Georgina's father gently sit down on the edge of her bed, taking one of her hands in his and raising it to his lips, kissing it softly.

"My poor little darling Georgina," he said quietly.

He sat there for some time looking down at his daughter. Eventually he stood up, pulling the comforter closer around her shoulders and they walked back to the lounge. Judge Harris asked.

"What time would you like me to come back to fetch her?"

"Um…if you have a few minutes, I can pack some of her

things and help you now get her to your apartment," answered Paul.

"Yes…that sounds like a good idea," replied Georgina's father. "Yes, let's do that."

Fifteen minutes later they had a very groggy Georgina in the car, and they headed to Judge Harris's home. When they had settled her in the guest room, Judge Harris offered Paul some coffee which he declined.

"Have you eaten son?" he asked.

"No, not for a while. I couldn't face anything to be honest." Paul said as he fished out a card from his jacket pocket.

"Here…here is my card with my contact details. Please keep in touch and let me know how she is doing. I doubt she will be going back to work for some time," said Paul.

Judge Harris took the card and walked over to a bureau. He scribbled his mobile number on a piece of paper and handing it to Paul he said.

"Call me any time Paul, day or night. And when you can, please come over to see her. She will need you as much as she will need me."

Paul nodded as he tried to imagine a future for Georgina without Simon. He then said.

"The investigators will want to interview her. I'll keep in touch with you in that regard too."

"Thank you. We are going to have to get her through a very difficult time. And I know how awful it is for you too. She so often talks about you. I am sure you know just how much she admires you," said Georgina's father.

Paul smiled and said, "It's mutual but Georgie is in a league of her own. I am sure I don't have to tell you that." Georgina's father smiled sadly.

"Are you sure I can't call for a taxi?"

Paul shook his head. "No please…not to worry but thank you for the offer."

There was a moments silence between them and then Paul shook Judge Harris's hand and turned to leave. Turning back, he said.

"It is a privilege to meet you Judge Harris…William. I am just so sorry that it's under these circumstances."

Georgina's father nodded at Paul and watched him walk to the elevators. Quietly he closed the door and stood there for some time, his mind trying to navigate why and how the whole tragic event had taken place. His mind swiveled to the evidence hidden there in his home. There had to be a connection, but it would have to wait. Helping Georgina deal with this trauma was his priority now and no doubt it would be for some time to come.

CHAPTER TWENTY

Police Commissioner Edward Baker was sitting at his desk deep in thought watching the news. His eyes narrowed as he leant forward, making sure he didn't miss a word. He flipped through the different channels. The narrative was eerily duplicated as though everyone had been given the exact same script. Something told him that this had been planned well in advance. It was also obvious to him that this alleged suicide was linked to what Harris and Damote were working on. They had mentioned a forensic scientist being involved and clearly, this person had hit a raw nerve. He reached for his intercom.

"Hillary, please get detectives Harris and Damote here for a meeting as soon as possible."

"Yes sir, will do." she replied, and the intercom clicked off.

He sat back again and stared out the window at the vast city below him. He felt an enormous weight on his shoulders, more so today than most days. Over time, law enforcement had become more and more convoluted with multiple shifting alliances and self-interested parties. How different it was compared to when he had been on the beat. Or was it? Perhaps it had always been like this. Perhaps one only became aware of how complex everything was when one moved up in the ranks. And now he was at the very top. He was ultimately responsible for everything. Everything pointed back to him, and he didn't have the luxury of a second chute. A sense of the inevitable crept into his mind and he had to ask himself the question…what legacy would he be leaving on his watch?

Go Len! Wyatt read the text from Sedgefield. *Well done buddy. We can all sleep easy now.*

Wyatt fumed. The presumptuous little prick. Even though it was in fact true, he had to squash this before anything could take seed. Nothing should ever be evidenced in text. Sedgefield really should know better!

Wyatt texted. *No idea what you're referring to.*

Alan replied. *The forensic chap. He is out of the way. Good riddance!*

Wyatt gritted his teeth as he texted back.

I had nothing to do with it! Don't ever mention it again!

Wyatt could see that Sedgefield was typing.

Hey man I'm sorry! I thought that given our conversation, this was your handywork.

Wyatt wanted to smack Sedgefield in the mouth.

IT WAS NOT ME! Never refer to this incident again.

Wyatt stabbed at the messages as he deleted them.

Hopefully that would be the end of that. Idiot! Then he remembered…keep your enemies closer. Wyatt sighed. He would have to apologize to Sedgefield for being so abrupt. Well, that could wait. He needed a drink. Now.

The Medical Examiner's report was conclusive. It was a homicide. The TV stations and newspapers were buzzing. Paul had asked Murphey if he could be appointed as the chief investigating officer, but Murphey had declined.

"You're too close to this and actually I want to keep you out of the firing line," said Murphey.

Paul opened his mouth to object, but Murphey raised his hand and continued.

"I have appointed detectives Les Johnson and Jordan Brown to head up the investigation but with specific instructions that you are to be part of the team…just not the face that the press or anyone else will see. They're good guys, and they won't shut you out."

Paul was quite taken aback at the turnaround of Murphey's attitude towards him. He was showing a side to him that Paul had never seen. He said.

"Thank you, sir. What you are doing makes sense."

Murphey looked at him for a while.

"Let's chat in my office."

Murphey led the way and shut the door.

"You are going to have to appraise them about the DNA link to Chad Levenstein. I have no doubt that is why Dr. Chevalier was murdered. I dismissed it at the time, but I shouldn't have."

Paul was surprised for the second time. However, he was still concerned about sharing this information.

"They will have to keep it under wraps don't you think?" Paul asked Murphey.

"Without a doubt," he replied.

"Won't the FBI want to take charge sir? ventured Paul.

"I'm not sure," said Murphey. "We'll have to see what happens. If they do decide to do that, my hands will be tied."

Paul nodded. "Okay let's see what pans out sir."

Murphey then said. "You told me at the time, that the FBI had removed all files and evidence regarding Levenstein's DNA from Dr. Chevalier's office. Has anything else happened subsequently that you or Detective Harris know about?"

Call it the instinct of a seasoned detective but Paul instantly felt his guard go up. He had learnt some hard lessons when he hadn't followed his intuition. Something was telling him to keep his cards very close to his chest, so he decided not to share anything further with Murphey.

"No sir. That is where we left everything. There have been

no further developments."

There was a long silence.

"Okay," said Murphey. "But I want to know everything as soon as it happens. I must be kept in the loop at all times."

"Yes sir. Will do," replied Paul.

He was lying and that was not conduct becoming of a detective. However, he felt that Murphey was lying too. Something told him that Murphey knew a whole lot more than he was letting on. Well, as they always say, know your enemy. At this point in time the jury was out as to which side Murphey was on and Paul wasn't taking any chances. He would never underestimate the people behind Simon's murder again.

Paul met detectives Les Johnson and Gordon Brown in one of the meeting rooms. He liked them and knew them well. They were good solid guys, never posturing or exhibiting one-upmanship. Real team players.

"Hey man we're really sorry about your friend," said Les.

"Thanks guys," said Paul. "He was more Georgina's friend. They were very close."

"Here's a copy of the medical examiner's report," said Jordan sliding a file across to Paul. He continued.

"They found a pin prick just inside the hairline on the back of Chevalier's neck. The toxicology report cited both paralyzing and inhibitor chemicals. So, the murderer had incapacitated Chevalier first and then strung him up to make it look like a suicide."

Paul felt sick inside.

"Would Chevalier have been conscious? Would he have suffered?" he asked.

"No, I don't think so," replied Jordan. "The concoction was pretty potent. Used a lot by the Russians. It's most likely that he was unconscious within seconds."

"I do hope that is the case. Any camera evidence?" asked Paul looking from Jordan to Les.

"We have someone there now pulling all the CCTV footage from the apartment building. The concierge will be coming in later to be interviewed. He was pretty shaken up, the poor guy," said Les.

Paul told them about the cameras that Simon had set up in his apartment. Perhaps forensics hadn't found them yet. Both Les and Jordan were surprised as nothing had been noted on the initial report about any surveillance inside Chevalier's apartment.

"We'll ask forensics to look again," said Jordan.

"I would prefer that we look ourselves and keep forensics out of it for the moment. I have my reasons," said Paul.

Les and Jordan exchanged looks.

"No problem Paul. We'll go back and look ourselves."

"Yes, we trust your judgement Paul," added Jordan. He went on. "We'll also need to interview Georgie too, but we'll wait until you think she's ready."

"I appreciate that guys. She has taken a real knock. She and Chevalier had been dating on and off for years. The truth be known, they only ever had eyes for each other."

"That's awful. Poor kid," said Jordan shaking his head.

"Look Paul, we…and I mean the three of us, are going to get this bastard and everyone else behind it," said Les. He continued. "Murphey said that you have some info to share with us?"

Paul then told them about the Starbucks cup they had found when they were watching Salome. He also told them about the FBI confiscating all the evidence. He could see that they were both shocked to learn that Levenstein was still alive. They were equally shocked by the actions of the FBI. But that was all that Paul told them. It wasn't because he didn't trust them; they were definitely trustworthy. It was more that he wanted them to get to a point where they would understand that some information simply could not be shared with anyone other than the three of them, especially not with Captain Murphey. When he was sure that they had reached that point, then he would tell them everything he knew.

"Wow! That is totally mind blowing! And it would be unbelievable too if it weren't coming from you Paul," said Les. Jordan looked thoughtful.

"Surely if the FBI had all the information, there was no need to go after Chevalier? And why was the FBI burying the information anyhow? It should have been all hands-on deck to hunt down that bastard Levenstein," said Jordan.

Les shook his head. "Jordan, you know what the FBI has become. They have masters in high places. They can't even be trusted to go anywhere near a playground."

The inference was clear. This was about child trafficking and too many powerful people being involved. Les's eyes were wide open.

"You're right," said Jordan. "Forgive me for my lapse of naivety. Must be because I haven't had my caffeine fix. Anyone for coffee?"

Paul and Les raised their hands.

Later that day, Paul was checking his emails when he saw the request for a meeting with the commissioner. He replied saying that he was available the following day but that he would be alone; his partner was still in shock and not at work. Five minutes later his email pinged confirming 16h00 the following day. Paul had no intention of informing Murphey about this meeting. He looked up and saw him talking intently on his phone. Something was worrying Paul. Murphey had seemed genuinely compassionate at Simon's apartment and even now, he was not being his normal obnoxious self. However, Paul was always suspicious when people acted out of character. Then an idea popped into his head. All the detectives were able to access the department's phone records. He waited for about five minutes after Murphey had finished his call and then logged on, entered the necessary codes, and up came the call log for the whole department. He noted the most recent number from Murphey's extension and then did a reverse search. He sat back in his chair, shocked. It was for the FBI headquarters in Washington. The worm! Paul shook his head. Well, forewarned is forearmed. He would have to watch Murphey very closely. The plan was now clear to him. Murphey would keep the FBI appraised on everything that the investigation team found and once they ascertained that they were too close to the truth, then they would march in and take the investigation over. It was so obvious now. Well, it can work both ways thought Paul. Information and misinformation were often closely related and indiscernible. This was going to be a chess game of note. Paul was certain of it, and he planned on winning.

The concierge looked very nervous when he arrived for

the interview. Paul moved to put him at ease.

"We are truly sorry Mr. Conte for what you have been through. However, we would like to commend you on your actions of calling 911."

"Thank you, sir," said Conte. "I just feel so bad for Dr. Chevalier. He was always so nice to me."

They all sat down. Les opened his file, shuffled through his notes, and then looked up at the concierge.

"We would like you to take us through everything from beginning to end. Please don't think that any small detail is unnecessary. Anything that you can tell us will help our investigation."

John Conte took them through all the events; the gas company scheduling a monoxide inspection, the guy who said he was Detective Damote, everything that he could remember.

"Did the gas company actually arrive for the monoxide inspection?" asked Jordan.

"Yes. It was just one guy. Not the usual guy who does the inspections, but the company does have a lot of staff. But I never saw him leave. There was so much chaos, so he possibly did exit the building, but I just didn't see him. He arrived at about six fifteen and I said he could go straight up to the 14th floor," answered Conte.

"Well, the CCTV footage will help us there," said Les as

he jotted down the times and details. Looking back up at Conte he said.

"Did you look closely at the badge shown to you by the guy who said he was Detective Damote?"

"No sir. I am very sorry. I should have done that," apologized Conte.

"It's okay Mr. Conte," said Paul. "As you said, Dr. Chevalier had told you that he was expecting me and Detective Harris. You had no reason to be suspicious." Both Les and Jordan nodded.

"Still sir, I should have been more thorough," said Conte anxiously.

"It's okay Mr. Conte," said Paul kindly. He continued.

"Dr. Chevalier was also expecting a third guest, a Brad Townsend. Did he mention him to you?"

"Yes, he did, but the guy never arrived…or perhaps he did but never went up. Everything was so chaotic and there were a lot of people milling around," replied Conte.

"Well," said Les, "I think we have gone through everything. If anything comes to mind, anything at all, please call us day or night."

They all stood up as Les handed him a card.

"Thank you for coming in Mr. Conte. You have been a great help."

"Oh, just one more thing," said Paul as he took something

out of his file. He showed Conte a photo of Stonehouse. "Was this they guy who posed as me?"

"Yes sir. Definitely. That's him," replied the concierge.

From behind the photo Paul slid another photo of Mullens. "And was this the gas guy?" he asked.

Conte leaned forward and peered at the photo. Les and Jordan exchanged looks.

"Yes sir. In fact, I remember being a bit perplexed because he had also been there the previous day for a suspected gas leak in Dr. Chevalier's apartment but that was for a different company. Perhaps he is a free-lancer and does work for both companies. His IDs did check out."

"It has transpired that his IDs and name were fake. We're still trying to identify him," said Paul.

"I am so sorry detective," said the concierge looking distressed. "I had no idea. The ID looked legit."

"It's not your fault Mr. Conte. Not at all," said Paul. "Thank you for coming in. We may call upon you again but for the moment, you have helped us enormously."

Conte turned to go but then looked back again at Paul.

"Will you send my best to Miss Harris please…sorry Detective Harris? Could you tell her how sorry I am?"

"Of course," said Paul inclining his head. Conte nodded, looked at Les and Jordan and then left the room.

After showing him out, Paul went back into the interview room. He could see that the photo of Mullens had thrown Les and Jordan, so he told them about how the gas guy was the same person who had been tailing Simon. He suspected that he was an FBI ghost and Georgina had managed to snap a photo of him. But at this point in time, they had no idea who he was. Paul also told them about Murphey and relayed the story about the FBI call.

"I'm sorry guys but I think we must be careful. Something is not quite right with Murphey, and I just need to know from both of you if you think I'm overreacting."

Both Les and Jordan were silent for a while, mulling over what Paul had just told them. Then Les said.

"Look, Murphey has always been an asshole. Why would that change now? I think we must close ranks and tell him only what we want to tell him." He turned to Jordan. "What do you think mate?"

"I concur with you both," said Jordan. "God knows how many times that guy has kicked my ass for no reason."

"Thanks guys. Glad we're in agreement on this."

Paul sat down just as Les and Jordan were getting up to go back to their desks. They exchanged looks. Paul looked up at them.

"Don't go anywhere guys. Get comfortable. There's a shit load more I'm about to tell you."

CHAPTER TWENTY-ONE

Georgina was sitting at the window looking out over Central Park when Les and Jordan arrived to interview her. They were shocked by her appearance. She looked gaunt and hollow; the spark completely gone from her eyes.

"I'll leave you be," said Georgina's father to the detectives. "You're sure you don't want coffee or anything?" he asked.

Les smiled. "Quite sure, thank you Judge Harris."

Georgina's father quietly closed the door of the living room and Les and Jordan sat down opposite Georgina.

Jordan whistled. "What a view! I've never seen Central Park from this height except in magazines."

He was about to snap a photo with his mobile but then thought better of it and slipped it into his jacket pocket. Georgina attempted a smile. She knew Les and Jordan well and held them both in high regard. Jordan was from Brooklyn, and she liked it that he was proud of his roots. So many people tried to distance themselves from their beginnings, but Jordan was simply comfortable with who and what he was. Les was much the same although he had come from a very affluent background. His family regarded him as a Harvard drop out. He considered himself a Harvard escapee. If only they knew what a brilliant detective he was.

"Guys…" Georgina began. "No platitudes please. Let's just get down to it if you don't mind."

"Sure Georgie," said Les. "Paul has brought us up to speed on everything, including Murphey. We are with him on closing ranks, keeping everything between the three of us. Actually…four, you included."

"Yes, Paul told me. He came over last night and told me about the concierge, Murphey etcetera. Thanks guys. It's good to know that we're on the same page," she said.

There was a silence. Les and Jordan were momentarily unsure of how to proceed.

"Les, Jordan…" started Georgina. She looked from one to the other. "I'm going to be out of the loop for a while and I know you both understand why. But in the interim I will answer any questions you have. Please just bear with me. My heart is totally broken. I don't mind telling you that."

Jordan leant forward and took her hand.

"Georgie…you take as long as you need. We will not rest until we have brought these psychopaths to justice. We've got you girl."

They then went through all the events with Georgina as she remembered them. It became clear that everything was somewhat hazy after she had discovered Simon. Shock can do that to one. The most difficult thing for her to come to terms with was how she had collapsed and had not been able to get up to try and cut Simon down.

"He may still be alive today if I hadn't collapsed. I'm a detective for God's sake! I'm accustomed to crime scenes. What was wrong with me!" Georgina said her voice quavering.

Her eyes were glistening, and Les and Jordan could see that she was battling to control her emotions.

"No Georgie," said Les gently. "The toxic chemicals that had entered Simon's bloodstream were fatal. He would never have survived. They wanted to make sure of that."

Georgina looked at Les for a long time.

"So, this was a professional hit, right?" she asked.

"Oh yes," said Jordan. "They knew exactly what they were doing."

Georgina nodded her head slowly.

"And I believe the man who said he was Paul was in fact Special Agent Stonehouse?"

"Yep. One and the same," replied Les.

Georgina got up and walked over to the drinks tray. Les and Jordan exchanges looks, eyebrows raised. It was way too early for a scotch. She turned and looked at them.

"Water anyone?" she asked.

They both quickly shook their heads, embarrassed at their presumption. She poured a glass of water from the crystal water jug, took a sip, and then looked directly at both of them, her eyes narrowed.

"So, he's the patsy," said Georgina as she walked back and sat down. Les and Jordan looked at each other again.

"Not that I feel too sorry for him…" she continued. "He is such a jerk. However, even jerks don't deserve to go down for a murder they didn't commit."

"Go on…" said Jordan, frowning.

Les was looking equally perplexed.

"Somebody in a position of power instructed him to pose as Paul. I'm sure of it. Somehow, they must have found out that the evidence the gas guy had taken from Simon's apartment the day before was bogus. I know that it was because Simon gave me the original evidence for safe keeping earlier on that same day. It is now safely in my father's freezer. Somehow, they must have found out that Simon had set them up…again…and so they needed to silence him." She continued. "Knowing that the suicide set up would most probably be proven to be a homicide, they needed someone in position to take the rap for it. They wanted an open and shut case. Something that could swiftly satisfy the American public's desire for justice and would be history within a few weeks."

Les and Jordan were silent. They were mulling over what she had said. Then Les said.

"Our consensus…Paul, Jordan, and me, is that the gas guy and Stonehouse were working together." Jordan nodded in agreement.

Georgina shook her head.

"Not a chance. Stonehouse is an idiot but he's not a killer. He is so incompetent that he would have botched it anyhow. Plus, the fact that he has a monumental ego…he would never share the credit. No…the gas guy is our killer, and he was working alone. Stonehouse wouldn't have even known about his existence let alone the fact that he was there."

They were all silent as Les and Jordan digested this hypothesis.

"You may be right Georgie," said Jordan. "The concierge said that Stonehouse was white as a sheet when he ran out of the building. He was in a total state of panic. Not really the reaction of a guy who had supposedly just carried out a premeditated murder."

"And the concierge didn't see anyone else leave the building?" asked Georgina. Jordan shook his head.

Les was looking out the window, lost in thought as he contemplated this scenario. He then turned to Georgina.

"Well, if you don't mind me saying Georgie, for a girl who

has been through an unbelievable trauma, you're still on top of your game."

Georgina smiled. But it was a sad smile. Both Les and Jordan's hearts went out to her. They got up to leave.

"Just one more thing," said Georgina. "Paul tells me that the cameras that Simon rigged up in his apartment have vanished. The entire murder would have been recorded if the cameras were still there at the time. I very much doubt Simon would have removed them."

"The forensic team have no record of any cameras or recording devices," said Les. "Nothing has been found and Simon's apartment has been gone over from top to bottom. We even looked ourselves."

"Yes, I know," said Georgina. "But there *were* cameras there. I saw the video myself of the gas guy looking for the evidence the previous day. Simon had sent it to me."

"Yes, Paul showed it to us too, but forensics have literally crawled all over that place. There is nothing. Someone must have taken everything."

"But who?" asked Georgina. "Who would have had access? The apartment has been sealed off to anyone who is not law enforcement. And I don't think the gas guy even knew that the cameras were there. The footage from the day before was testimony to that. So, I doubt it would have been him who removed them."

Georgina walked to the window and stared down at Central Park.

"Someone else other than Paul and I knew about the cameras. We need to find that person."

Both Les and Jordan were silent. For now, they didn't have an answer.

"We'll keep digging Georgie," said Les. "We will find something."

Georgina turned and looked at them both for a while.

"I do hope so guys," said Georgina. "Stonehouse's life is going to depend upon it.

Judge Dermot signed off on the arrest warrant for Special Agent Stonehouse. Paul, Les, and Jordan agreed that they had to go through the motions. They had to make it look as though they were following the evidence and that the case would be a prosecutor's wet dream.

"When do we tell Stonehouse that we know he didn't do it?" asked Les.

"We don't," said Paul. "He will be screaming it from the roof tops. We simply cannot afford for that to happen."

"I know he's a prick, but it doesn't sit comfortably with me that with him being FBI, he's going to have a really bad time in the klink," said Les.

Jordan sat back and sighed.

"Whoever said this job was easy. The convoluted layers of subterfuge are exhausting but necessary."

Both Paul and Les turned and stared at him.

"What?" said Jordan looking from one to the other.

"Well fuck me. Isn't he quite the philosopher!" said Paul.

"Hell, I didn't even know you knew such big words!" laughed Les.

Jordan gave them both the finger.

"Hey! I'm a Brooklyn boff! Stick with me boys. You may learn something."

The blood drained from Stonehouse's face. Four NYPD officers were walking straight towards his desk. The whole office became silent as everyone watched the event unfold. They stopped in front of his desk.

"Special Agent Stonehouse?" asked one of the officers.

Stonehouse couldn't even answer. His heart was thumping in his chest and his mouth was as dry as the Nevada desert. One of the officers moved behind him and helped him stand up. His legs were shaking like jelly, and he felt his hands being moved to behind his back. A voice very far away was reading him his rights. His mind seemed to be blocking out parts of what was being said to him. He remembered the words *for the murder of...* but everything else seemed to drift up into the ether.

He felt as though he was floating. Faces were moving past him in slow motion as they walked him to the elevators. An unmarked van was waiting in the basement, and he remembered wondering why this was necessary. He was totally dazed and was sure that any minute now he would suddenly wake up from this nightmare and would be back safe and sound at his desk, eating Molly's sandwiches. It was lunch time, wasn't it? His mind couldn't compute anything. This could simply not be happening to him. But it was. The nightmare for Special Agent Stonehouse was only just beginning.

That afternoon at 15h00, Director Len Wyatt of the FBI walked to the podium. The room was bursting to capacity with the press and the cacophony of chatter was almost deafening. This was a show they weren't going to miss. It's not every day that an FBI agent is charged with murder. Wyatt raised his hands and the room finally fell silent. He cleared his throat as he scanned the press. This was good he thought to himself. The quintessential who's who of the media were present and he would be guaranteed of the coverage he wanted. He then began.

Ladies and gentlemen of the press, thank you for attending this briefing. This is indeed a dark day for the Federal

*Bureau of Investigation…*Wyatt glanced around the room, taking his time, then continued…*We pride ourselves on upholding our motto, fidelity, bravery, and integrity…and we are equally proud to serve the American people every day of our lives, even if that requires us putting ourselves at risk. I would like to imagine that all of you will understand, and perhaps even sympathize, as to how disturbing it is for us that one of our own…*and for effect Wyatt put his hand to his chest…*someone we trusted, and someone you, the American people trusted, has betrayed all that we stand for.*

He paused for dramatic effect. Nobody moved or said a word. One could hear the proverbial pin drop. Everyone was waiting for him to continue.

As of two hours ago, Special Agent Stonehouse, who has been with the FBI for over ten years, has formally been charged with the murder of Dr. Simon Chevalier. He is presently being transferred from Washington to New York where he will be indicted and will stand trial. As you are all aware, the initial assumption was that it was a suicide. However, we now have proof…beyond reasonable doubt… that it was in fact murder at the hands of Special Agent Stonehouse.

There was a swell of chatter and camera flashes popped. Wyatt was reveling in the moment. Talk about guilty before proven innocent. It was no accident that Wyatt was using courtroom words. He was putting Stonehouse on trial in the courtroom of the press which in turn would translate into guilt in the eyes of the American people. He looked around the room making eye contact with key journalists, to flatter them by visually seeking them out. He could see that he had them spellbound, exactly where he wanted them. He was a master manipulator. When he felt that he had paused long enough, he continued.

Many of you will be asking how this possibly could have happened, with all the checks and balances we have in place in our organization...an organization which has been fighting crime for over a century. However, now, and then, something like this does happen... Wyatt spread his hands in a deprecating manner...*And this case is not without intrigue. The victim himself, Dr. Chevalier also had compromised his position as someone who should have been trusted in one of the most exacting and important aspects of our justice system, that being forensic science. Whether his recent errors were intentional or merely mistakes, he too failed the American people. However, no one...no matter his or her failings, deserves to have their life taken from them with such brutality. And I for one, will do whatever it takes to see that justice is served.*

Right at the very back of the room, hardly visible in the crowd, stood Agent Brad Townsend. He stared at Wyatt, his jaw muscles working, his fists clenching and unclenching. Every fiber of his being wanted to launch himself at Wyatt, to knock him from his pinnacle of smug superiority and it took all his resolve to remain where he was, to force himself to listen to the most duplicitous morally corrupt human being he had ever known. The fire of vindication for Simon that was burning inside of him was turning into an inferno. He would use this rage. He would wait patiently and plot for the day when Director Wyatt would suffer the worst humiliation at the feet of the American people. He would personally shame him publicly for the whole world to see.

Wyatt loved his own oratory talents, making the press wait for his final words of wisdom. He then delivered his trump card raising his voice.

This, ladies and gentlemen, has been an FBI agent gone rogue! And I promise you… I will fix this!

Press briefings seldom solicit applause, but the press got to their feet an applauded Wyatt. He had won them over. And most importantly, he had given them the line he wanted them to quote. Every newspaper and TV station the following day had the headline he had planned on.

FBI AGENT GONE ROGUE.

One had to admit that Wyatt was brilliant, and that brilliance was further evidenced in how he had seized the opportunity to put himself centre stage, to be the one everyone could trust to *fix* this terrible event. He had told them as much and they had been suckered right into the vortex of his deception. Brad fumed. Fix this? What…was he now going to elevate himself to deity status and bring Simon back to life? He turned away from the applauding crowd, sick to his stomach by Wyatt's unadulterated manipulation and by how easily the press, who called themselves journalists had been taken in. Not one person had raised the question of the cornerstone of the entire justice system and that was that one was innocent until proven guilty. What had this country come to? He pushed his way to the exit, intent on getting as far away as possible from Wyatt and these sycophants. He felt utterly outraged by what was nothing more than a dog and pony show.

The following morning in the New York State Supreme Court, Special Agent Stonehouse entered a plea of *not guilty*. The whole process from the time he had been brought up from the cells to when the cuffs were removed from his wrists and his cell door was slammed shut, was no more than ten minutes. He sat down on the hard blue plastic mattress, nursing the red welts where the handcuffs had chaffed his wrists. He knew that they had set the cuffs as tightly as possible. This was only the beginning of how they would punish him subtly and frequently. He put his head in his hands and allowed a loud sob to escape from deep within his chest. He was shattered. Never in his wildest dreams could he ever have envisaged such a nightmare for himself. How many times had he seen perpetrators in the same position and how many times had he been glad of their suffering. For the first time ever in his life, he wondered if any of them had perhaps been innocent and had been carelessly flushed down the toilet of a fallible justice system.

The attorney appointed to represent him had advised that he enter a plea of guilty with a view to possibly receiving a reduced sentence. Stonehouse had just stared at him open-mouthed. He couldn't believe what the asshole was suggesting.

Shrugging, the attorney had said, "I'm just saying…it may be the best course of action at this juncture."

"I AM NOT GUILTY!" bellowed Stonehouse.

He had slammed his fist down on the table, his eyes wild with rage. The attorney had jumped with fright and gathering up his briefcase, had hastily left the interview room, mumbling something to the effect that he would be back in the morning. Stonehouse stared after him, absolutely seething at the indifference and incompetence of his counsel who seemed to be afraid of his own shadow. He had hoped Molly would visit him sooner rather than later, but she had told the attorney to tell her husband that she and the kids had gone to stay with her parents for a while until this whole nonsense had blown over. This was a low blow for Stonehouse. He needed her now more than ever and he suspected that it was more a case of her not being able to face the other mothers at the school. She had been something of a showoff, boasting that her husband was a special agent. Well clearly, he thought to himself, she was not going to give them the opportunity to snigger as to how special he was now. He sat back against the wall and tried to fathom any way that he could possibly prove his innocence. He racked his brain to find one thing that could cast doubt on his guilt, but he couldn't come up with anything. Nothing. Everything pointed to him. He had walked straight into a trap, and he was now sure that Wyatt had set him up. But why? What was he hiding? Why would he throw him to the wolves? What could possibly be his motivation? He must have fallen asleep because he jerked awake with the loud clang of the holding cell door being opened and a guard banging down a tray of food onto the floor. He was stiff and sore. He looked at the slop masquerading as food in the bowl and wanted to throw up. He couldn't even face the lukewarm anemic looking cup of coffee. For the first time in his life, he thought about suicide. There were a lot of *firsts* for him now. But how would he do it? They had taken everything away from him. Even the means to end this horrific nightmare. He kicked the food tray away and turning to face the wall, he curled up on the hard vinyl mattress, covering his ears with his hands to block out the clanging noises and the guards yelling abuse at the inmates.

CHAPTER TWENTY-TWO

Paul apologized to Commissioner Baker for Detective Harris's absence explaining to him that she had been close to Dr. Chevalier and was still in shock and off work.

"I understand," said Baker. "And I am truly sorry for her pain and for the tragic loss of one of New York's finest forensic minds."

"Well sir," said Paul, "It looks like Agent Stonehouse will be convicted for the crime he clearly committed."

He was testing the waters.

Baker glanced at the newspaper on the side of his desk with the glaring headline, *FBI Agent Gone Rogue* and looked back at Paul. He then said pointedly.

"We both know that is a load of hogwash Detective Damote. Could we perhaps cut to the chase and get down to why you are here?"

Paul allowed himself a small smile and reaching across, placed a file in front of the commissioner.

"Sir, everything is in there. The whole sorry, sordid story."

Baker opened the file.

"Let's move to the sofas," he suggested. "We can spread everything out on the coffee table."

Two hours later, Baker stood up and walked to his desk.

He buzzed his personal assistant.

"Hillary…may we have more coffee please before you go home?"

"Right away sir," came the reply.

Then he hesitated, looked at his watch and turning to Paul, he said.

"Hell, a scotch would be more appropriate…and most definitely welcome."

He turned back to his intercom and cancelled the coffee. He opened one of the drawers of his desk and pulled out two glasses and a bottle of scotch and walking back, placed them on the coffee table. Paul shifted in his seat, feeling somewhat uncomfortable. After all, this was the police commissioner.

"Oh, don't look so worried Detective Damote! Sometimes even I can break the rules. We still have a lot of work to get through this evening. Five minutes from now, everybody will be gone."

He poured scotch into each glass, looked at Paul and said.

"We are both just cops you know. I just happen to have a lot more scrambled egg on my shoulders, that's all."

Paul laughed nervously and they clinked glasses. Slowly he started to relax and after a few more sips of the best scotch he had ever tasted, he felt the tension in his shoulders ease.

After another hour of going through all the evidence Baker put down his glass, stood up and with his hands on his hips, surveyed the paperwork spread out before them.

"This is a hornet's nest I prayed would never happen on my watch," he said. Paul waited for him to continue.

"The truth be known, at the time I harboured suspicions about Levenstein. But there was no way that I could prove it. This…" and he picked up the copy of the DNA report "…changes everything. This is something people will kill for. And have killed for. They're only getting started."
He sat down again and continued.

"Our strategy going forward has to be watertight…we simply can't have anyone else paying the ultimate price." Paul understood exactly what the commissioner was inferring. He himself had worked on a number of high-profile Mafia related cases, and he knew only too well how quickly the bodies could pile up.

"This…all of this will bring a few people down," he continued, "but it will only be a consolation prize. If we can't identify Levenstein, we would have won a prize for only running half the race."

Paul nodded. "That is more or less what I said to Detective Harris when we were deliberating if we had enough of the puzzle to bring to you or not. So, I agree with you sir. It's imperative that we identify Levenstein as he looks now."

Baker stood up and walked over to the window, deep in thought. He turned around, the sky behind him was a soft blend of pink and orange and the lights of New York were starting to twinkle.

"Detective Damote…people think that I sit up here in an ivory tower removed from everything below, breathing rarified air, endlessly signing off on initiatives. But that's not the case. When I said that I'm just a cop…I meant it." He walked over to the couch and sat down again, the leather creaking as he leant forward to pick up his glass. He swirled the scotch around, studied it for a moment and then taking a sip, continued.

"I was once an undercover operative, for many years in fact. I learnt how to blend in, how to be the proverbial chameleon. That experience has stood me in good stead." Paul sensed that something important was coming, that Baker was moving towards something significant that he wanted to share with him. Baker went on.

"There is a child trafficking ring that goes all the way to the top in this land of ours, a perversion that has crept into the upper echelons of big tech, the highest political appointments and even law enforcement. A perversion that is so disturbing that sometimes I have to remind myself that it's real. But it is real, and it is festering within our society. It is shocking what humans are capable of."

Paul sat dead still. He was aware that he was hardly breathing. He said nothing, not wanting to disturb the momentum that was building. Baker looked long and hard at him.

"I am going to share something with you that simply cannot go further than this room. I need to have your word detective."

Paul looked Baker straight in the eye.

"You do sir. You have my word."

Baker stared at Paul for a few moments.

"Okay. Here it is." He placed his glass on the table. "Detective Damote, I have been working under cover for the last six months."

He registered the look of absolute shock on Paul's face.

"Sir?" said Paul. "I don't understand."

"No surprise there detective. Who has ever heard of a police commissioner working under cover. It does sound rather weird come to think of it."

He then appraised Paul of the club at the top of the Sheldon Wagstaff building and he didn't spare any of the details. Paul was spellbound. This kind of thing only happened in the movies, or so he thought. On reflection Paul realized that no other law enforcement operative could possibly have gained entry to such an exclusive club to carry out surveillance. Baker had used his position and influence and had gotten the qualifying referrals. He was in.

"But how in the world do you pay the exorbitant fees?" asked Paul incredulously.

"With great difficulty detective. I have had to move money around this department like a merry go round. I could make the worst of the money launderers pale in comparison to my skills. I've had to ensure that the money can never be traced back to this department, otherwise the game will be up and they will go to ground."

Paul shook his head in amazement. Baker continued.

"Most of the guys who belong to this club are actually quite harmless. They have massive egos and they like women. A lot. Hardly a crime. But there are those who are different. Their tastes…shall we say…are not what we would ever call normal. They like them young. Way too young. And this club offers this service to them too. Most of the members have no idea that this goes on. They would be disgusted and horrified. Most of the guys have kids themselves. What you need to understand is that this level of perversion is not as prevalent as one would think. It's rare in terms of the overall population. But it is there and it's sickening none the less and I know exactly which members of the club are involved. I also believe that it is linked to a massive money laundering scheme. And I have suspected for a long time that their supplier of underage minors and the kingpin of the money laundering is one and the same. He is simply invisible now."

Paul was speechless. He hadn't moved. His glass was still halfway to his lips. It was as if he had been frozen in time. Baker laughed. "I am sorry detective. I am not being trite. It's just that your face is such a picture of shock."
He threw up his hands. "I have no idea why I am finding this so funny."
Finally, Paul was able to speak. "Perhaps it's just a release of tension sir."
Baker nodded and sobered. "Yes, Damote…this has been a very hard journey. I have had to allow unspeakable crimes to take place in order to continue gathering intel."
"Sir, I am having extreme difficulty in discerning which is more shocking. The pedos of the elite or the fact that the police commissioner of the New York Police Department is an undercover operative!" Paul started to laugh too. "It's absurd! Who would ever have thought such a thing was possible."
"I know," said Baker. "Ridiculous isn't it! But please know this…" he said, his expression becoming serious, "You are now one of two people who knows about this. In time, I will reveal why and who the other person is."
Paul was quiet for a few moments. He looked up at Baker.

"Thank you for trusting me, sir. It is a great privilege to be in your confidence."

For Baker it had been an enormous relief to be able to share the burden with another man. Because that was what it had been; a massive burden of knowledge whilst being powerless to act on it. It had been heart breaking to know that underaged kids were being abused and that he had to let it happen so that he could gather all the evidence. Now, in this office, on this day with Detective Damote, all this had changed.

"Detective Damote…we are going to bring the whole cabal down if it's the last thing we do."

"I'll drink to that sir," said Paul.

"Well then I guess I'd better top you up," said Baker smiling.

Paul held out his glass and for the first time in a long time, he felt that there was hope on the horizon.

Two hundred miles away in Washington, Wyatt poured himself a double and sat down on one of the sofas that flanked the fireplace in his home office, settling back against the plush upholstery. Life was good and he found himself smiling. Things had been tough for a while, a bit of a touch and go scenario but he had handled it and to all intents and purposes, the Levenstein issue was now history. He watched the flames flicker in the fireplace and felt a wonderful sense of contentment wash over him. The press briefing the day before had been a total success and Stonehouse was as good as convicted. Picking up his mobile, he sent off a cryptic text message to Sedgefield and Turner, nothing that could be defined.

We are home and dry chaps! Crack open the champers!

He sat back and savoured the warmth of the fire and the taste of the single malt whiskey as its heat spread though his body. Yes, he thought to himself. Life is good.

Back in New York, there was a loud buzzer sound, and all the cells were plunged into darkness. Stonehouse heard the voices of the guards fade down the corridor and an overwhelming sense of despair descended upon him. This was his first night of incarceration in Rikers. He had been denied bail at his hearing, not that he could afford it anyhow. How long would it be? And what fate would be waiting for him at the end of it all? In the darkness, he lay down on the hardest mattress he had ever felt and pulled the rough blanket over himself. The cell was cold, and the blanket offered very little warmth. Pulling his legs up into a fetal position, the tears started to flow, and Special Agent Stonehouse literally cried himself to sleep.

CHAPTER TWENTY-THREE

Paul, Les, and Jordan were using one of the interview rooms and were going through the forensic photos they had received. They had also gone through the tedious task of watching all the surveillance footage compiled from the public areas of Simon's apartment building.

The gas guy's peak cap had been pulled low over his face, so he was not identifiable via the cameras. However, the concierge had identified him as the same person in the photo that Paul had shown him, so they knew that the man who had been tailing Simon and the gas guy were one and the same. Now they had to put a name to the face. And then there was the issue of how he had escaped after the murder. The CCTV cameras had recorded him entering Simon's apartment building twice over a two-day period, but only exiting once. And at no time had he used either of the elevators.

Paul sat back in his chair and throwing up his hands, said to Les and Jordan.

"How in the world did he get out?"

"The same way he got in," said a female voice.

They all looked up surprised. There stood Georgina behind Paul.

She smiled. "Hi guys."

Paul jumped up. "Georgie! What are you doing here? You should be with your father…"

Georgina pulled out a chair and sat down.

"I can wallow in self-pity, or I can get back into the saddle and vindicate Simon's memory. It's not a hard choice."

They all exchanged glances.

"Good on you Georgie," said Les high-fiving her.

"Yes, welcome back," concurred Jordan smiling at Georgina.

"Thank you," she said. She looked at each of them. "Right! I have fresh eyes. I'll see if I can spot anything."

"Coffee? Anyone?" Paul asked.

"Good idea!" said Georgina. "And make it snappy."

Paul laughed. "Oh dear! She's back!"

Wyatt had organized an informant in Rikers so that he could keep tabs on Stonehouse in case he did something stupid like claim that he had been set up, or worse, talk about Leventstein. The trial date had been set for three months' time. This allowed plenty of time to pressurize Stonehouse into committing suicide. However, the sooner he did it, the better.

Give him a rough time... Wyatt texted to his informant, who was one of the guards in Stonehouse's block.

No problem sir, came the return text. *Plenty of inmates interested in his fat wobbly ass.*

Wyatt frowned. Too much information you idiot he muttered to himself. He sat back in his chair, slowly rotating from side to side. He decided to mentally count off the issues at hand.

So, first off Chevalier was taken care of and was now out of the picture. The evidence of Levenstein's DNA had still not been found but he wasn't particularly worried, as it probably never would been found. Mullens had been paid and was off the radar for a while until he needed him again. Collins had nothing to report about detectives Harris and Damote. Besides, it appeared that Detective Harris was consumed with grief and Captain Murphey had assured him that Detective Damote was in hand. He had also confirmed that the investigating team were satisfied with the overwhelming evidence that Stonehouse was their guy. A slam dunk case. Great.

His thoughts then turned to the police commissioner Ed Baker. No need to worry there he thought. It had been an awkward meeting a few weeks ago but when he had seen

Baker at the Wagstaff a few days ago, he was his normal friendly self. Stonehouse was a gonner of that he was sure. He would receive a minimum of twenty-five years, and Wyatt had made sure that the attorney representing him would never allow Stonehouse to testify and blurt out anything about being set up, or about Levenstein. Hopefully Stonehouse would kill himself before the court case. The only loose end he could think of was Agent Brad Townsend. He was unsure of what to do. By all accounts, Townsend was regarded as a tenacious and extremely bright agent. Perhaps this was a case of letting sleeping dogs lie. He didn't want to attract any unnecessary attention to himself. Yes, he would leave that be for the moment and just keep tabs on Townsend from a distance.

"Bingo!" said Georgina. "Got him!"

Paul, Les, and Jordan got up from their seats and huddled around Georgina. She was looking down at one of the photos taken in Simon's apartment by the forensics team. "What are we looking at?" asked Paul as he stared down at a photo which had been shot from a low angle of the edge of one of the chairs in Simon's lounge. Les and Jordan were equally puzzled.

"All I can see are possibly some fibers?" ventured Jordan. Paul glanced at the inventory list of forensic photos.

"Yes, it's a record of fibers on the chair," he confirmed.

"No." said Georgina shaking her head. "Look at the background." They all leaned in closer.

"What, the open door of Simon's apartment?" asked Les.

"Look closer!" said Georgina impatiently, pointing at something with her fingernail. "Look beyond the door." Then they all saw it. The glass window of the fire escape door was just visible on the extreme right of the photo and although it was blurry, they could none the less clearly see a face with the hood of a white forensic suit, peering through the glass.

"The bugger! That's how he got out! exclaimed Paul. "He made himself look like one of the forensics team!"

"Clever girl!" exclaimed Jordan looking down at Georgina.

"Clever boy," said Georgina tapping the face of the gas guy with her fingernail. "No one would have even questioned him. He would have sailed right out of the front entrance of the building totally unnoticed."

"That photo must have been taken a good few hours after the murder. It would have been a while before the forensic team arrived," said Les.

Georgina sat back in her chair deep in thought. Then she said.

"That means he would have been hiding somewhere in the

building during that time. We need to go back and look thoroughly. We may get lucky and find something."

Paul then said. "I'll get hold of forensics. But how are we going to keep this from Murphey?"

"We can't," said Les. "So, we're going to have to do it ourselves. If we engage the forensics team again, he'll know that we're looking for something."

"Well, we'll need someone who knows how to process the scene," said Georgina looking from one to the other.

"I still have a load of gear from my days in forensics," said Jordan. Everyone exchanged looks.

"Well, aren't you full of surprises! Good one Jordan," exclaimed Paul. Jordan grinned.

"Looks like our Sunday is sorted then. I'll bring the gear. You bring the beer."

The memorial service for Simon was set for Thursday at 11h00 at the All Saints Catholic Church in Manhattan. A funeral as such could not take place as the body had not yet been released to the family. Georgina knew Simon's parents well. They were devastated to have lost their son and only child. They had travelled from Maryland and were staying not too far from her father's apartment. Georgina and her father had hosted them for dinner the previous evening and it had been a very sad and somber affair. They were both elderly, having had Simon in their forties but none the less, Georgina was shocked to see how they had aged, and she felt helpless as to how to ease their pain. The truth be known, she was still trying to work through her own.

Paul was unable to attend. One of his daughters had injured herself at school and he needed to get to the hospital. Nothing too serious but none the less, he needed to be there for his family. The church was packed to capacity. Simon's parents asked Georgina to sit with them and she gently held Simon's mother's hand which felt so frail and vulnerable in hers. The eulogy was heartfelt, and tears prickled in Georgina's eyes, but she was determined to maintain her composure. When the service finished, Simon's parents were taken to the entrance of the church so that the mourners could file past them and offer their condolences. Georgina hung back and decided to wait until everyone had gone before she would join Simon's parents at the wake.

As she looked around, she saw Director Wyatt make his way to the exit. Just watching him made her skin crawl. She instinctively felt that this was due to more than just the fact that he had denigrated Simon at the press briefing.

Call it her detective radar but she did find herself wondering if he was perhaps the one behind this whole tragic saga. The FBI had done everything in its power to protect Levenstein and go after anyone who wanted to expose him. As they say, it usually comes from the top.

Brad Townsend stepped behind one of the pillars and kept himself screened from Wyatt's line of vision. He knew that sooner or later Wyatt would make his move to ensure that he was also brought to heel, but for the moment he was keeping a low profile. The mourners processed past Simon's parents at the entrance of the church, shaking hands and offering their condolences. Brad watched Wyatt take Simon's mother's hand in both of his and no doubt he was reeling off a whole lot of platitudes. Her watery eyes looked up at him and she made an effort to smile and thank him for being there. He then shook Simon's father's hand and Brad had to look away. The hypocrisy was simply too nauseating. Simon's parents had no idea that this man standing in front of them, a week or so ago, had trashed Simon's reputation in front of the press and thus in front of the American people. The cheek of him attending Simon's memorial service and pretending that he even gave a damn. Brad was glad that they were none the wiser. They had enough pain to deal with presently.

Georgina bent down and picked up one of the printed memorial pamphlets. She looked down at Simon's photo and an overwhelming sense of grief welled up inside of her. A voice behind her suddenly interrupted her reverie.

"Detective Harris…?" Georgina spun round. A handsome, clean-cut man was looking at her.

"I'm Agent Brad Townsend. I was a friend of Simon's from university days. We were meant to be having dinner the night of Simon's murder," said Brad as he extended his hand.

"Oh!" said Georgina taken aback. She shook his hand. "Simon had told me that he had reconnected with you recently…and yes, Detective Damote and I had been looking forward to meeting you that evening…" her voice trailed off.

The church was almost empty now and as she looked at the entrance, she saw Simon's parents being ushered towards the car that had transported them there. She looked back at Brad who then said.

"Firstly, may I say that I am truly sorry for the terrible loss you have suffered Georgina. May I call you Georgina?"

"Yes of course Agent Townsend," she replied.

"Please…call me Brad."

Georgina smiled and then said.

"Thank you for being here Brad."

He was silent for a while as he looked at her, and then said.

"I have the camera recordings."

Georgina was totally taken aback and was speechless for a moment, her eyes wide. He continued.

"I went back to Simon's apartment late that night and removed the cameras and recording device. I knew that forensics would be back the next day. It was too late in the evening for them to have completed all their work, so I was hoping they hadn't discovered the cameras yet. Simon had shared the video with me of the gas technician who had been looking for the evidence the previous day. I have an FBI badge, so it was easy to gain access. I was lucky. Everything was still there, so I took it."

Georgina continued staring at Brad, at a loss for words.

"Simon and I were good buddies at university. He was someone I truly admired and although we hadn't seen each other for a long time, the friendship was just the same as it always had been."

Her eyes welled up with tears. She felt a flood coming that she knew was going to be almost impossible to hold back and she saw immense compassion in Brad's eyes. He moved closer to her and gently held her upper arms with his hands.

"The Micro-SD card is in your left jacket pocket. Please give it to your partner. I do not want you to watch it."

His hands tightened around her arms to convey the seriousness of his request.

"Promise me Georgina that you won't watch it. Not now, not ever."

She stared at him, her expression shocked but the urgency in his voice caught her attention and she nodded, tears starting to spill down her cheeks. Slowly, she lowered herself down onto the pew. She was feeling dizzy and nauseous, and she leant forward putting her head in her hands. She remained like that for a few seconds trying to regain her composure. When she looked up again, he was gone. She looked around perplexed and wondered if she had imagined the entire thing. She slowly stood up and started for the exit, wiping the tears from her cheeks as she walked. She slipped her hand into her left pocket.

It was unmistakable. The card was there.

CHAPTER TWENTY-FOUR

Stonehouse shuffled in the queue for supper with his tray. He had already lost weight; prison food was not exactly haute cuisine and he longed for a home cooked meal. He held out his bowl, not making eye contact with the chef standing behind the counter. The chef dipped the ladle into a steaming, lumpy grey looking stew but instead of tipping it into the bowl, he slopped it all over Stonehouse's arm. Stonehouse jumped back yelling with pain, dropping his tray and coffee as he grabbed his burnt arm.

"Hey fatty!" exclaimed the chef with a smirk. "Look at the godamned mess you've made!"

One of the guards marched over and grabbed Stonehouse by his shirt.

"You had better fucking clean that up, you moron!"

He then pushed him hard in the direction of a mop and bucket placed in the corner a few feet away. With the force of the guard pushing him, he lost his footing and fell headlong into the wall, smashing the side of his face. The mop and steel bucket went flying, spilling dirty water onto the floor. Everyone in the canteen was laughing, enjoying the impromptu comedy show. The guard stalked over and kicked Stonehouse in the ribs and threw the bucket at him.

Stonehouse ducked and the steel bucket ricocheted off the wall with a loud clang and then bounced onto the floor, spinning around. The guard turned around to his audience and said.

"Looks like our fella here can play the cymbals!"

Everyone laughed and the guard raised his hands like a conductor. Turning towards Stonehouse he yelled.

"Pick it up you idiot and clean the whole godamned canteen! You have one hour to do it!"

Stonehouse wiped the blood from his face and slowly stood up. Before long, the last of the inmates had filed out and the canteen was empty. So were all the food dishes. The hunger pangs gnawed at his stomach as he mopped and cleaned the floors and tables.

An hour later, the guard returned dragging two wheely bins with him. Without even looking at Stonehouse, he tipped all the trash onto the floor. At that moment a senior warden walked in and surveyed the mess.

"Well, I would say that this inmate has no clue how to clean! Never seen such a godamned mess, have you?" he said turning to the guard, who shook his head, his expression somber.

Stonehouse stood there, sweat dripping off his face saying nothing. His one eye was now so swollen and blue that it was almost closed, and he had a long, bloodied graze down the side of his face.

"Well…no pressure moron. You've got the whole night to get this place cleaned up. Better get to it sonny," said the warden and he turned on his heel and walked out.

The guard followed him and as he went through the canteen door, he flipped the light switch on the outside and Stonehouse was plunged into darkness. A key turned in the lock and then there was silence.

He stood there feeling utterly helpless. He slowly stepped backwards feeling for the wall and then slid down onto the floor. There was nothing he could do in the pitch dark. Within a few minutes the floor was so cold that he got up and fumbled his way to one of the benches and lay down. He must have eventually dozed off because he turned in his sleep and suddenly rolled off the narrow bench, crashing to the floor. He yelled out, writhing in pain clutching his shoulder, scrambling into a seated position. Eventually he realized that his shoulder was dislocated. The pain was excruciating. He cupped his elbow with his one hand to minimize any movement and shuffled on his knees towards the wall. He leant against it, turned slowly, and sat back. He started to sob. He knew without a doubt that he was not going to be able to take much more of this.

It must have been five in the morning when a hint of grey showed through the high-set grilled windows and slowly the canteen became lighter. Stonehouse was numb with cold, but he willed himself to stand up and start the hard task of picking up all the trash with his good arm. Every time he bent forward, the searing pain made him want to cry out, but he willed himself to continue. Then with one hand, he mopped the floor and after an hour, he was finished. He emptied the bucket and placed it with the mop where it had been the evening before. Slowly he sat down on one of the benches, sweat pouring down his face, even though he was shaking with cold. Or was it pain. Everything just seemed to blur together. He was vaguely aware of the sound of a key turning in the canteen door lock, but he didn't even bother to look up.

"Well, looky here! Whoopy doo! Looks like we have ourselves one hellava good cleanin' boy!" exclaimed the guard, his hands on his hips as he surveyed the canteen. "Best you apply for the job buddy. Pay's lousy but who cares!" he burst out laughing at his own poor attempt at a joke. He continued. "You'd better get yourself cleaned up sonny before inspection else you're gonna be in shit street again. Now you run along darlin'…" he drawled.

Stonehouse stood up slowly, saying nothing. As he walked towards the door, the guard sneaked his foot out and tripped him up. Stonehouse fell forward, crashing down onto his dislocated shoulder, screaming in pain.

" Get up you idiot!" yelled the guard.

Stonehouse tried to stand up. The room started to spin and in the next moment, he fainted, his legs buckling under him as he fell backwards, the back of his head smacking hard, bouncing on the concrete floor.

Wyatt cracked the top of his boiled egg with the back of his spoon and prized off the top. Good. The yolk was nice and runny. Helen was preoccupied with her muesli and the kids were both glued to their mobiles, eating their waffles absentmindedly. Wyatt's mobile buzzed. He put down the spoon and scrolled to the text message.

Our boy is in the infirmary. Had an accident...

Wyatt smiled. He texted back. *Well done. Keep up the good work.* He closed his mobile and picked up his spoon. Helen looked up.

"Anything interesting?" she asked.

"No nothing. Just work," mumbled Wyatt.

He picked up the newspaper and screened himself from her vision. Things had become somewhat icy in the Wyatt household. He was not quite sure what was going on, but he had an inkling that she may have found out that he was banging her best friend. These women had state of the art radar antennae when it came to infidelity. After a while, he put the newspaper down, finished his egg and was about to excuse himself when Helen said.

"So, it's not Stella, my ex-best-friend sending you boob or butt shots?" she asked bitterly.

"Seriously?" exclaimed Wyatt. "In front of the kids?"

"They can't even hear us. They were born with those air pods stuck in their ears. When do they ever listen or even speak to us anyway," said Helen looking disdainfully at their children. Wyatt shook his head and stood up.

"See you this evening," he said as he passed her. "Bye kids." They didn't even look up.

Paul, Les, and Jordan were watching the video footage from the card Brad had slipped into Georgina's pocket. It was horrific. The absence of any audio made it all the more surreal. They watched as the gas guy pushed his way into the apartment and threw Simon onto the sofa. Simon got up, tried to grab him but the gas guy twisted away. A heated exchange ensued between them and then Simon started gesticulating as he walked towards the intercom. He leaned in close obviously talking to the concierge, glancing momentarily over his shoulder and then away again. The gas guy moved like lightning. Simon would not have had a chance to defend himself. It was pitiful watching Simon collapse, clutching at his killer but the worst of it was still to come.

The gas guy worked quickly, climbing onto the dining table so that he could rig the rope up onto the light fitting ceiling hook. He then dragged Simon's paralyzed body and hauled it up, putting the rope with its preset loop around his neck. He then pulled hard on the rope three or four times, hoisting Simon up, his feet just resting on the dining table surface. He climbed up next to Simon and knotted the rope. After jumping down, he pushed the dining table away quickly and Simon's body jolted downwards and one could see his neck twist sideways, his body jerking right to left.

"Oh Christ," said Paul, his voice quavering. "Georgina must never see this."

Les and Jordan exchanged looks; both of their expressions grim. They were hardened detectives, but both felt sickened to their stomachs. The gas guy looked around quickly, grabbed his toolbox and headed for the door. He carefully left it slightly ajar and then disappeared in the direction of the fire escape door, away from the elevators.

Nothing happened for a while but a minute or two later, they watched Stonehouse tentatively enter the apartment.

He walked slowly into the lounge towards the kitchen. At first, he didn't see Simon but when he did, his extreme shock was evident. He fell backwards onto the parquet floor, scooting backwards frantically on his buttocks. His facial expression was one of absolute horror and when he reached the apartment door, he rolled over trying to get up and fell again as he scrambled to get away, heading in the direction of the elevators.

The room was deathly silent as the three detectives continued to watch the footage. For about twenty seconds nothing happened. Then Georgina ran into the room. Les glanced across at Paul who was leaning forward, his fists bunched. At first Georgina looked around, her mouth opening and closing as she was calling Simon's name. And then they watched her do a double take, as she looked to the right where the dining room was. She staggered forward a few steps, her mouth wide open in a soundless scream, her arms reaching out in front of her. Her legs then caved in under her and she collapsed onto the floor. She was reaching up, her eyes wide and terrified but she couldn't stand up. Her limbs were simply not functioning. Her mouth was opening and closing, almost like a fish gasping out of water. She fell forward, her shoulders heaving while she was crawling towards Simon.

Beads of perspiration lined Paul's forehead as he watched the nightmare play out. He watched himself enter the apartment a few minutes later and run towards Georgina, grasping her shoulders. And then looking up he saw Simon. He ran out of frame momentarily and then appeared again with a knife in his hand. He grabbed a chair, scrambled up and was frantically slicing at the rope. Next thing both he and Simon came crashing down while Georgina was slowly crawling towards them. He was leaning over Simon, shaking him and then he became aware of Georgina tugging at him. He turned to look at her. Her mouth was open, imploring, desperate. He jumped up, sweeping her up into his arms and moved towards the lounge.

Paul pressed pause. He couldn't watch any more.

"Sorry guys…I need to get some air," he said, his voice shaky. He turned and left the room.

Les and Jordan looked at each other and then looked at the frozen image of Paul with Georgina in his arms. Les ran his hand through his hair.

"This is beyond evil…" he said shaking his head.

Jordan reached over and switched the machine off.

"How will Georgina ever get over this?"

Les shook his head slowly and said, "She won't."

The following day, Paul and Georgina were having breakfast in a coffee shop close to the precinct. They were discussing Paul's meeting with the police commissioner. He left out the bit about Baker being under cover; that was for Baker to tell Georgina if he so wished to.

"We need to see him again," said Paul. "The camera footage changes everything."

Georgina stirred her coffee lost in thought for a while. Then she said. "I presume we'll go via his personal assistant?"

"Yes, most definitely. We can't have Murphy know anything about this. I'll set it up Georgie."

She nodded and looked out the window lost in her own thoughts. Paul watched her. Even though she was back at work full time and was mostly her usual spunky self, today it seemed to him that some part of her was absent. Not surprising. Grief is a terrible thing. There would be good days and then there would be bad days. The finality of loss was entirely debilitating.

CHAPTER TWENTY-FIVE

Paul, Les, Jordan and Georgina set off early on Sunday morning for Simon's apartment building. They did however take a circuitous route. They drove to a parking garage about three miles away and then got into a van Jordan had borrowed from a friend. They then drove to Simon's apartment building and after Georgina had punched in the access code and the garage security gate had opened, they went straight down into the underground garage. They waited a full fifteen minutes before exiting the vehicle to be sure that they hadn't been followed. They took the elevator from the basement straight up to Simon's floor and then split up. Simon's front door still had the crime scene tape sectioned across it.

Les and Paul searched the fourteenth, fifteenth and sixteenth floor lift areas and fire escapes for any place the gas guy could have hidden, whilst Jordan and Georgina did the same working their way down. Nothing on the thirteenth, twelfth and eleventh floors. And then they found a cleaning closet on the tenth-floor fire escape landing. Georgina immediately texted Paul. He replied. *We're coming down.*

They stood outside the closet and discussed the best course of action. First off, they would open the door and peek in. If they felt that it required further inspection, Jordan would don his forensic gear and go in to investigate. He put on a latex glove and opened the door carefully. It was a small closet but large enough to house cleaning materials, a vacuum cleaner, mops, buckets etcetera. And a person if necessary. They all peered in.

Nothing looked out of place but none the less this closet represented the closest and quickest place the gas guy could have escaped to, especially knowing that Stonehouse was minutes away. So, it clearly warranted a thorough examination.

"I'm going in guys. This may well be where he was hiding," said Jordan. They all nodded in agreement. He backed away and started to unpack his forensic gear.

"I'll let you know if I need any bags and then you can just pass them to me," he said to Georgina.

Once Jordan was kitted out, he turned on his headband torch and went into the closet. Paul, Les, and Georgina sat down on the stairs and waited.

Brad was sitting in front of his state-of-the-art computer at home. One could easily mistake it for an intergalactic spaceship's control console. He had three large, curved computer screens and the hard drive spec was probably one of the most powerful private desktop computers money could buy. He had multiple firewalls and intrusion detections, and he could navigate by stealth anywhere he wanted to whilst constantly maintaining invisibility. He liked to work in a darkened windowless room. It helped him move though the cyber layers as if he were creeping up on the enemy on a dark moonless night. He could feel that he was getting closer to his prize. He was a hunter peering through the dense binary foliage looking for the slightest hint of cyber spoor. And then suddenly there it was. Right in front of him. Like bubbles rising to the surface, the deleted files he had been searching so hard for appeared. And this would lead him straight to the front door of the parties who were hiding them from the world.

"I have something," said the muffled voice of Jordan. They all jumped up and peered in through the door. "Bag please."

Georgina slipped a latex glove on and fished a bag out of Jordan's forensics bag. She leaned in through the door and handed it to him. He carefully opened it and hovering a pair of tweezers above the opening, he let a syringe cap fall into the bag. He then sealed it carefully and handed it to Georgina. They all looked at it in amazement. Syringe caps most definitely do not constitute standard cleaning equipment. Jordan spent another half an hour combing the closet but couldn't find any other evidence or fingerprints. Finally, he emerged exhausted. He had been in there for over an hour. The concentration required for forensics was grueling. He divested himself of his suit and goggles and wiped the sweat off his face and neck with a small towel from his bag. He was hot and tired but exhilarated. Les cracked open an ice-cold beer from the small cooler box and handed it to him. Jordan's eyes lit up.

"Beers for everyone!" Les said passing them around.

"Time for a toast!" he said, and they all clanked cans.

Paul then said somberly. "To Simon, our friend and hero. We will avenge your passing."

They were all silent for a while. Georgina looked at all of them and raised her beer can.

"Thank you. To a team like no other."

They all headed back to Jordan's apartment. Now they had a problem on their hands. How were they going to get the syringe cap processed and analyzed without anyone knowing.

"Well, Levenstein had his own private lab rat. Guess we'll have to find one too," said Jordan. "I know how to do the analysis, but I don't have a lab."

Les looked at Georgina and asked.

"Was there anyone in particular that Simon ever mentioned to you Georgie? Someone who he held in high regard at his lab. Someone he trusted?"

Georgina thought for a moment before replying.

"Yes, in fact there was. A technician by the name of Sophie. I remember him saying that she was top class at her job plus she was very loyal to him."

"Hmmm…" said Paul thoughtfully. "Let's contact her discreetly and see if she will assist us."

"What about asking Brad Townsend to do it? He seems to be very good at doing things under the radar," ventured Georgina.

"Sounds worth a try," said Les. "Do you want to reach out to him?"

"No, I don't think I should," said Georgina. They're still watching me. You…perhaps not so much."

"Okay. Leave it to me. I'll contact him." said Les.

It was Monday morning and Police Commissioner Baker had been informed about Stonehouse. He immediately sent one of his officers to conduct an investigation and to report back to him. The prison guards had closed ranks and all that he came back with was a vague report from the prison doctor regarding Stonehouse's injuries which he stated had been self-inflicted. Yeah right.

Baker pressed his buzzer.

"Hillary…"

"Yes sir?"

"Get me the Inspector General of Prisons please," he said.

"Right away sir," Hillary answered.

Baker drummed his fingers on his desk while he waited. Two minutes later, Hillary buzzed him.

"Line one sir."

"Thank you." Baker pressed the button and was through to Inspector Warren Taylor.

"Warren…," said Baker.

"Yes, hello Ed. How are you keeping?" asked Taylor.

"All good thanks Warren. Have you got a couple of minutes?"

"Yes of course. How can I help?"

"It's about Special Agent Stonehouse who was arrested on suspicion of murdering the forensic scientist. As you know it's been all over the news."

"Yes. Not good for the FBI. Wyatt must be somewhat embarrassed," mused Taylor.

Baker sensed that there was no love lost between the inspector and the director of the FBI.

"Well, there seems to be an issue with some injuries that

Stonehouse has suffered in one of your prisons. No doubt you're aware that he is presently in Rikers," said Baker.

"Yes, I am aware of that. What kind of injuries?" asked Taylor.

"Well, that's just it. The doctor is being obtuse, and the guards have closed ranks. Which is why I am calling you." Taylor was silent for a while and then he said.

"Would you like me to look into it?"

"I would be most appreciative Warren. Look, I know this may sound somewhat left of field, but I am not entirely convinced that Stonehouse is the murderer. I think there are parties who want him convicted swiftly. Too swiftly." Taylor remained silent. Baker continued.

"I also think that he's possibly a suicide risk. He is not tough enough to deal with prison. Now if he is proven guilty, then he belongs in prison for a very long time. But…if he is not…" Baker let the sentence hang in the air.

"Yep. I got you," said Warren. "Most perpetrators claim that they are innocent when they are not. We all know that but there are exceptions. We can't have a situation where a potentially innocent man is driven off the edge. So yes, I will look into it. Give me a little time though. I think you can appreciate that one can't go head-to-head with these guards. They're a breed of their own."

"Well, I really appreciate it, Warren," said Baker. "And

thank you for your time."

"My pleasure Ed. I'll get back to you…soon," said Taylor and with that, he rang off.

Brad Townsend sent an email to Sophie de la Motte posing as a good friend of her recently deceased cousin. He said his name was Ben Jones and that he hoped she wouldn't find it intrusive, but would she like to meet for a coffee? He was in New York visiting family. He would however understand if she refused as obviously, she had never met him. A day later he received a reply that she was happy to meet with him. Perhaps they could meet at her local coffee shop? He replied saying that was perfect and please would she say when and send him the location. He added.

"I very much look forward to meeting you, Sophie. It will be nice to reminisce about Rory."

That was the advantage of being a hacker. Finding info on anyone was dead easy. The meeting was set for tomorrow at 15h00 at a coffee shop called *Time Out* close to the lab. Great. Now to convince her to help them.

The following day, Brad arrived early at the coffee shop. He stood up when she entered, knowing exactly what she looked like from her police clearance photo on the law enforcement data base. The fact that she was very pretty did not go unnoticed by him. He waved to catch her attention. Seeing him, she walked over to the table and shook his hand, smiling.

"Lovely to meet you Sophie," said Brad.

"Likewise, lovely to meet you Ben," she replied as they both sat down.

There was a moments awkward silence and then Brad said tentatively.

"Except I am not Ben…"

She immediately made to get up, but he reached out and gently touched her arm.

"I am…was…a close friend of Simon's. I need your help Sophie which is why I contacted you."

She hesitated, unsure of what to do. Brad continued.

"We are in a public place Sophie. I can't hurt you. I'm sorry for the subterfuge but we…my friends and I think that we can trust you. You were very loyal to Simon."

She slowly sat back down again. "Why the lies Ben…or whoever you are?" she asked.

"Brad. My name is Brad Townsend, and I'm an FBI agent." He immediately saw the wariness in her eyes. He added quickly. "But I am a good FBI agent. Oh God…that sounds so cheesy," he said shaking his head.

Suddenly Sophie smiled.

"Yeah…very cheesy. You could do better than that."

"All right…" replied Brad. "Let's start all over again. Hello Sophie. I am Brad and I'm a dork!"

She stared at him for a moment and then suddenly laughed. Tilting her head, she said.

"Okay…Agent Dork, what's this all about?"

So, Brad told her all about the team and then about Stonehouse taking the rap for something he hadn't done. And then finally he got to the evidence they had found in the cleaning closet.

"Simon spoke highly of you Sophie to Detective Harris. We need your help in processing the evidence…without anyone knowing. We are all being watched, and we simply can't log the evidence in for processing through the standard means."

She looked away lost in thought, her expression sad. Brad said nothing waiting for her to continue.

"I miss him," she said looking back at Brad. "I miss Dr. Chevalier. He was exceptional. Not only in his work but also how he interacted with everyone. He was really kind. And he was the brightest person I have ever known."

"I know," said Brad. "Even at university, no one could come close to him. He was always ahead of the game. He came to me a few months ago asking for help. He was onto something big and when he told me what it was, it amazed me how fearless he was."

Sophie was silent for a while and then she said.

"I'll help you. I know how rubbish the FBI has become. Oh sorry…not you Ben…Brad," she was fumbling her words, feeling embarrassed. Brad chuckled.

"Now who's being the dork! But it's okay. You're right Sophie about the FBI. I know only too well. I am right in the middle of it."

They looked at each other for a while and then Sophie became serious.

"Okay Brad. Tell me what you want me to process," she said leaning forward, her elbows on the table.

And in her eyes, Brad saw something of Simon. A determination and a fearlessness. Yes, he thought to himself. This girl was made of strong stuff, and he instinctively knew that he could trust her.

Ed Baker's line buzzed.

"It's Inspector Taylor for you sir," said Hillary.

"Put him through please." There was another buzz and he picked up. "Warren. Thank you for calling."

"Hi Ed. I have information for you. It seems that someone from the outside is pulling strings in Rikers. Someone wants Stonehouse singled out for rough treatment."

"Hmmm. I thought as much," said Baker.

"I have arranged for him to be transferred out to another facility. And the guards concerned have been reprimanded and are on probation. It's a never-ending battle with these guys. They are a law unto themselves."

"Yes, I know. I have my fair share of overzealous police officers." said Baker. "Well, thank you very much Warren for your help and intervention. I want this guy to have a fair trial. And it would help if he remained in one piece."

"Yes Ed. Exactly. No need to worry. He's being sent to a secure facility in Albany County, and they know that I'm watching them."

"Thank you. I really appreciate it," said Baker.

"My pleasure. All the best Ed," said Taylor.

"You too Warren," and Baker ended the call.

Well, well, well! Not hard to guess who was behind the bullying. It was a good move by Taylor transferring Stonehouse to another facility.

His intercom buzzed again.

"Detective Damote has asked if he can make an appointment to see you sir," said Hillary.

"Yes Hillary. Please schedule it in. We will need at least two hours. And please ask him if Detective Harris is back at work and can be present."

"Will do sir," she replied.

He sat back in his chair contemplating the events and machinations over the last few months. All the threads that had been floating around aimlessly, unattached and fragmented, were now coming together as if by some gravitational force, slowly coalescing into a group of intertwined fibers that would eventually twist and turn to form a very strong rope. He looked out over the sprawling city and beyond, wondering just how many co-conspirators would be metaphorically swinging at the end of it, when all of this was over.

CHAPTER TWENTY-SIX

Stonehouse awkwardly climbed the steps of the bus, his arm in a sling. He couldn't have handcuffs on, so a police officer had his hand firmly around Stonehouse's good arm. The officer helped him into a seat halfway down the bus and then turned back to take a seat at the front. Looking around, Stonehouse saw that he was the only inmate on the bus. It lurched forward and the gates of Rikers swung open. Stonehouse had been surprised when he had been told that he was being transferred. He realized that something must have happened because the guards wouldn't even look at him as he was escorted down to the ground level to be processed for transferal.

Through the steel mesh on the bus windows, he watched the cityscape slowly slip away and after some time, the suburbs gave way to small towns and then farmlands. He had no idea where he was going to and after a while, he stopped speculating. He thought about his wife and children on her parent's farm. His previous life was now so very far away. He was even having difficulty in visualizing his children's' faces. He couldn't even remember what his comfortable bed felt like at home. But he did know how he felt by his wife's betrayal. Where was her support when he needed it most? One thing he knew for sure, no matter what the outcome of his trial would be, his marriage was over. Molly had proven to be someone who could not be counted on when a tornado came into town. Because that was just what had happened. He felt as though he had been violently sucked up and was endlessly swirling around in its vortex, alone and terrified.

What the fuck do you mean he was transferred out?!!! texted Wyatt to the guard in Rikers.

Dunno. He's gone and I'm on probation, the guard texted.

You idiot! Where has been taken to?

The reply came back. *Dunno.*

Wyatt snapped his mobile shut and he sat there fuming. Whatever happened Stonehouse could not be given the opportunity to ever get into a courtroom. He had been hoping that he would do himself in and he was pretty sure that it would have happened had he not been transferred out. In fact, he had instructed the guard to make sure Stonehouse had access to something that he could kill himself with when he came back from the infirmary. This was starting to look like a shitshow all over again. He would have to take matters in hand. But first he had to find out where he was being held. Time for Murphey to deliver.

Sophie carefully looked around before extracting the small forensic bag from her pocket. She gently tipped the syringe cap onto her workbench and began to process it. She fully understood just how vital this evidence could be. It may well be the only physical link to the true murderer, other than the camera footage Brad had mentioned. The problem with the footage he had said, was that the peak cap limited the capabilities of facial recognition and although they had tried running the photo Paul had of the guy tailing Simon, nothing came up. To this end, Brad was not convinced that a jury would be satisfied with the grainy images as being definitively one and the same man. Thus, they needed something exacting. She couldn't afford to make the slightest mistake. So, for the next three hours, she systematically went through all the protocols to maximize evidence and minimize any deterioration of the evidence once it was exposed to the necessary processes.

Paul contacted Ed Baker's personal assistant again and asked her if she could check with the commissioner if he thought there was any merit in him meeting the whole investigation team, explaining to her that there were four of them in total. She asked him to hold while she checked with the commissioner. He held on for a couple of minutes. He heard the receiver being picked up again.

"Yes, Detective Damote, he thinks that would be a good idea. May I have the names of the other two detectives please?"

"Detectives Les Johnson and Jordan Brown," Paul replied.

"Thank you, detective. One other thing, the commissioner has asked me to tell you that Agent Stonehouse has been transferred out of Rikers. He'll tell you all about it tomorrow."

Paul was surprised.

"Thank you ma'am. We were unaware of this," said Paul.

"We shall see you at 14h00 tomorrow," confirmed Hillary.

"We'll be there. Thank you," said Paul before replacing the receiver. Well…he thought to himself. Something must have happened to Stonehouse in Rikers.

He had made the call from one of the downstairs desks. He was simply not risking Murphey or his little informant Monica overhearing anything. He then went back upstairs and indicated to Les and Jordan to join him in one of the interview rooms. They followed him in. Georgina was presently out so he would bring her up to speed when she got back. He then appraised them of the meeting he and Georgina had scheduled for the following day.

"I suggested to the commissioner that you two attend the meeting since you are the key investigators. And by the way, he's on the same page as us guys," said Paul.

"Well, that helps," said Les. "It can't hurt to have the police commissioner on your side."

"There has been a development," said Paul. "Stonehouse has been transferred out of Rikers."

Les and Jordan looked surprised.

"Really? Why?" asked Les.

"No idea. The commissioner will appraise us tomorrow," said Paul. "We need to go to the NYPD Headquarters separately for tomorrow's meeting since we don't know if we are still being watched or not. Georgie and I are working on a fraud case, so we have good reason to go there. You guys need to come up with something that will cover your tracks."

"Sure, no problem," said Jordan. "It just happens to be my specialty!" he grinned. "14h00 tomorrow on the 15th floor, right?"

"Right," said Paul. "You guys are in for a few surprises. Baker is far more than what one expects. He's one of us, a dedicated cop…not someone sitting up on high barking orders to his minions."

"Good to hear it," mused Les. "Can't say the same of our friend who heads up the FBI."

As they were returning to their desks, Murphey stood at

his door and ordered them to come into his office. They all filed in.

"Where is Detective Harris?" he asked.

"She's collecting a document on the insurance fraud case. She should be back here quite soon," replied Paul.

There were only two visitors' chairs, so Paul remained standing while Les and Jordan were directed by Murphey to sit down.

"How is the investigation on Stonehouse going, hmmm?" Paul pursed his lips. This guy really grated on him. Les took the lead.

"Well sir, there's not much more for us to do presently. The evidence against Stonehouse is overwhelming and conclusive, so now it's a matter of waiting for the trial."

"And you haven't found any other evidence to contradict Stonehouse being the perpetrator?" asked Murphey.

Les looked around at the others and shrugged. Paul took up the baton.

"We've looked at the CCTV footage and have interviewed the concierge. Plus, Stonehouse's fingerprints were in the apartment. The evidence is solid."

The room was silent. Then Murphey asked.

"And have there been any other developments?"

"No sir," answered Paul.

Murphey looked from one to the other. He had been

around long enough in law enforcement to know when he was being stonewalled. He would have to watch them all even more closely than he had been doing.

"Okay," he said. "Keep me posted."

"Yes sir," they all said in unison.

Les and Jordan stood up and the three of them left Murphey's office.

Ten minutes later, Paul did a number check and sure enough, Murphey had made a call to the FBI in Washington. Paul shook his head. No surprise there.

Wyatt was feeling uneasy after Murphey's phone call. It was time to recall Mullens, so he sent him a text asking him to get in touch. There were too many loose ends again and Murphey was taking way too long to find out where Stonehouse had been transferred to. Something told him that Ed Baker was somehow involved in all of this. Plus, Murphey's comment that the investigating team were possibly holding out on him was also concerning. His phone pinged. It was Mullens.

Looking for me?

Wyatt texted. *I need you back here. Now.*

His mobile pinged. *In Bali. Will take first flight back.*

Wyatt closed his mobile. Mullens had better get back fast. No ways could he rely on Collins to do his dirty work.

Georgina arrived back and Paul told her about the impromptu meeting with Murphey and how he had told him all was on track with getting Stonehouse convicted.

"We told Murphey that we are basically treading water now. Not much else to report," said Paul casually.

Georgina understood what he was doing especially with Monica in earshot. Later, when they were walking down to the canteen, he told her about Stonehouse being transferred out of Rikers.

"Gee," remarked Georgina. "There must be a very good reason for that. Guess we'll have to wait until tomorrow to find out."

"Yep," said Paul. "And I did a call check too…Murphey called the FBI in Washington straight after the meeting." Georgina shook her head.

"Are you keeping a record of all his calls?" she asked.

"Oh yes partner. I will ensure that his actions come back to haunt him," replied Paul.

Georgina was silent for a moment and then she said.

"He's shrewd Paul. We must be careful and not assume that he doesn't know that we're holding out on him. Also, he may well have other sources of information."

Paul nodded in agreement.

"Yes, I feel the same. We need to keep one step ahead of our slippery captain."

The syringe cap was a literally a gold mine of evidence. Whoever had removed the cap had been careless and had done so with his teeth. There was also a saliva deposit on the outside of the cap in addition to the teeth imprints on either side of it. There were no fingerprints partial or otherwise, so Sophie assumed that the perpetrator had been wearing gloves. But there was still more to come.

Inside the cap Sophie found traces of a chemical solution. She imagined that it must have been from a droplet from the glass vile from which the solution had been extracted via the needle. The perpetrator must have prepared the syringe in advance and then replaced the cap over the needle. She started to process the evidence, duplicating the slides as Simon had taught her to do. *Always have insurance he had said to her.*

Brad had warned her not to run any DNA through the standard system. They couldn't afford anyone being alerted in any form or manner. He had the expertise to do the search incognito. What he didn't tell her was that he also wanted to protect her. He knew how dangerous these people were and he was not going to let anyone hurt Sophie. The truth be known, he had found her attractive the moment he saw her enter the coffee shop. Something about her had resonated with him and he found himself harbouring romantic notions about her.

Sophie looked at the printout analysis of the chemical traces she had found inside the syringe cap. She felt sick inside. Simon would have had no chance. What had been injected into him was a combination of Succinylcholine and Midazolam. The former would have caused paralysis, and the latter would have slowed and inhibited his breathing. The combination would have been fatal within minutes. She had always been horrified how Midazolam had been administered to hospitalized Covid patients. No surprise that so many of them died. What it had been in reality, was *assisted dying* without the consent of the patient or the family.

Brad had given her a private number on which she could send him encrypted messages. She texted him saying that she had hit the proverbial forensic lottery. Within minutes he responded asking her if she could come over to his apartment as soon as possible with the analysis.

Sure, she texted. *It's not like I would have any reason to feel unsafe with a guy called Agent Dork.*

That made him smile. He was liking this girl more and more by the minute.

CHAPTER TWENTY-SEVEN

Brad opened the door to Sophie. She smiled at him, and he felt his heart squeeze. For goodness' sake he thought to himself! What was going on with him? He stood back and ushered her in. He had done a major blitz on the apartment. He couldn't have her come into a place looking like a nuclear fallout.

"Wow! It smells clean in here! Been spring cleaning?" she asked him.

Brad rolled his eyes. "Busted!" Sophie burst out laughing. "I am a forensic analyst you know," she said shaking her head.

They both laughed and then he offered her coffee…or wine…or whatever she wanted.

"Well…perhaps a Bronx or a Cuba Libre?" she ventured.

Brad stared at her. He had no idea what she was talking about.

"Just kidding!" she said. "A coffee will be fine. We have work to do. Wine or cocktails can come later."

Brad's heart skipped a beat. That sounded promising.

They headed into the kitchen, and he made them both Cappuccinos. Then they moved to his computer room. She looked around and said.

"Maybe I should be worried. This place looks like a cyber dungeon!"

Brad wiggled his eyebrows and said in a deep scary voice.

"Welcome to my Data Den…"

Sophie gave him a *seriously* look and rolled her eyes.

"It takes a lot more than that to scare me."

Brad laughed pulling out a chair for her.

"Now. Down to work," he said.

"I have all the info here," she replied handing him the file.

He sat down in front of his computer station and grinning, he made a show of cracking his knuckles and wiggling his fingers, ready to dive into cyber territory. He then became serious and focused on entering all the information into the data base, ensuring that nothing would show up on any laboratory or law enforcement platform. He took his time, being very careful and precise. Once everything had been entered, the system started to analyze the DNA. He pushed his chair back.

"Now we wait," he said. "Usually these hitmen have criminal records, so perhaps we'll get lucky," said Brad.

"May the forensic gods smile upon us," Sophie replied pressing her palms together.

They weren't sure how long it would take. It could be anything from one to four hours, maybe more, so she handed him the report on the Succinylcholine and Midazolam solution that had been present in the syringe cap. Even though Brad was well aware what Simon had been injected with since the coroner had analyzed the blood samples, he was still shocked when he saw it in black and white. This linked what was inside the syringe cap definitively to what was in Simon's blood stream. When he finished reading the chemical analysis, he turned to Sophie frowning.

"I will be mighty annoyed if we don't get a match to the perpetrator."

Sophie sighed. "Well, if nothing comes up now Brad, we will eventually be able to tie him to the murder when we find out his identity. The coroner's report ties up with the syringe cap. And the saliva ties the syringe cap to the perpetrator. Sooner or later, we'll identify him. And once we do that, we have all that is needed to convict him for Simon's murder."

Brad nodded. He then said.

"I have been in the FBI for several years, and I have had my fair share of witnessing what humans are capable of. But this really gets to me. A guy who was a pillar of society, who had dedicated his entire adult life to forensics was just simply eliminated to protect a bunch of utterly vile perverts. And the FBI is part of it. It beggars belief."

Sophie looked at him and reached out, touching his shoulder and then said tenderly.

"He was your friend Brad, and I am truly sad for you." The gesture caught him off guard. He turned to her and what he saw was simple kindness. It was all there, in her eyes. She held his gaze.

"Sophie…I…," Simon stammered. She placed a finger over his lips.

"Sshhh…," and she leant forward and put her arms around him. He nuzzled into her hair and breathed in her scent, savouring the moment. After a while, he pulled back and cupped her face in his hands, looking at her beautiful features, her soft ivory skin, and deep blue eyes. She was simply perfect.

"Sophie de la Motte…I am going to be totally unprofessional now," he said, and he pulled her towards him and kissed her long and hard, his heart quickening at how she responded. He eventually pulled away and looked intently into her eyes. She smiled and said.

"Well, I can't let you be the only unprofessional one around here," and with that she leant forward and kissed him with equal passion. As cheesy as it seemed, Simon's thoughts were that he felt as though he had died and gone to heaven. Yep, he thought to himself. I'm a dork.

It was two in the morning and Brad carefully moved his arm out from under Sophie and got out of bed. He quietly put on boxers and a T-shirt and tiptoed through to his computer room. He peered at the screen and felt his stomach flip. There it was! A DNA match!

"Oh wow…" he whispered to himself as he quickly sat down and scooted closer to the screen. They had gone from the lottery to the jackpot. There on his screen was a photo of the same guy who had walked uninvited into his office at the FBI and who had posed as the gas technician on two occasions. His name was Ryder Mullens. Brad called up another site and Mullen's illustrious career as a violent offender came up…that was until three years ago when he literally disappeared from the radar. But what was just as worrying was how much of his file was redacted. And there was no known present address either. He transferred all the information into a folder on his desktop and then printed out the DNA document. He then saved the files to an external hard drive as an extra safety measure. Lastly, he sent both files to Les via an encrypted email. It would require a code from Les to open it. There was going to be one seriously happy team! He powered off his computer and taking the printed page with him, he quietly closed the door.

He was too wired to sleep so he sat down on the sofa, put his headphones on and watched a movie. Eventually, the morning light started to creep into the apartment. He got up and went through to the kitchen to prepare breakfast for Sophie, closing the doors so that the coffee machine would not wake her. Twenty minutes later he walked through to the bedroom with a tray. Sophie was just starting to stir. He quietly placed the tray down next to her on the bedside table and gently kissed her forehead. Her eyes opened and on seeing him she smiled, stretching like a contented cat.

"Morning Agent Dork…" she said sleepily, her voice a little croaky.

"Morning my Forensic Goddess," he replied smiling.

She slowly sat up and he puffed up the pillows for her and then handing her a coffee he said.

"No sugar since I consider you to be way too sweet for my own good." Looking amused she shrugged and said.

"Well, that's obvious."

He picked up his cup and sat down next to her on the edge of the bed.

"Now, I have prepared two breakfasts for you. I want you to lift the lid on that one first," said Brad pointing to the plate closest to her.

She looked at him quizzically and reached for the upside-down plastic bowl covering the plate.

"Quite the stylish cloche," she commented.

"A what?" said Brad confused.

"Never mind," said Sophie shaking her head laughing.

Then she saw the DNA print out. She gasped and sat bolt up straight almost spilling her coffee. Snatching it up, her eyes widened as she read the report.

"Brad!" she exclaimed. "We've got him!"

"That we do!" he replied grinning. She quickly put her coffee down and flung her arms around him.

"One more piece of the puzzle is in its place," she said beaming at him.

He simply couldn't believe how beautiful she was.

"Hmmm…," said Brad. "Perhaps I need to put you in your place too…"

"Oh yes…? And how do you plan on doing that?" she asked with a coquettish smile.

And with that he pushed her back gently onto the pillows and breakfast was long forgotten.

When Les read Brad's email he sat back in his chair, stunned. This was simply the best news. He punched the air with his fist.

"Yes!" he said to himself.

He knew that he couldn't mention a thing in the office; too many ears, so he printed it out and slipped it into the file for the meeting with the police commissioner. He felt like a schoolboy who had made the first team but couldn't tell a soul about it. He replied to Brad congratulating him and Sophie on their amazing work.

It was half past one and Georgina made a show of reminding Paul that they needed to lodge some more documents on the fraud case at the NYPD headquarters.

"Should I just go?" she asked Paul.

"No, I'll come with you," said Paul getting up.

As they passed Monica's desk, Monica said.

"You don't have to do that anymore you know…"

They both turned to look at her.

"And what is that, Monica?" asked Georgina quizzically.

"You know what I mean," said Monica and then she looked over at Murphey's office. "I'm never helping that jerk ever again. He is such a user. And I am such a fool."

Georgina and Paul exchanged looks.

"He can rot in hell," mumbled Monica as she turned back to her work.

Georgina raised her eyebrows at Paul, and they left without saying a word.

Les and Jordan were already there when Georgina and Paul arrived on the 15th floor of the NYPD headquarters.

Hillary showed them into the Baker's private boardroom.

"The commissioner will be with you shortly," she said.

And then smiling at Georgina and Paul she added.

"I know you two love coffee. How about you detectives?" she turned and looked at Les and Jordan.

"Thank you, ma'am," said Les. "That would be greatly appreciated." Jordan nodded his affirmation, smiling.

As soon as she had left the room, Les turned to the rest of the team and said.

"Have I got good news for y'all! Brad and Sophie have identified Simon's killer. His name is Ryder Mullens."

They looked at each other, totally taken aback, huge smiles spreading on their faces.

"That is incredible news!" said Paul beaming.

"Go Brad and Sophie!" exclaimed Jordan.

Then they all looked at Georgina. She was smiling, but it was a sad smile and she looked away for a few moments before she said.

"I want that guy thrown in a hole so deep that he will never see daylight again."

"Georgie…" Les began but at that moment the police commissioner entered the room. They all stood up and stood to attention.

"As you were," Baker said.

He nodded at Paul and Georgina.

"Harris, Damote, hope you are both well. Especially you Detective Harris. I am truly sorry for your loss," he said, his expression one of kindness and caring.

"Thank you, sir," said Georgina.

Baker then looked at Les and Jordan.

"Good to have you both here detectives," he said taking a seat at the head of the table. "Detective Damote has appraised me that you are the key investigators into Dr. Chevalier's murder."

"Yes sir, we are…but detectives Harris and Damote are as much part of the team." Les answered. "Thank you, sir, for including us in this meeting."

"Right," said Baker. "Let's get down to it. May I suggest that we go through a recap of the events in order, followed by what evidence we have and thereafter we can brainstorm a way forward."

"I have prepared a bullet point list on both counts sir," said Les as he handed out copies to the commissioner and the others.

"But there is one more recent point of evidence that is not on the list sir. As of last night, we were able to identify Dr. Chevalier's killer. One Ryder Mullens."

Baker looked up surprised.

"Well, you have been busy! Congratulations!"

"We have his DNA and evidence linking him to the

murder. Watertight. Nothing circumstantial sir," said Jordan.

"Okay…well then let's hear it," said the commissioner leaning back in his chair.

Les took the commissioner through the evidence they found in the cleaning closet on the tenth floor of the Simon's apartment building, the analysis of the syringe cap and DNA identification, and then he told the commissioner about the surveillance footage in Dr. Chevalier's apartment and why Chevalier had installed cameras. Baker listened intently as Les appraised him that the entire murder had been recorded and that they now had the recording in their possession. They were all silent for a while. Then Baker said.

"Someone has been directing this entire thing. This Ryder Mullens and Agent Stonehouse would not have acted off their own bats. Has this Mullens character been seen at any other time other than what we have now?

"Yes sir," said Georgina. "He was tailing Dr. Chevalier. He also paid a visit to an agent at the FBI called Brad Townsend who had been friends with Dr. Chevalier for many years; they went back to university days. This is the same agent who has identified the DNA."

"There was also another person tailing Detective Harris

and me," added Paul. "We haven't identified him as yet sir, but we don't think he has been as active as Mullens." Baker was thoughtful. Then he said.

"Okay…take me through all the events from beginning to end. Pretend I know absolutely nothing. This way we can all have a helicopter view of all the events and timelines." Les looked at Paul and Georgina and said.

"Damote, Harris…it's probably best one of you take the lead on this."

Georgina indicated that Paul should do the honours. He cleared his throat and began.

"The whole saga began when Detective Harris and I were on a stake out. We were hoping to obtain DNA evidence on a perp. Three blocks down from the Starbucks, the said perp threw away a Starbucks coffee cup which Detective Harris fished out of a trash bin. Except it wasn't his cup. It was someone else's. It was awkward for her to reach in to retrieve the cup. She obviously felt around and retrieved what she thought was the perp's cup."

Baker looked from Paul to Georgina. He smiled at her, wanting to make her feel at ease.

"We took the evidence to Dr. Chevalier and asked him to fast track it for us. And that was when all the alarm bells started ringing. The DNA lifted off the cup was that of the late Chad Leventstein, which meant that he was in fact not *late* at all but very much alive. The FBI stormed into Dr. Chevalier's lab and confiscated everything. And I mean everything…they took every bit of evidence that Dr. Chevalier was working on at the time, so several unrelated high-profile cases were subsequently thrown out of court. A travesty given the extent of police work that had been required to bring some heinous criminals to court in the first place."

The police commissioner interjected.

"So, if I am to understand you correctly, multiple unrelated cases were destroyed through the actions of the FBI?"

"Yes sir. Special Agent Stonehouse was the FBI agent involved. He confiscated every single file and piece of evidence from Chevalier's laboratory. He even took his personal mobile and forensic security ID. It was six weeks before Chevalier was allowed back to work. Furthermore, Stonehouse also told Chevalier's superiors that the reason for his absence was due to a nervous breakdown."

Ed Baker shook his head in disbelief.

"I am almost tempted to leave Stonehouse to rot where he is." exclaimed the commissioner. "Except we have much bigger fish to fry. Go on," said Baker.

Paul nodded. "After Stonehouse had raided Chevalier's

lab, he interviewed us at our precinct and threatened us with criminal charges if we so much as talked about the incident. He said that as far as we were concerned, the whole thing had never happened."

Baker raised his hand to halt Paul momentarily.

"Well, you will be interested to know that the director of the FBI Len Wyatt himself came to see me, and he asked to have both of you transferred out of New York."

Georgina and Paul exchanged looks.

"And what was your response if I may ask sir?" asked Paul.

"I simply said no." answered the commissioner. "He refused to give me any details as to why he wanted the transfers. I don't think he was particularly happy that I wouldn't cooperate."

"Well, he would have been even more unhappy if he had known that due to Chevalier's quick thinking, the DNA evidence was replaced with bogus evidence seconds before Stonehouse walked into the lab, so what they confiscated was of no use at all. However, it is clear now that somehow they found out about this. The day before Dr. Chevalier was murdered, Ryder Mullens gained access to his apartment and found the evidence in the freezer and took it. What he didn't know was that once again, it was bogus evidence planted there by Dr. Chevalier himself.

Detective Harris had already been given the original bona fide evidence by Chevalier earlier that day for safe keeping. It seems that this was not his first rodeo with the FBI. So, now Detective Harris has the original evidence plus the printout confirming the DNA match," said Paul.

Baker looked at Georgina and asked.

"So, this evidence is absolutely safe? I presume it's not lodged in Brooklyn?"

"That is correct, sir," Georgina replied.

Baker looked at Les and Jordan and asked. "And neither of you were involved at this stage?"

"No sir," replied Jordan.

"So, if this Ryder Mullens had the evidence, or thought he had it, why did he murder Dr. Chevalier?" asked Baker.

"That we simply don't know sir. Perhaps they found out that they had been duped again. How they found out, will probably remain a mystery," replied Paul. "We can only assume that this no doubt led to the demise of Dr. Chevalier."

"Okay," said Baker. "If I am understanding you correctly, the FBI thought that that they had the real evidence three times and were outwitted on each and every occasion?"

"It would appear so, sir," replied Paul.

Baker was pensive. They were all silent for a while.

"That would explain why Dr. Chevalier had to be

eliminated. And why Stonehouse would have been set up in case the suicide scenario didn't cut it."

They all nodded.

"I doubt Stonehouse would have been the brains behind this. In my opinion, this goes a lot higher," ventured Baker.

"We would all agree with you sir," said Les. "The camera footage from Dr. Chevalier's apartment supports that. Stonehouse was clearly deeply shocked when he saw Dr. Chevalier's body. We are certain that he didn't even know that Ryder Mullens had been there."

"And you say that all of this was recorded?" asked Baker.

"Yes sir," replied Les.

"I would like to see that footage," stated Baker. All three detectives surreptitiously glanced at Georgina.

Baker immediately picked up on it and hastily added.

"Not now of course. Another time."

Georgina was looking down at her hands in her lap and Baker's heart went out to her. He looked at Paul.

"How did you obtain the footage detective? asked Baker.

"It has become clear now sir, that Dr. Chevalier had also shared the footage of Mullens stealing the so-called evidence from his freezer with Agent Brad Townsend. Townsend then approached Detective Harris at the memorial service and gave her a memory card. Being FBI, he had been able to gain access to the sealed off murder scene late the night of the murder and had removed the cameras and recording device before it could be found by forensics. He knew that the moment the FBI learnt about the footage, it would have disappeared," Paul concluded.

"Good that he had the presence of mind," said Baker.

"Yes sir, he is with us on everything. After we found the evidence on the 10th floor of Dr. Chevalier's apartment building, we then approached Agent Townsend to make contact with a forensic technician by the name of Sophie de la Motte who had worked under Dr. Chevalier and was very loyal to him. He enlightened her that Stonehouse was probably not the perpetrator and asked her to process the evidence under the radar as it were. This she did. The rest is history."

"Well, we have quite the undercover team, don't we!" exclaimed Baker. He and Damote exchanged looks both knowing that Baker was including himself in that too.

"But where does Captain Murphey stand in all of this?" asked Baker.

Everyone looked at each other. They were all silent for a while. Then Paul said.

"Sir, I have been doing a check on outgoing calls from Captain Murphey's office…sorry to say…without his knowledge. Virtually every time we have had updates with him, he has called the FBI headquarters in Washington directly afterwards."

"So, sir, we have not been keeping him in the loop for that reason. To tell the truth we don't trust our captain," added Les.

"Yes, perfectly understandable," said Baker. "He may well regret the side he has chosen. I have been concerned about Captain Murphey's loyalties for some time now hence why my personal assistant has been in direct contact with you two," and he tilted his head towards Paul and Georgina. Everyone nodded in agreement.

"So…let's recap. We have the original DNA evidence of Chad Levenstein, we have the footage of Dr. Chevalier's murder, and we have the identity of his killer. There are two key things that we don't have. Who is pulling the strings, although we do have our suspicions but that is not good enough and we need proof…and then most importantly we have not identified Chad Levenstein as he looks now," concluded Baker.

"Yes sir," said Les. "We could proceed with all that we have, but all that it will result in is Mullens going away for life. Levenstein will go to ground, and we will never apprehend him and all his pedophile associates."

Baker decided not to reveal at this point in time his knowledge that Director Len Wyatt was one of the pedophile friends. And he knew that Damote wouldn't have said anything to any of his colleagues about the pedophiles he was monitoring at the Wagstaff club, not even to Detective Harris.

"Sir," said Georgina. "We know that we can't sit on this forever and the longer we take to prosecute Mullens, the more likely those behind the scenes will cover their tracks. May I make a suggestion?"

"Yes of course Detective Harris. By all means," said Baker nodding.

She frowned for a moment, hesitated and then once she had her thoughts in order, she began.

"Stonehouse is a liability for whomever is orchestrating everything behind the scenes. Attempts have been made to push him over the edge but that has now been scuppered with him being moved to another facility. I imagine that the kingpin behind this does not want Stonehouse to ever testify that he was set up as a patsy or even to mention the Levenstein DNA. He would not want even a hint of such a thing to enter the minds of a jury. In fact, he doesn't want Stonehouse near a courtroom. It is only a matter of time before he will move to have Stonehouse eliminated in prison and will make it look like he was merely collateral damage of prison violence. Or suicide. And it is also only a matter of time before he finds out where Stonehouse is being held. I think we need to lay some bait and draw out the kingpin to act prematurely."

They all pondered Georgina's words and then Baker said. "What bait do you have in mind Detective Harris?"

"Stonehouse needs a different voice sir. New counsel. There is no doubt in my mind that it was no coincidence that Steve Morrison was appointed as his defense counsel. He is probably the most incompetent attorney money can buy. Stonehouse needs someone who has not been vetted for his incompetence, but rather someone who literally gives prosecutors sleepless nights. Stonehouse needs to appoint Roland Radcliffe as his defense attorney."

They all exchanged looks. Wow. That was aiming high.

"I can see where you are going with this Detective Harris but how in the world could Stonehouse afford him? He is after all the highest profile defense attorney in the state…and probably in the country too. And the most expensive. Only moguls and movie stars can afford hiring him to get them off the hook."

"Well, can Stonehouse afford *not* to have him?" Georgina asked. "There are many ways to skin a cat sir," she added smiling.

She is quite the strategist, Baker thought to himself.

"So, take us through the sequence of events as you see them please detective," said Baker sitting back in his seat.

"Well sir, we persuade Stonehouse to engage Roland Radcliffe. I suspect that Radcliffe would not be able to resist such a high-profile case no matter the financial rewards or lack thereof. We then need to get Radcliffe to make a public announcement that he has evidence that Stonehouse is innocent. Proof beyond reasonable doubt. He can use Director Wyatt's words that were so utterly effective with our incompetent press. That will set the cat amongst the pigeons sir."

Baker was impressed by Georgina more and more by the minute.

"Would this not put Stonehouse in mortal danger?" asked Jordan.

"Yes, it would. But that is exactly what we want. And it is our job to protect him," said Georgina.

The commissioner nodded and then said.

"I know Radcliffe well. We've been sworn enemies forever and a day but there is none the less mutual respect between us. I'll have a word with him."

Paul grinned and looked around the table.

"Oh, to be a fly on the wall…"

Baker chuckled. He then continued.

"Right. So now we have lured our kingpin and gotten him rattled, but we still have no idea who he is. Where do you see it going from there Detective Harris?" asked Baker.

"Nowhere. Yet. We wait and see if he makes a move sir. Whoever is behind this is very clever and very powerful. However, we do know that there is *never* honour amongst thieves, so Mullens may well panic and want to do a deal. He may suspect that he's been given up by his paymaster. Radcliffe's announcement will definitely rattle his cage and I believe he may possibly seek immunity from prosecution if he tells us all. It's a long shot but it's not impossible," said Georgina. She paused and then said.

"In the interim we do whatever we can to identify Levenstein sir." She then concluded, "On that score, I am stumped. I do hope between all of us we come up with something…real soon."

The room was silent for a while. Baker was going through all that Georgina has said in his mind. It did make sense. Prosecuting the real killer would not deliver the prize they really wanted which was Levenstein and whoever was protecting him with such vigour. Rattling cages was all they could do for now.

"Okay," said Baker. "I think we follow Detective Harris's lead on this but only if we are all in agreement. I need to know if anyone has a better idea or can see holes in this one. We need to tread very carefully."

"Is Stonehouse safe where he has been transferred to?" asked Jordan.

"Probably a lot safer than Rikers," said Paul. "However, whoever was behind Chevalier's murder has a very far reach. He may well find Stonehouse, so we must be vigilant."

"What about perhaps having someone on the inside to protect Stonehouse and to watch for anything that may indicate that the secrecy of his location has been compromised?" asked Georgina.

Baker contemplated her suggestion and then said.

"That makes sense. I'll ask Warren Taylor, the Inspector General of Prisons to see if he can help us there. And I'll set up a meeting with Radcliffe and brief him. One of you must go and see Stonehouse and get him to play ball and appoint Radcliffe asap."

He stood up and they all immediately stood to attention.

"Let's say we reconvene in a few days' time and review our progress," suggested Baker.

"Thank you, sir," said Les on behalf of the team.

Baker left the room, and they filed out after him, thanked Hillary for the coffee and headed to the canteen to discuss the meeting before splitting up to return to the precinct.

CHAPTER TWENTY-EIGHT

Stonehouse had been put in a single cell. He noticed that the guards seemed to avoid him, and he wasn't being subjected to any of the usual jibing and bullying. Odd he thought. Someone had obviously intervened which had resulted in him being transferred out of Rikers. But why?

"You have a visitor Stonehouse," said the guard looking at him through the bars.

This particular correctional facility, which was situated in the country still had the old-fashioned bars as opposed to the steel doors of the more modern urban detention centers. Stonehouse looked up surprised as the guard unlocked the cell.

"Stand up. Turn around," instructed the guard.

Stonehouse complied and automatically put his hands behind his back. The guard slipped the handcuffs on and then turned Stonehouse around, holding onto his arm as he escorted him to the interview room. Stonehouse's shoulder was still painful but at least he was out of the sling and that was progress.

The attending guard opened the door to the interview room and Stonehouse was steered to a chair in front of a table.

The guard removed the cuffs, told Stonehouse to sit and then re-cuffed his hands to a steel bar on the table.

"Ten minutes," said the guard to the visitor who was standing in front of the window with his back to the room, his form silhouetted against the sunlight streaming in through the bars. The escort guard then turned to leave, nodding at the attending guard who closed the door and leaning against the wall, took his mobile out of his pocket, clearly disinterested in inmate Stonehouse and his visitor. Stonehouse blinked and squinted his eyes against the light as the figure turned around and walked towards the table. It was Detective Damote.

"Seriously?" said Stonehouse. "You've come all this way to gloat, hmmm?"

"Stop with the hmmming and pay attention," said Paul as he pulled out the visitor's chair. Stonehouse looked away feigning disinterest. Paul sat down and leant forward.

"I want you to really concentrate Stonehouse. This is an opportunity you do *not* want to miss."

Stonehouse turned his head and looked at Paul but said nothing. Paul noted the residual bruises and the long dark red scab on Stonehouse's face. He shook his head and then slid a piece of paper across the table to Stonehouse.

"You are to fire your attorney and appoint this guy," he said tapping his finger on the handwritten name and number. "And you are to do this asap," added Paul.

Stonehouse stretched his cuffed hand and picked up the paper. He scrutinized it for a moment and then tossing it aside, looked up at Paul and said.

"And why would I replace one useless son of a bitch with another?"

Paul was silent for a while.

"Because you can't afford not to," he replied.

"You know nothing of what I can or can't afford to do," sneered Stonehouse.

Paul raised his eyebrows, saying nothing. He then stood up and headed for the door nodding to the guard. Stonehouse watched him go and then raising his voice he asked sarcastically.

"Why would you care what the fuck happens to me anyhow?"

Paul turned and looked at him for a few seconds, a hint of a smile on his face.

"I don't. But I do care about justice. Suit yourself."

The attending officer opened the door and Paul walked out. Stonehouse sat there dazed.

"Let's go," said the guard as he moved towards Stonehouse who reached out for the piece of paper and closed his fist around it, unsure of what to make of the conversation that had just taken place. The guard bent forward and released the cuffs from the bar. He helped Stonehouse stand up and holding his arm, he took him back to his cell.

Roland Radcliffe was a natty dresser. His suits were made in Saville Row in London. His game show host teeth were so white they could dazzle a mole. He had a collector's time piece for every day of the week, each of which cost more than what an average executive earned in a year. He owned five homes and enough cars to open his own showroom. Women desperately vied for his attention and yet he remained single. He was so high profile that even celebs asked for his autograph. They wanted to keep him sweet just in case one day they needed him to get them out of a jam. He was known to be picky.

The elevator doors opened on the 15th floor. Hillary was waiting for him. Everyone turned to look at the man who instilled fear in even the most ruthless of prosecutors.
"Mr. Radcliffe, right this way please," she said politely.
He gave her one of his signature dazzling smiles and once she had shown him into the police commissioners office, she quietly went back to her desk, took her sunglasses out of her bag, and put them on. The rest of the staff on the floor were rolling about laughing.

"Mr. Radcliffe…" said Baker as he got up from his desk, extending his hand.

"Police Commissioner…to what do I owe this pleasure?" Radcliffe drawled as they shook hands.

"Murder," said Baker spreading his hands. "What else."

Radcliffe chuckled. "Well, I guess that is my specialty," and then narrowing his eyes he said.

"Somehow I think this has something to do with the forensic scientist's murder, am I right?"

"Dead right. No pun intended," replied Baker.

"Let me guess…Agent Stonehouse was given a brain-dead defense attorney, no pun intended either, so that a guilty verdict would be guaranteed. And you don't want that, am I right?" said Radcliffe.

"Right again," said Baker. "I'm impressed. But then again, you wouldn't be here if I didn't think you had worked that out already."

Radcliffe looked a Baker for a while.

"Okay. I'll do it," he said.

Baker raised his eyebrows, surprised.

"Please do sit down…" he said gesturing to one of the seats in front of his desk as he moved to sit down himself. But Radcliffe cut him off.

"No need. I know exactly what must be done."

"Okay…" said Baker, straightening up, rather surprised.

He continued. "I do however have one request…"

"And that is?" asked Radcliffe.

"When you make your announcement to the press that you have evidence that Agent Stonehouse is innocent, please use the words *beyond reasonable doubt* somewhere in your dialogue."

Radcliffe's smile broadened. "Now I wonder where I heard those same words not so long ago."

Baker picked up a file marked confidential on his desk and handed it to Radcliffe.

"It's all here. Knock yourself out. Oh, and one bit of advice…don't let Stonehouse know anything of what's in there," he pointed to the file. "He will blurt out everything and that will be your case done for. We can't have the famous Radcliffe lose a case, now can we?"

Radcliffe laughed. "You know…for an absolute pain in the arse you have a good sense of humour Commissioner."

"I have to. How else would I cope with defense lawyers like you," said Baker chuckling.

They shook hands, both grinning at the absurdity of them being on the same side for the first time ever and then as Radcliffe turned to go, he hesitated and said.

"I have one question Commissioner…"

"Shoot," said Baker.

"Is your personal assistant single?" he asked with a

twinkle in his eye.

"Would it make any difference?" asked Baker.

"Nope," said Radcliffe grinning and he left the room.

Baker shook his head and sat back down at his desk.

No one expected Radcliffe to be leaving so soon, so Hillary was caught off guard when the police commissioner's door suddenly opened, and Radcliffe breezed past her desk. Out of the corner of his eye he noticed her sunglasses, then stopped and turned back looking at her quizzically.

"My smile too bright for you?" he asked her.

"Yes sir," she answered, her face dead pan.

"May I ask you out on a date?" he asked.

"No sir," she replied without a hint of animation.

He nodded and then tilting his head as he looked her up and down.

"Not yet that is," he said with a smile.

Hillary slowly removed her sunglasses and looked up at him. Smiling sweetly, she said.

"Not ever sir. Goodbye Mr. Radcliffe."

Turn on the news…now… was the text Wyatt received from Mullens. Wyatt grabbed the remote and clicked onto CNN. A plastic looking brunette who clearly had been under the surgeon's knife once too often and whose fire engine red lipstick made her look like a character from Salvador Dali's inferno, was talking about the Stonehouse Chevalier murder case.

In a shocking revelation today, Roland Radcliffe who is Agent Stonehouse's newly appointed defense attorney, briefed the press late this afternoon stating that he had proof beyond reasonable doubt of the innocence of Agent Stonehouse and the identity of the true killer of Dr. Chevalier. This has sent shock waves through the law enforcement sector who assumed that this was an open and shut case. After reports of brutality towards Agent Stonehouse in the Rikers detention facility, he has been moved to an undisclosed facility and it has been said...

Her voice faded as the reality of what had transpired hit Wyatt like a ton of bricks. Just the name Radcliffe struck terror into his heart. He was probably the shrewdest and most successful defense attorney in the US and his personal investigating team behind him were so good that they could unearth evidence even if it was buried on Mars! This was a shit show on steroids. His mind started to race. He texted Mullens. *Get here now!*
On my way, came Mullen's reply.

"Damote, Harris, Johnson, Brown! In my office now!" bellowed Captain Murphey.

They all exchanged looks from their desks and simultaneously got up, heading for Murphey's office but he marched out and led the way to one of the interview rooms. They all filed in.

"Sit!" he commanded. They all sat down.

"What the hell is going on, hmmm?" he yelled, his hands on his hips, looking from one to the other.

"Radcliffe has been appointed as Stonehouse's counsel and he says that he has proof beyond reasonable doubt that Stonehouse is innocent!" Murphey was mad as a snake.

Les opened his mouth but Murphey cut him off. "And he says he has proof as to who the real killer is!"

Nobody said anything.

"Well don't just sit there! I want to know what's going on and don't even think of stonewalling me!" threatened Murphey.

Les, Georgina, and Jordan looked at each other nervously but Paul was entirely focused on Murphey.

"Well sir…" said Paul calmly. "If you don't want us to stonewall you, then stop calling the FBI every time we have a briefing."

Everyone's eyes widened with shock as they turned to look at Paul. They couldn't believe what he had said.

Murphey looked as though he was going to have a heart attack, his face was purple with rage.

"I will have you suspended for that!" he yelled slamming his hand down hard onto the table. Everyone jumped except for Paul.

"Go ahead sir," said Paul evenly.

Nobody said a word. The ticking of the clock on the wall was the only sound they could hear. Even all the ambient office noise seemed to have faded to nothing. Murphey knew the game was up. Time for damage control.

"You've no idea what you are talking about Damote. How dare you question my integrity!" Murphey demanded.

"I never mentioned integrity sir. But you did," said Paul quietly.

There was another long silence. Paul continued to look at Murphey, his stare unrelenting.

"Have you been spying on me Damote, hmmm?" asked Murphey indignantly.

"Yes sir, I have." replied Paul in a matter-of-fact tone.

Murphey was totally blindsided. He had not expected that. A denial, yes, but not an admission. Paul continued.

"I've been checking the phone records sir, and that is how I know that you've been calling FBI Headquarters in Washington on a regular basis."

"And what makes you think those calls were related to this

case, hmmm? Bit presumptuous of you don't you think?" Murphey asked, feeling confident that the lie was clawing back some high ground.

"The timing sir. The calls were made to the same number after every meeting we've had on this specific case." Paul's voice was disturbingly calm.

"I had to report everything to the FBI. I had no choice," said Murphey now playing the victim. "And just for the record I do not have to report to you Damote!" He spat Paul's name to emphasize his contempt.

Paul held his gaze and then said.

"This is *not* an FBI case. So, no sir, you did *not* have to report to them. But I am sure it is all above board so the records will be no threat to you sir, or the FBI." said Paul. Murphey knew that he had been outwitted. This was humiliating beyond words. It was slowly dawning on him that Damote was a formidable enemy and best he get him back on sides.

"Okay…okay. I get your point. I can see how this must look," said Murphey in a conciliatory tone of voice. There was a trickle of sweat running down his temple.

"I have been keeping tabs on what the FBI knows."

The lie slipped so easily off his tongue.

Paul sat back in his chair and folded his arms.

"So may we hear it please sir… that is if you are *now*

willing to share it with your own investigative team?"
The sarcasm was not lost on Murphey.

Murphey didn't tell them anything that they didn't know already. But what Paul had done was to put Murphey on notice that they knew what he was up to. It was a warning shot and if Murphey had any sense, he would desist with what he was doing and concentrate on his precinct. The message was loud and clear. However, the standoff had also invited in a conflict of interests, and he was now in an invidious position. The investigating team clearly did not trust him now but providing Wyatt with information had created a nice little revenue stream on the side for Murphey. What was he to do?

He called a close to the meeting and asked Paul to remain behind. Closing the door after the others had filed out, he turned on Paul.
"How dare you humiliate me in front of the other detectives?" his voice was low and threatening.
Paul said nothing, his expression neutral.
"I am your captain and you had better remember it!" Murphey hissed.
Without missing a beat Paul said, "Then act like one."
Murphey's mouth opened and then closed. Paul continued.

"You may have a higher rank than any of us do, but that does not mean that respect is mandatory. You have compromised us as a team by choosing to inform the FBI on what we are doing. Furthermore, you know only too well that the FBI is blatantly protecting the most heinous criminals and you are okay with that. Well, we all have a very big problem with that sir, and when all of this is over, all four of us will be applying for a transfer to another precinct. And you will be left to explain why four of your top detectives no longer wish to serve under you."

There was a long silence. Both men stared at each other. Eventually Murphey spoke.

"You have crossed a line Damote."

"Yes, sir I have. And so have you. The moment you decided to inform on your own detectives."

Paul stood up, his expression one of disgust. He pushed in his chair and as he got to the door, he turned and looked at Murphey.

"Do you know what my greatest strength is sir?"

Murphey rolled his eyes.

"No…pray do tell…" he said sarcastically putting his hands into his pockets assuming a disinterested stance.

"My greatest strength is that people like you underestimate me."

He stared at Murphey for a moment, then walked out and

headed back to his desk. Murphey was at a complete loss as to what to do. He simply was not going to take this lying down, but he also knew that if he called Damote's bluff then a whole load of shit would come tumbling down onto his head. He needed help and his thoughts turned to Wyatt. He would know what to do. He would call him but not from the precinct. That was no longer an option. He would call him from the privacy of his home that evening.

CHAPTER TWENTY-NINE

"Police Commissioner…" said Lela Hinton silkily. "How are you this evening?"

"Very well Lela and all the better for being here as you know," said Baker looking up at her from his newspaper.

"I understand exactly what you mean Commissioner. This club…" and she looked around at the various men seated, chatting or reading as the *Nymphs* glided around discreetly, "…is something of a second home to many of these gentlemen. Somewhere to escape to after a hard day of endless responsibilities and pressures." She then tilted her head and asked sweetly, "What can I get you to drink Commissioner?"

"Hmmm…let me think. Perhaps an Abelour 16-year-old? That will do me fine if you have that particular one?" Baker ventured.

"Of course. Coming right up. Will you be having dinner here? asked Lela.

"No, not tonight thank you," Baker replied.

"And would you like your usual? Tanya is here and I can have her wait for you in your favourite room when you are ready…" Lela said her face a picture of innocence.

"That would be lovely Lela. Thank you," said Baker.

She turned to go, hesitated, and then looked back at Baker. "You know Commissioner, I think you may just be in love," she said with a twinkle in her eye. "You only have eyes for Tanya." Baker smiled at her.

"I am something of a one-woman guy…well, two women guy if you count my wife," he chuckled. Lela's laugh was like tinkling glass.

"I understand perfectly," she purred. "She'll be waiting for you, and I shall get that Abelour right away."

She turned on her heel, clicking her fingers at one of the *Nymphs*, murmuring her instructions discreetly. She then drifted over to some of the other men to shower her charms over them like shards of glass.

Baker continued to read his newspaper, but he wasn't really taking in any of the news. His mind was on the strategies that he and the detectives were working on. It would only be a matter of time when the walls of the Sheldon Wagstaff club would metaphorically come tumbling down. Hopefully Lela Hinton would find herself slap bang in the middle of the ruins. Her complicity in the underage sex that took place on her premises was simply unforgivable.

Brad Townsend was lost in thought. Now that he knew

where all the evidence on Levenstein had been taken to, how was he going to get his hands on it before they could move it again? There were three critical elements that would bring the whole cabal down. Firstly, the video evidence Levenstein had gathered of all the men and women, who had participated in the underage trafficking. Secondly, the DNA evidence that Levenstein had secretly collected from the participants and thirdly, the identity of Levenstein himself, as he appeared now. There was no guarantee that any of the points in isolation would be strong enough in a courtroom to nail the lot of them, but the combination of all three would be fatal. Sophie was coming over to his apartment later so perhaps he could brainstorm with her. The more he got to know her, the more apparent her intelligence and strategic mind became. How did he get to be so lucky to meet someone like her, he thought to himself. He vowed that he would keep her safe. No one was going to get within an inch of Sophie. He had never verbalized to her the sense of protection he felt over her, but he was pretty sure she knew already. Nothing got past Sophie de la Motte.

Baker walked down the east wing passage of the Wagstaff Club to Room 12. He looked up and down before he entered. The corridor was quiet and deserted. He opened the door, stepped in, and closed it quietly, locking it.

Tanya was standing at the window, wrapped in one of the fluffy white bathrobes from the sumptuous bathroom. The rooms were the epitome of luxury with every possible detail present for an amorous liaison. She turned as she heard the door open. Walking towards Baker, she removed her mask, and stood to attention.

"Good evening, sir," she said.

"Good evening Officer Davidson," said Baker. "As you were."

Tanya relaxed her stance. Baker continued.

"How are you bearing up?"

Putting the mask down on a side table she said.

"Well, I'm not sure how much longer I can do this sir, but I think we are getting closer to our goal. Pity some of the other female police officers can't take over from me. Walking around naked all day is not my idea of police work but then again, this job is full of surprises," she laughed shaking her head.

"Ah but the other police officers wouldn't get past *go* with Lela Hinton let alone *collect two hundred*," said Baker dryly. "Not often a woman can say that her extreme good looks are a disadvantage. That is to you, not to the NYPD. I am indeed grateful to you for taking on such a difficult assignment."

Tanya smiled at the compliment and then said.

"I am more than happy to serve sir." Baker nodded.

She went on. "Lela has been hinting that my exclusivity for you sir is starting to annoy the other members. It's hard enough being undercover but going under the covers with these entitled tossers is simply not going to happen."

Baker laughed. "I so enjoy your English terms. *Tossers!* I suppose in our lingo we would use the word *schmucks.* Anyway, I would never let it get to that Tanya. Lela thinks I'm smitten with you so clearly our strategy is working."

He walked across to the drinks tray and poured two scotches and two mineral waters. He passed one of the water glasses to her and he took the other one.

"So now, is there anything new that you have you been able to find out?" Baker asked settling down in one of the armchairs.

Tanya walked across and sat down on the sofa.

"Quite a bit sir. Lela has installed secret cameras in another two rooms. I have found out where her safe is and that is where she keeps the surveillance memory cards. And I am homing in on the vicinity of her lock up where she keeps the bed linen etcetera," said Tanya.

"Good work. That is great progress. And you are absolutely sure there are no cameras in this room?" Baker asked.

"Quite sure sir. I have gone through it with a fine-tooth comb. This week three underage girls were brought in through the basement garage. One was rejected outright by Lela. The second one…it was discovered that she wasn't a virgin so there is going to hell to pay for someone. The third one was given to Sedgefield. He is a monster. That poor little thing."

Baker winced. It was very hard for him to hear this.

"Officer Davidson, I think we're only a few weeks away from blowing this whole thing wide open. And no mercy shall be shown to any of them."

Tanya nodded, lost in thought. Baker knew about the sexual abuse she had suffered as a child and his admiration for her bravery in not only reliving the nightmare of her childhood but also putting herself at great risk in this undercover operation, was way beyond the call of duty.

"If you know where the memory cards are kept, what chance is there of you swopping them out?" asked Baker.

Tanya contemplated his question. He continued.

"We need the originals. If Lela gets a hint of things going south, she'll move those cards at the speed of light. I've no doubt she thinks they're her *get out of jail card*."

Tanya nodded in agreement and then said.

"I will first have to see what they look like so that I can plant identical ones. That means I need to access the safe.

It's a combination type lock and I doubt I will find the code anywhere in her office."

"I can bring in a safe expert," suggested Baker. "Do you think you can smuggle him in?"

"Let me work out a plan sir. I know that the chef is going off for a few days and Lela's usual stand in chef has jetted off to LA after some drag queen boyfriend, so perhaps I can suggest to Lela that I know someone who can temporarily take the helm. I'll give it a shot. I hope your safe breaker can cook," she added smiling.

"Well, I guess he's going to need a crash course," said Baker. "And her lock up? Will you be able to identify an exact location?"

"I have been thinking about it sir. Tailing her is too risky as would planting a tracking device on her vehicle be too. She is no fool. However, what we could consider is accessing the onboard computer. It's a recent model so the GPS data should be accessible remotely. Do you have someone who could do that sir?" she asked.

"Oh yes, most definitely," replied Baker. "That's a good solution Officer Davidson. "

"Okay, sir. I will get the make and car registration number to you as soon as possible."

There was a long silence, both of them going over the possible scenarios in their own minds.

"Well," said Baker looking at his watch. "We have at least another hour of supposedly being *busy* so how about our usual form of entertainment?"

"Good idea!" said Tanya. "She got up and walked over to a cabinet and pulled out the Backgammon set. She sat back down, curling her legs under her and set out the pieces.

"Clearly one of the perks of the job. Thrashing the police commissioner at Backgammon!" she said grinning.

"Hey, you have only won the last three games!" exclaimed Baker.

"And we've only played four!" retorted Tanya. "So there's plenty of opportunity for you to redeem yourself."

Baker shook his head and said "Don't get overconfident. I've been letting you win because you've been doing such a great job."

"Yeah, right sir!" Tanya said dryly.

Baker flipped a coin and he got to go first. Twenty minutes later, he was truly beaten.

Back in Washington, Wyatt listened to Captain Murphey as he recounted the meeting with his four detectives that afternoon. He held the mobile away from his ear and rolled his eyes as Murphey rattled on and on about how humiliating the whole saga had been for him. Eventually Wyatt interrupted him. He was not going to be able to take much more of this whining monologue.

"Do nothing!" he interjected. For a moment there was a glorious silence. And then Murphey said.

"What? How can I do nothing? They need to be brought to book, all of them! I can't allow my detectives to think they can challenge me!"

Wyatt shook his head. Idiot he thought, he has no idea how to manage minions.

"Suit yourself Captain but in my experience, it's better to do nothing and rather wait for an opportunity to arise, then you can then exact revenge. Something always comes up." Wyatt looked at his fingernails and made a mental note to fire his manicurist. Murphey was silent for so long that Wyatt eventually said.

"You still there?"

"Yes sir," was the curt response. Murphey sounded like a petulant child. Suddenly Wyatt lost patience.

"I'll tell you what is a whole lot more important than your little spats with your boys and girl scouts and that is what information they have! I want to know why Radcliffe is claiming Stonehouse is innocent. I'm going to give you two days to find out! I am not paying you to be a whinger Murphey. I'm paying you to be an informant. And while you're at it, I want to know where they're keeping Stonehouse. Now get the job done!"

And with that Wyatt snapped his mobile shut. What was wrong with that idiot he raged to himself. Murphey had given him nothing. Zilch. Nada. Fuck all!

Baker threw up his hands and exclaimed.
"I give up! I have been humiliated enough!" He gathered up the pieces on the board and packed them away. "Besides, I would say it's safe to call it a day...or a night."
"Agreed sir and thank you for being such a monumental loser," said Tanya grinning.
Baker attempted to give her his best disapproving stare with zero effect. Then standing up he said.
"On a serious note, please be careful Officer Davidson. These people are dangerous."
"Yes, sir," said Tanya immediately getting up and standing to attention. "I understand. And I am being very careful sir."
He laughed. "You have no idea how ridiculous you look standing to attention in a fluffy dressing gown!"
Shaking his head, he chuckled as he headed to the door. "See you next week."
"Night sir," replied Tanya.
He unlocked the door and left the room. Taking the lift directly down to the basement, he got into his Lincoln and headed for home, longing for the haven of normality with

his family, far from this crazy upside-down world. Tanya saw the funny side of how she must have looked. She laughed to herself as she took the two glasses of scotch and poured them down the basin. She switched the shower on, poured out some shower gel and dampened two towels and the bathmat. She switched the shower off, made the bed look as though it had seen action, closed the drapes, and flattened a couple of the sofa cushions. She ripped open a couple of condoms, threw the packets in the bin and flushed the condoms down the toilet. This process was repeated every week. She did it in five minutes flat.

In between their weekly clandestine meetings, she appeared to be the perfect *Nymph* whilst conducting surveillance on all the comings and goings. Lela constantly changed their masks so the only place that a hidden camera could be housed, was in a navel stud. Lela did not approve of this type of jewelry, and it had been a close shave when she had held out her hand, demanding that Tanya remove it and give it to her. Tanya demurred, insisting that Baker loved it. After appraising Baker of this rather tense moment, he made sure that he dropped his fondness of navel jewelry into a later conversation with Lela who immediately gave it her seal of approval. Tanya removed the robe, tossed it on the bed and put on her mask.

After glancing around the room to check that she hadn't forgotten any small detail, she slipped out the room and headed back to the public areas, assuming the cat like walk that all the girls were instructed to adopt.

When she entered the drawing room, all the men turned to look at her. They were mesmerized. Her perfectly upturned breasts swayed slightly as she moved, and the ambient lighting emphasized her tiny waist and the flare of her hips flanked by the seductive indentations on either side of her smooth rounded buttocks. She was without a doubt the most beautiful of all the *Nymphs* and many of the men were deeply envious that she was an exclusive reserve. That meant that she was strictly off limits. Someone had obviously paid a substantial amount of money to *own her*. She smiled sweetly at the men as she took their orders for the next round of drinks. When she returned, not one word was spoken as the men watched spellbound, how the weight of her breasts shifted and moved as she bent forward and placed the drinks before them. No doubt each and every one of them yearned to caress her soft dusky skin, but none dared. It was an unspoken rule in the club. If a *Nymph* was privately owned, then no other man could lay a hand on her.

CHAPTER THIRTY

"Tell him that if he doesn't come and see me in the next twenty-four hours, he is fired!" Stonehouse yelled down the phone at Radcliffe's secretary.

"He is a very busy man…" began the secretary.

"I don't care! I am a very innocent man! Now just get him here!" Stonehouse slammed down the call box handset.

"Hey…easy man," said one of the inmates. "We all need that phone."

"Go fuck yourself!" barked Stonehouse as he stormed off. He had gotten more and more brazen since it had become apparent that there was a *hands-off* order from on high. Gone was the frightened tearful inmate. He was back to his old usual self, bullying anyone he could.

Four days later Radcliffe came to see him. As Stonehouse berated and ranted at him, Radcliffe occupied himself with picking off miniscule bits of fluff from his £5000 silk suit.

"You finished yet?" asked Radcliffe smoothly, looking up at Stonehouse. Before Stonehouse could even answer Radcliffe suddenly uncoiled with the speed of a cobra and his whole demeanor changed, snapping into focus his long-forgotten Bronx roots.

"Now you listen you pathetic little weasel. Rich people, *very* rich people queue up for my services, so why I am bothering with such a short ass'd runt like you is obviously a major fucking lapse of judgement. One more fucking insult from that measly little mouth of yours and I'm outta here and you'll not see the outside of this place for a minimum of twenty-five years. Do I make myself clear, punk?"

Stonehouse was speechless, eyes wide. Radcliffe bulldozed on.

"And don't even dare utter one sound you fuckwit. From now on you will nod only. Comprende? C'mon…show me how you can nod weasel…"

Stonehouse nodded, his mouth clamped shut, as tight as a nervous sheep in the outback.

"Good…" said Radcliffe smoothly, exhaling deeply, suddenly calm and collected, the cobra slinking back down into a tight coil.

"So now that we have a good understanding, we can begin," he said, opening his Aspinal of London notebook and uncapping his Boheme limited edition Mont Blanc pen.

Stonehouse stared at him, trying to comprehend the sudden and swift change of personality. What he didn't appreciate was that this was how Radcliffe shredded his opponents in court. He simply took no prisoners, and his lethal reputation preceded him. Radcliffe looked up at Stonehouse and asked.

"Now…are you innocent?"

Stonehouse nodded.

"Were you set up?

Stonehouse nodded again.

"Do you know who killed Chevalier?"

Stonehouse shook his head.

"Are you an idiot?"

Stonehouse stared at Radcliffe totally perplexed.

"Because if you were set up that means you are an idiot. So, I am going to ask you again. Are-you-an-idiot?" Radcliffe emphasized each word.

Stonehouse nodded vigorously.

"Good," said Radcliffe tilting his head in approval.

He then looked long and hard at Stonehouse and said.

"I have no proof of your innocence. I have no proof that you were set up. And I have no proof of who murdered Chevalier." he lied. "I just made that stuff up to rattle the press. But I do know that you are too much of an idiot to have done it and I will make sure the world knows it."

Stonehouse's eyes widened but before he dared open his mouth Radcliffe said.

"Keep your mouth shut in here. Say nothing to anyone.

You do that and I will get you out of here a free man. You stuff up and open that big trap of yours, then you're on your own. And don't test me Stonehouse," said Radcliffe his eye's narrowing. "My bite is much, much worse than my bark."

Radcliffe stood up, gathering up his things. "Guard!" He turned on his heel, marched to the door and then was gone.

Stonehouse sat there, as dazed as he had been when Director Len Wyatt had yelled at him. He thought to himself *do I look like a punch bag?* And a voice in his head said, *Dah!* because clearly everyone was taking a shot at him.

Late that night Wyatt and Mullens met at their usual place, the pool house. Helen and the kids had gone to sleep some time ago, so Wyatt crept out of the house and made his way down over the manicured lawns. Suddenly the sprinkler system came on and Wyatt yelped as he dodged the sprinkler heads and sprinted towards the pool house, cursing, and shaking water droplets off his pajama pants when he finally made it.

"Stupid gardener," he muttered. "I'll fire his ass."

Mullens emerged out of the shadows.

"Sir…" Wyatt looked up.

"Yes, sorry…hi…damn sprinklers."

"Sorry sir," said Mullens.

"Let's go inside," suggested Wyatt and they went into the pool house. Wyatt switched on a lamp and they both sat down. Wyatt got straight to the point.

"Mullens…my informant at the Midtown North Precinct has advised me that Agent Stonehouse was transferred to the Albany County Correctional Facility. He has to be silenced. He can't even so much as see the inside of a courtroom."

"I have a contact at Albany sir. What time frame are you looking at?" asked Mullens.

"I want this guy pushing up daisies like yesterday," replied Wyatt.

"I'll get onto to it straight away sir. I should be able to organize it within twenty-four hours."

"Good," said Wyatt. "Get it done. I want to see it on tomorrow evening's news."

"Yes sir." Mullens got up to go, but then hesitated.

"Do you know anything about Stonehouse's new lawyer? That he claims to know who killed Chevalier? That he has proof?"

"I think he's bluffing. That's Radcliffe's style…bluffs his way to create hype," said Wyatt a little too brightly. "I really wouldn't worry about it. There's no chance he would have anything on you."

Mullens was thoughtful. He noticed that Wyatt was avoiding eye contact and that he had said *you*…not *us*.

"Right. Okay then sir, I'll text you when it's done."

"Thank you Mullens."

They both got up and headed out the door.

Wyatt turned to say something to Mullens, but he was gone. He looked around, perplexed. How did he disappear so quickly? He had always found it quite unnerving how silently Mullens moved and how he seemed to materialize and then vaporize. Mullens was a good ghost to have but if the police came knocking at Wyatt's door, he would throw him under the bus in a heartbeat.

Early the next morning, Mullens contacted one of the guards at the Albany County Correctional Facility. He told him exactly what needed doing. The guard asked for a couple hours and said he would come back to him. By ten he texted Mullens saying that it was sorted and that he and one of the inmates were standing by. It was going to cost a pretty penny, but Mullens knew that would never be an issue. Wyatt was rolling in it. Besides, he was too shrewd to use his own resources. Wyatt knew exactly how to manipulate the system and how to use FBI money to do his dirty work. Mullens texted back. *Get it done. Today.*

His mind then turned yet again to Radcliffe's announcement claiming Stonehouse's innocence. It was gnawing at him. How did he know? What did Stonehouse tell him? All perps claim they are innocent, but Radcliffe was no fool. He would never have attained the height of success if he merely bluffed his way and took the word of every entitled prick he defended. No, somehow, he had information and Mullens had to find out what, where and how. If Wyatt had set up Stonehouse, then he could just as easily set him up too, thought Mullens. If push came to shove Mullens was under no illusions, Wyatt would give him up in an instant. So, Stonehouse had to be eliminated as soon as possible so that he would never have an opportunity to even mention in a courtroom that Wyatt had sent him to New York and thus all speculation would cease. Mullens concluded in his mind that Radcliffe had vital information and Wyatt was brushing him off, of that he was sure. It made him very uneasy indeed.

Inmate 14677011 was watching Stonehouse closely. All the prisoners were in the exercise yard, and he observed Stonehouse walk over to a concrete bench and sit down. He waited a while, then looking around he casually sauntered over and sat down next to him. Stonehouse looked up at him and shifted sideways.

"Hey man…I'm not going to bite you," said the inmate laughing.

Stonehouse looked away. He was not interested in engaging with anyone. Nor did he trust anyone. Who could in a place like this.

"I hope your trial goes well. I don't think you did it," ventured the inmate. Stonehouse turned to look at him, his expression hostile.

"What would you know?" said Stonehouse. "Besides I don't want to talk about it."

They were both silent for a while and the inmate watched the other prisoners milling around, enjoying a bit of sunshine, shooting the breeze.

"Wanna piece of gum?" he offered, extending a packet to Stonehouse.

"No thanks," mumbled Stonehouse looking back down at

his feet. He was shifting stones around with his one foot, arranging them in a circle, his thoughts drifting to Radcliffe's visit.

"Guess this place is much better than Rikers, eh?" said the inmate.

Stonehouse froze, his eyes sliding sideways.

"What makes you think I was in Rikers?" asked Stonehouse warily.

"Oh, a little birdie told me," he replied smiling cryptically.

"Why don't you just fuck off," said Stonehouse, angry now as a sense of panic started to rise up inside of him.

The inmate's smile faded and shaking his head, he said.

"You know Stonehouse, I have no idea why so many people are trying to protect your sorry ass. You sure don't deserve it."

Stonehouse was staring at him. What did he mean? So many people?

The inmate held Stonehouse's gaze, his expression hard and then he glanced over his shoulder, and something caught his eye. One of the prisoners was moving towards them from behind, his right hand obscured, tight against his side. The inmate tensed and watched him, assessing his body language, his senses on high alert. The prisoner accelerated his speed slightly and the inmate saw the guy's right shoulder tense up. Suddenly he realized what was happening. The prisoner leapt forward, his arm arching up high with a sharp object in his hand. At that moment, the inmate reacted with the speed of a reptile and struck Stonehouse hard between the shoulder blades, pushing him with a force that only an adrenalin rush could produce. Stonehouse went hurtling forward as the blade flashed on a downward and sideways trajectory. It was too late for the assailant to halt the momentum or direction of the weapon. Instead of plunging into the side of Stonehouse's neck, the sharp blade sliced through the air and sunk deep into the throat of Inmate 14677011.

An arterial mist of blood sprayed over Stonehouse as he landed on the ground, skidding on his stomach in the dirt. He leapt up screaming, stumbling backwards, his eyes wild with terror. The pulsating arc of blood from the inmate's jugular rained down on the sand and a dark black pool of blood started to form. The guards were blowing their whistles as they were running towards them. The prisoners in the yard stood frozen unsure of what was happening. The inmate momentarily stood up clutching his neck, the blood squirting between his fingers as he staggered towards Stonehouse, an expression of terror on his face. He finally collapsed, face down onto the ground, his hands scrabbling in the dirt. His movements started to slow, and Stonehouse watched in disbelief as the inmate slowly rolled over onto his back, a strange gurgling sound emitting from his throat, his life force slowly ebbing out of him. His body twitched a few times and then finally he was motionless, lying in an expanding pool of his own blood, his blue eyes open to the sky.

Total silence descended on the yard. Stonehouse stared horrified at the scene before him, rooted to the spot. Slowly he looked up. Through the crowds he saw the assailant slip through a gate that was standing ajar on the far side of the yard and within seconds he had disappeared from view. The guard look around and then quietly closed it, and in the silence, Stonehouse heard the faint click of a padlock. The guard walked away slowly, glancing back only once as he too disappeared from view.

There has been yet another bizarre twist in the story of the alleged killer of Dr. Simon Chevalier. A few hours ago, an attempt was made on the life of Special Agent Stonehouse who was recently transferred to Albany County Correctional Facility after a reported case of brutality at Rikers Island State Penitentiary. An undercover police officer who had been assigned to protect Agent Stonehouse, died during the attack.

The blonde reporter then turned to Roland Radcliffe who was standing next to her on the steps of the New York State Supreme Court building, his face grim.

Mr. Radcliffe, what do you make of this shocking turn of events? she asked pointing the microphone towards Roland Radcliffe. He turned and looked directly into camera and said.

This attempt on my client's life underpins the fact that he is innocent, and clearly there are unseen forces who do not want him to ever testify in a courtroom. They will stop at nothing to silence him. Well, I am simply not going to allow that to happen. Special Agent Stonehouse will have his day in court. Mark my words.

The reporter then asked.

Are there plans to ensure that Agent Stonehouse will be moved to safer custody since obviously he was not safe in the Albany County or Rikers Island?

Radcliffe nodded.

As we speak Agent Stonehouse is being transferred to an undisclosed destination. It appears that no prison is safe in America. The American people should be asking why this is? They should be asking who gains by killing Agent Stonehouse? This was not a prison fight. This was an organized hit. What machinations are afoot in our land? It's time for hard working American citizens to start asking the present administration some really tough questions.

The reporter moved the mike back to herself and said.

Thank you, Mr. Radcliffe, for your comments.

Radcliffe nodded. Then turning to the camera, she said.

The identity of the undercover police officer who lost his life is being withheld until his family has been notified. There will be an update as soon as new information comes in. And now…back to the studio.

Police Commissioner Ed Baker stared at the screen, appalled by the turn of events and that the undercover police officer assigned to protect Stonehouse was now dead. He had been informed within minutes of the attack and had immediately mobilized to have Stonehouse transferred to a witness protection safe house. Normally a transfer would be a convoluted affair with mounds of paperwork. But there was no luxury of time, so he pulled rank and made it happen within half an hour. He would hear from his team when the transfer was complete and when Stonehouse was safely ensconced in a place far from the reach of those who wanted him dead.

Across town, Georgina, Paul, Les, and Jordan sat in shocked silence. In Washington, Wyatt was rooted to the spot, seething that Stonehouse had yet again gotten away and he knew now that he had to cut all ties to Mullens. In turn, Mullens was mortified that the whole plan had gone awry and was expecting a call from Wyatt at any moment. That call never came. Captain Murphey sat watching the news cast, terrified that he would be found out for providing the information as to where Stonehouse had been held. And now he had the blood of an undercover police officer on his hands and the thought petrified him, not due to any sense of conscience but through fear of the possible consequences. Brad Townsend immediately texted Sophie, asking her to stay with him that night at his apartment. Clearly information was leaking like a sieve, and he would not risk her safety for anything or anyone.

Stonehouse was seated in the back of an unmarked police van. There were no windows and no inner latches, so any hopes of escaping were scuppered. Besides, he was handcuffed to the rails on either side of the only seat which was positioned in the middle of the van. There was one small light in the roof and given the fact that he could hardly hear the engine, he suspected that it was a bullet proof vehicle. He looked down and in the dim light he could see that he was still covered in the inmate's blood. After everyone had realized that the inmate was dead, chaos had erupted. The guards had grabbed him and rushed him inside, down multiple corridors to one of the solitary confinement cells. As they pushed him inside, two guards took up positions on either side of the cell door. Within the hour, the steel door opened, and he was helped up, handcuffed, and led via a different route to the waiting van, its engine running. Ten seconds later the sliding door of the van was slammed shut and the vehicle lurched forward causing the handcuffs to cut into his wrists. He yelled out but there was no one to hear him.

Wyatt looked down at his buzzing mobile. It was Mullens. He cancelled the call. He no longer needed him or wanted contact with him. He had screwed up, simple as that. Stonehouse was still alive. Besides, the time had now come for a more military style operation, and a private briefing at a location far from prying eyes had already been scheduled.

Mullens sat back and muted the TV. The Stonehouse incident was the hot story on all the TV stations and there was no doubt in his mind that Stonehouse was now totally out of reach. To make matters worse, Wyatt was ghosting him, and this made Mullens laugh out loud. A ghost being ghosted! No matter. He would bide his time and see what panned out. The thing about professional ghosts, is that they always have some form of insurance. If Wyatt threw him under the bus, he would drag Wyatt kicking and screaming straight under with him.

Brad took Sophie into his arms as she walked through the door. She smiled up at him.

"And for what reason have I been summonsed so hastily by Agent Dork?" she asked laughing.

Brad frowned at her. "You know damn well why Sophie de la Motte. I have to ask you again. Are you absolutely sure that there is nothing linking you to the processing of that syringe cap at the lab?"

Sophie became serious.

"Yes Brad. I am one hundred percent sure. Nothing can ever be traced back to me. I would tell you if I had any doubts. All records are password protected and the syringe cap itself is buried under a mountain of other evidence in the secure storage. You are the only other person who knows where it is."

Brad looked down at her. It had been quite an ingenious idea of Sophie's to hide the syringe cap in the evidence box of a cold case file in the cold storage of the lab.

"Okay. Sorry for being a worry wart," he said pulling her towards him against his chest as he gently cupped the back of her head in his palm.

"It's okay Brad. No girl with half a brain would complain about a man like you looking out for her," she said smiling up at him.

"So…young lady, I want to ask your opinion on something," he said, leading her into the lounge. "Wine? And then I will make you some din dins."

"Lovely. Let's sit in the kitchen," she replied. They walked through to the kitchen and while he poured them each a glass of wine, he told her that he had found out where the Levenstein evidence had been taken to. Her eyes widened.

"Well done, Brad! My goodness…quite the cyber sleuth!"

"I hope so. It is my job after all!" he laughed. "So, if I know where it is, do you have any ideas as to how I could get my hands on it?"

Sophie was silent for a while, mulling over Brad's question. She looked up at him and said.

"You don't. You can't walk in there and simply take possession of the evidence. But the NYPD can. They can get a search warrant from a judge and raid the location."

"It won't be that easy. The FBI is the official custodian. No one can trump that," countered Brad.

"Yes, you are right. Quis custodiet…" began Sophie.

"…ipsos custodes," said Brad completing the quote. They

both said in unison. "Who guards the guards."

Sophie was quiet for a while and then she said.

"No Brad…actually on reflection I don't think the FBI would even know about this location. Only the people trying to bury this from the public eye would know, and they would use the status of the FBI as a smokescreen."

"Yes, you may well be right sweetheart. I think perhaps I should discuss this with the investigating team. Neither of us would be able to get anywhere near the evidence but as you say, the NYPD could possibly do it if they can circumvent any checks and balances that the kingpin would have in place," said Brad thoughtfully.

Whilst they chatted further, he whipped up a quick pasta and they ate sitting at the kitchen counter. When they had finished, she helped him clear everything away and then they had a coffee. Conversation was easy and it felt as though they had been together for a lifetime. It was getting late. Brad stood up and took Sophie's hand.

"And now my darling Sophie, you know what you were saying earlier on about possession…I think I might just take possession of you. That okay with you? After all…" he said grinning, "I am FBI."

"Ah, well, in that case…if you're FBI, I would be deeply disappointed if you didn't," replied Sophie, her eyes wide. Laughing, they both headed to the bedroom.

Lela Hinton had taken up Tanya's offer to assist with a stand-in chef given that Tanya said she could vouch for his discretion. Very fortunately, Officer Cooper who would pose as the temporary chef enjoyed cooking, so the combination of his own experience plus a crash course under the tutelage of a top chef resulted in his cooking skills and menu being good enough to pass muster. Besides, it wasn't like he was cooking for La Boheme, and it was only for three days. This represented the only window of opportunity they had to get into the safe, identify the type of memory cards that Lela Hinton used, arrange bogus replacement cards, and get the real cards out. All this was dependent on Lela Hinton being off the premises for a while and that was where the big gamble came in.

On the first day, Lela was at the club the entire time that the stand-in chef was on duty. He couldn't exactly hang around after his shift ended. The second day was not looking good either but then shortly after lunch, Lela told the *Nymphs* that she had some errands to run. Tanya walked into the kitchen and poured herself some water nodding imperceptibly at Officer Cooper. They had no idea how long Lela would be out and they also had to make sure that none of the other *Nymphs* saw any strange behaviour. Lela always locked her office when she went out and she even locked it when she was interacting with guests. However, a few days before, Tanya and the other *Nymphs* had been in her office being briefed on a new member who had recently been admitted to the club. The office key had been lying on Lela's desk. Tanya pretended to be adjusting the strap of one of her high heel shoes and leaned in as close as she dared, memorizing the engraved code on the key whilst Lela was looking away answering a question.

They probably had a ten-minute window before the other staff in the kitchen would wonder where the chef was. As soon as they were sure that Lela was at least already downstairs in the basement garage, Tanya and Officer Cooper made their way to Lela's office and turned the duplicate key in the lock. It opened. They both breathed a sigh of relief. After slipping in and closing the door, Tanya showed him where the safe was and as he started to work on the combination lock, she watched the camera monitors showing the basement, corridors, and public areas. She watched Lela get into her car and reverse out and disappear from view. The afternoons were generally quiet so there were only two members still in the dining room and only two other *Nymphs* on duty. She didn't take her eyes off the monitors. Her anxiety levels were rising as the Officer Cooper turned the dial back and forth, and she listened to the whirring of the inner cogs. Eventually after what seemed like an eternity, Tanya heard the magical click and the safe door swung open. Office Cooper knew exactly what he was looking for and he carefully searched amongst the various envelopes and boxes in the safe. He found the memory cards in a small black plastic box, and he then set about taking photos of them so that they could be matched perfectly. There were thirty-one in total and each one had a piece of tape on it and had been numbered with a black marker in Lela's handwriting. No sweat. They would just transfer the labels when they replaced the memory cards. He worked swiftly, replaced the cards exactly how he had found them and closed the safe. Tanya checked the corridor screen. All clear. They slipped out. He went back to the kitchen and Tanya headed back to the guests. Within ten minutes Officer Cooper had sent photos of the memory cards to the police commissioner. An hour and a half later, Cooper received a text that another officer was waiting for him at the small green grocers one block away with the replacement cards. He made an excuse that he needed a particular ingredient from the local store and left the kitchen. Ten minutes later he was back. Before he went back into the kitchen, he alerted Tanya through her wireless earpiece that he had the replacement cards and that he would meet her back at the office. At that moment, Tanya heard the ting of the lift and Lela emerged and walked directly towards her office.

"Miss Hinton…" called Tanya. Lela turned around.

"Yes Tanya?" replied Lela, her eyebrows raised. Behind her Tanya saw the chef walk towards Lela's office, then on seeing Lela talking to Tanya, he halted immediately, made an about turn and hurriedly disappeared back up the corridor around the corner. The kitchen staff were never allowed to set foot anywhere near the public areas in case the identities of club members were compromised.

"Um…are we expecting the commissioner this evening?" asked Tanya.

Lela looked perplexed. "No…why should we? He is only ever here on Fridays," she replied frowning.

"Oh…my mistake. I thought he had mentioned that he may be here this evening," replied Tanya.

"No…not that I know of." Lela looked at her quizzically and then she turned and walked to her office. She glanced back at Tanya who quickly smiled before walking away to the drawing room.

Lela only emerged from her office about two hours later. Her demeanor seemed fine, so it appeared that she was none the wiser that anyone had been in there. This was nerve-racking. Those memory cards were absolutely vital to the whole operation. They could only hope that an opportunity would present itself the next day for Cooper to swop them out.

The following day, one of the *Nymphs* knocked on Lela's office door and advised her that one of the members was complaining loudly. Lela immediately got up from her desk and followed the *Nymph* to remedy the situation. It was rare that she ever left her office open. Tanya hot footed it to the kitchen and caught the eye of Officer Cooper through the glass window of the door, gesturing to him urgently. He made the excuse that he was going to the gents and the two of them were in Lela's office within twelve seconds.

Tanya kept watch on the monitors, while Cooper worked frantically to enter the combination to the safe. The door opened and he grabbed the memory card box. He had 31 labels to replace, and he worked frantically. He had four more to go.

"Oh Christ! She's coming back!" Tanya exclaimed, total

panic in her voice. She glanced back at Cooper and then back at the monitors. Lela was probably ten paces away when Tanya heard the safe door click and the cupboard door shut. Cooper jumped up, swiftly grabbed Tanya, and shoved her towards the window, positioning their backs to the door. Lela walked into her office and stopped dead, shocked to see Tanya and the chef standing there.

"What are you two doing in my office!" she exclaimed her eyes wide.

They both turned around and Cooper lifted his hand. Tanya looked down and saw that he was holding a bloodied tissue around his thumb.

"I cut myself and asked Tanya if she knew where the first aid box was. We were just looking at the wound in the light…waiting for you," and he gestured towards the window. "She said that she was pretty sure you would have one in your office."

Lela looked at them both suspiciously.

"Let me see…" she said walking towards Cooper and Tanya.

Cooper opened the tissue and there was a deep cut in his thumb.

"Oh my!" exclaimed Lela. "That does look bad! Wait a moment…" and she went around to her desk and opened a draw. She withdrew a small first aid box and extracted some plasters and bandages.

"I'm not very good with blood," she said. "Would you help the chef please Tanya?"

"Yes of course. Perhaps it may be an idea to keep a first aid box in the kitchen?" she ventured.

"But there is one there Tanya, you should know that," Lela replied.

Tanya felt her mouth go dry. Lela went on.

"I am sorry, chef. I should have shown you where it is kept when you got here. My apologies."

"No, it's my fault Ma'am," he replied. "Sorry for being so clumsy. I guess it's an occupational hazard," he added laughing.

"No problem," said Lela. "Just ask the kitchen staff. They will tell you where it's kept…in case you are clumsy again." She smiled.

Cooper thanked her and he and Tanya left the office. When they got to the kitchen Tanya whispered to him.

"How the hell did you manage that?"

"I like to be prepared in case things go pear-shaped," he replied.

Tanya shook her head. "That was a close call. Wow! You're good."

She suddenly realized that whenever she spoke to him, he would be looking away. Then she clicked. She was semi naked. He was being respectful towards her.

She added. "And thank you for not ogling!"

He smiled and said. "Strict instructions from the commissioner. He has sworn me to secrecy. I understand that nobody else in the department knows about this. They think you've gone back to England."

Tanya nodded. "Yes…indefinite leave."

Taking the bandages from her, he said.

"I've got this. I'll manage it from here."

Tanya smiled at him and left the kitchen to resume her duties.

Lela looked around her office, feeling uncomfortable about what had just happened. She checked her draws and then the small cupboard where the safe was kept. Everything seemed in its place. She then opened the safe to be absolutely sure and saw that all the contents were there, just as she had left them. She looked around once more, shrugged and closed the safe and cupboard and then sat down at her desk. She opened her ledger and started going through the accounts.

When Cooper had finished bandaging his thumb, he discreetly took the small paring knife out of his pocket and threw it into the garbage bin. When he had completed his shift, Lela paid him, and he thanked her for the opportunity of the three-day job. Thereafter he went straight to the NYPD Headquarters and handed over the thirty-one memory cards to Police Commissioner Ed Baker.

Mission complete. A job well done.

CHAPTER THIRTY-THREE

Everyone was gathered in the police commissioner's private boardroom, but this time Agent Brad Townsend was included in the meeting. He appraised Baker of what he had found.

"Sir, I have managed to trace the location of all the Levenstein evidence. There is one location, two units. One is a standard lock up and the other is a refrigerated unit. The storage company is called First Storage and it's in Columbus, Ohio," said Brad.

"Well, that's interesting. How did you find that out Agent Townsend?" asked Baker.

"The paper trail had been destroyed and the computer records had been deleted. But as we all know sir, nothing is ever really deleted. I managed to intercept a private email address and that is how I found the deleted files and location." Brad explained.

"And the email address? Where did that lead to?" asked Baker.

Everyone turned and looked expectantly at Brad.

"Director Len Wyatt, sir," answered Brad.

The room was silent. It is one thing suspecting someone, it's another thing getting confirmation.

"Well, at least we know now for sure who is pulling the strings," said Baker, his expression grim.

"But why would he do that, sir?" asked Jordan, perplexed. "What is his motivation?"

Baker and Damote exchanged looks. The room was silent. The commissioner sighed and then said.

"It's time I brought you all up to speed, but this is not going to be easy for you all to hear, especially you Agent Townsend, being FBI."

He leant forward and spread his hands on the boardroom table, gathering his thoughts. He looked up and said.

"Len Wyatt is a pedophile, and he was closely associated with Levenstein."

Everyone except Paul was stunned. Baker continued.

"I have been running an undercover operation for some time now which is why I know about Wyatt and others like him. I thought they were all just carrying on without Levenstein. But of course, the DNA match has changed everything."

Baker then told them all about the Sheldon Wagstaff Club. He told them what went on there and about him being a member in order to carry out surveillance. He also told them about Officer Tanya Davidson who posed as a *Nymph,* and how she and Officer Cooper had managed to obtain all the original memory cards of the underage sex that was secretly filmed, from Lela Hinton's safe.

Everyone was totally spellbound. Paul realized that Officer Davidson must be the other person Baker had referred to when he had confided in him about being under cover. Baker continued.

"We have overwhelming evidence to bring most of the cabal down, but we are missing one key component and that is Levenstein's present identity. We would prefer not to move until we have that, but we may have to act, given that people are now losing their lives."

Georgina maintained her composure but only just. She was still grieving for Simon and a part of her always would grieve for him. She missed him more than words could express. Baker looked over at her.

"Detective Harris…your pain must be overwhelming. If you would prefer not to be part of all of this, it would be totally understandable. There is simply no pressure from me or anyone else."

Everyone nodded in agreement. Baker's expression was one of such kindness and concern that Georgina's eyes started to prickle.

"Sir, that is very kind of you, but I am going to do whatever I possibly can to bring these psychopaths to justice. I would prefer to remain part of the team please sir." she said.

"Fair enough," said Baker inclining his head. "But please know how much you are valued Detective Harris," he added.

"Thank you, sir," said Georgina.

Baker looked around at the rest of the team.

"Right…we must make a decision. I propose that if by the end of the week we have not been able to identify Levenstein, then we proceed with blowing the whole thing wide open." He paused and then continued.

"We have the recordings of what has been going on at the Wagstaff Club and who the pedophiles are. That is just the tip of the iceberg. There are a lot more out there who publicly distanced themselves from Levenstein, but who are still without a doubt involved in pedophilia. We now know, thanks to Agent Townsend where all the evidence on Levenstein is stored plus the evidence he had on all his perverted associates. We know who Dr. Chevalier's killer is, and we have DNA proof that Levenstein is alive and well. And now we have Stonehouse in a safe house, the address of which is only known to key people. What we don't know is who gave up Stonehouse's location in Albany County, but we do have our suspicions that it was Captain Murphey. However, for the moment, our focus is on identifying Levenstein," Baker concluded.

After a moment's silence, Paul then suggested.

"If we could retrieve all the CCTV footage of the street where we were trailing Johnny Salome, which may be in the Ohio lockup, then we may see an image of Levenstein throwing his Starbucks cup into the same trash bin," suggested Paul.

Baker shook his head.

"The facility is in the name of the FBI even if only Wyatt knows about it. The moment a judge signs off on a search, we can't be sure that Wyatt won't find out about it and then he will be aware that someone knows what is stored there. All the evidence will disappear faster than Casper the ghost and we can't risk that".

Everyone was nodding in agreement. Baker continued.

"In the interim, I have a few more questions. Where is the syringe cap evidence right now and where is the footage of Dr. Chevalier's murder being kept? Perhaps we need to consolidate all our evidence."

Brad spoke up.

"The syringe evidence is buried in a cold case file at the same laboratory where Dr. Chevalier worked."

"The recording is with us in the lock up at our precinct," added Les.

"And the original DNA evidence and print out?" Baker

looked at Paul and Georgina.

"The printout is in my father's safe sir, and the DNA evidence is in his freezer," said Georgina.

Baker did a double take. "And he knows about this?" he asked incredulously, his eyebrows raised.

"He knows that I am storing some things there, but he has no idea what they are sir. He said that he doesn't want to know for obvious reasons," replied Georgina.

"Yes of course," said Baker. "It would be considered a breach of conduct if he did know."

"He has no idea sir, and he will never ask," confirmed Georgina.

Baker nodded and was quite for a moment. Then he said.

"You know, Judge Harris's apartment is probably the safest place in the world right now. Do you think the rest of the evidence could be stored there too? I know it's totally contrary to standard protocols, but then there is nothing standard about the events of the last few months."

"Yes sir, I can definitely arrange to get everything there," said Georgina. "And I think we can all agree that it would be the last place anyone would even think of looking. Besides, getting a warrant to search a judge's home would be more than a challenge if anyone suspected anything," concluded Georgina.

Baker nodded in agreement and then said.

"Okay, let's do it. Everyone, please assist Detective Harris and let me know when the *eagle has landed*," he said with a wink and a smile.

Everyone laughed. Baker stood up and they all immediately jumped up and stood to attention.

"Good work everyone. As you were," he said and then he left the room.

They all relaxed and gathered their notes together.

"Should we go to the canteen and sort out who does what?" suggested Les.

They all agreed and filed out of the boardroom, making their way down to the fifth floor.

When Georgina and Paul got back to the precinct there was a message waiting for them. It was from a person they had interviewed who worked in the area where Johnny Salome had been operating before his disappearance. A Mrs. Belmonte who ran a pizza joint had spotted Salome and had immediately called the precinct. Georgina and Paul didn't even take their jackets off. They told Les and Jordan where they were going and set off immediately. Georgina noticed that Murphey studiously avoided eye contact as they walked past his office.

When they arrived at the pizza shop, Mrs. Belmonte told

them where she had spotted Salome. He had walked right past her shop window and had then turned up West 35th Street.

"I jus' happened to look up 'cos I'm bored with mixin' pizza dough and all when the dumb ass walks straight past my window. I jus' spazzed out, but like you tol' me, I didn't make no shoutin' or yellin' after the lowlife. He just kept rollin' along like he owns the godamned street," said Mrs. Belmonte putting her hands on her ample hips.

"I jus' ran to the door and kept my peepers peeled where he was headin'. Straight up West 35th was where he was strollin', the sleazeball."

"Approximately what time was this Mrs. Belmonte?" asked Georgina.

She squeezed her eyes shut and thought for a while.

"Mus' a bin twelve thirty or so. Ol' Simmons always picks up his order then. He'd jus' bin in," she concluded.

"And you are absolutely sure it was him?" asked Paul.

"Hell yes!" she exclaimed. "I'd know that rat ass scumbag anywheres!"

"Well thank you very much Mrs. Belmonte for contacting us. We really appreciate it," said Paul.

"You wanna piece of pizza? On the house?" she asked picking up two greasy slices with her pudgy hands. Both Georgina and Paul smiled but declined.

They walked around the area hoping to spot Salome but no luck. Eventually they headed back to the same Starbucks they had seen him in all those months ago and asked around, but no one had seen him.

"Well, if he's in the area, hopefully someone else will spot him sooner or later, and we can check any surveillance cameras." added Georgina.

"It certainly seemed to me that Mrs. Belmonte was sure it was him," said Paul.

Georgina nodded. "Let's head back."

They started to cross the street and waited for a bus to pass. Georgina's thoughts went back to the poor girl Selina Chapman who had been waiting at that exact same bus stop, unaware that Salome had been watching her. As the bus passed Georgina, she looked up at the driver, then continued to cross and stepped up onto the pavement. Suddenly she stopped dead in her tracks. She turned and watched the bus continue down the road. She reached out and touched Paul's arm. He looked at her, puzzled by her demeanor.

"Hey Paul…did you see that?" she asked looking at him.

"See what?" he asked, perplexed.

"That bus," Georgina replied pointing down the road. "The one that just passed us."

"Yeah, what about it…" he said frowning at her. "It's just a bus."

She looked up at him, her eyes wide.

"Paul, there was a dashcam mounted just in front of the driver!" she exclaimed.

"And what of it…" began Paul but then he stopped as he twigged what she was saying.

"My God, Georgie!" he said. "There will be surveillance footage! How long do you think they keep their recordings for?"

"We need to find that out asap!" Georgina said. "These buses drive up and down all day. What if one of them recorded Levenstein throwing his cup into the trash bin? It was on top of all the other trash so it must have been happened some time close to when Salome tossed his cup in there."

Paul turned and headed to the pole on which all the bus timetables and bus numbers were mounted.

"Okay so the buses that run up and down here are buses M11, M20, M50 and QM24," said Paul. "We need to get hold of the bus company." He got out his notebook and jotted the numbers down.

At that moment another bus pulled up. Georgina waited for the automatic doors to open, and then she skipped up the steps onto the bus. She flashed her badge and asked the bus driver if he knew how long the dashcam recordings were kept for. He looked at the one mounted in front of him, sat back and thought about it for a while.

"I think for about six months, certainly not less than that officer. There were new laws introduced after that marathon attack. I would say that anything between six months and a year," he concluded.

"Do you have the bus company's contact details on you?" asked Georgina.

"Yes Ma'am." He bent down and fished out a card from a side pocket. "Everything's here officer. We all fall under the Metropolitan Transportation Authority. They'll be the people to contact."

Georgina took it and examined it.

"Thank you very much," she said smiling at the driver. "You've been a great help."

"My pleasure Ma'am," he said inclining his head.

And with that she turned, got off the bus and walked to where Paul was standing. The brakes hissed and the bus pulled away. She pulled her mobile out of her pocket and dialed the MTA, tapping her foot as she worked through all the automated options. Finally, she got through to a real human being. They moved off the street into a shop away from the street noise so that they could hear more clearly.

Georgina put her mobile on speaker phone. After explaining what information she was looking for three times, she was finally put through to someone who seemed to have half a brain.

"You will need a warrant I'm afraid," said the woman on the other end. "I don't mean to be difficult but it's all these new privacy laws."

"I understand," said Georgina. "I will have it by tomorrow. To whom am I speaking?" and she indicated to Paul to write it down. He quickly pulled his notebook out of his pocket and waited, pen poised.

"It's Mrs. Alcott," said the woman spelling it out.

"Right got that. May I have your direct line please?" asked Georgina.

"Yes Ma'am," and she gave Georgina her direct number.

"I'll advise my supervisor," she confirmed. "See you tomorrow, Ma'am."

"Thank you, Mrs. Alcott. I appreciate your assistance."

Georgina rang off and looked up at Paul, her eyes shining.

"This may be the break we have been praying for Paul," she said excitedly.

"Clever girl Detective Harris!" said Paul as he high fived her. "I don't think either of us are going to get any sleep tonight, not if there's a chance we may be able to identify Levenstein."

"May the dashcam gods be with us!" said Georgina happily, looking heavenwards. They both laughed and as they walked towards the car, Paul started to imitate her saying *to whom am I speaking* repeatedly in a lah-di-dah voice. Georgina gave him a playful slap.

"Stop it! Stop it now!" she exclaimed.

"Very posh Ma'am," said Paul baiting her.

"Well, I can't help it if you're such a neanderthal and you have zero command over the English language!"

Paul laughed repeating *lah-di-dah, lah-di-dah* as he minced to the car. Georgina shook her head. Paul was an odd one. Full of surprises.

CHAPTER THIRTY-FOUR

By nine the next morning they were sitting on a bench waiting outside Judge Wilcock's chambers. Paul nudged Georgina and she looked down the corridor.

"Here comes the grumpiest judge on the bench," commented Paul.

They both stood up as he drew near. He didn't even acknowledge their presence as he unlocked his office. As he pushed the door open, he gestured curtly with his hand for them to follow him. Georgina and Paul exchanged glances and they both followed him into his office.

"Sit," he ordered. "I don't know why you think it's acceptable to be bothering me before I've even had my first cup of coffee," he added grumpily.

They said nothing. He removed his jacket and hung it up on a coat stand in the corner and after fishing out his spectacles from one of the pockets, he eventually sat down at his desk. Then for the first time he made eye contact with them.

"So, what is it that you want detectives? Yes, I know who you are," he said stabbing a finger at Georgina. "You're Harris's daughter. You are certainly better looking than he is. Dead ugly your father is."

Rich coming from you, thought Georgina.

"How is your father?" asked Judge Wilcock.

"He is extremely well, thank you," she replied politely.

"Hmmph. Not that he deserves to be. Right, what do you two want?" he demanded. Paul then said.

"We would like a warrant to view footage from the dashcams of some buses run by the Metropolitan Transportation Authority. We are hoping to find evidence of a perpetrator who has been attacking young women."

"How many has he attacked?" asked Wilcock, peering at Paul over his spectacles.

"Fourteen that we know about," answered Paul.

"Well, you can't be any good at your jobs if it's that many!" exclaimed Wilcock. He reached out. "Give."

Paul handed him the warrant ready for signature.

Wilcock picked up his pen and started to read the document. Grumbling, he applied a flourish of a signature and handed it back to Paul.

"Now stop messing around and arrest the guy," he added grumpily.

"Yes, Judge Wilcock. And thank you," said Paul standing up. Georgina stood up too.

"And you..." he pointed at Georgina, "tell your father that he is the most hopeless Bridge player I have ever had the misfortune to play with. Now scram!" he said waving his hand at them.

"Thank you, Judge Wilcock," said Georgina sweetly. "I'll be sure to convey your message to my father."

Once they were out of Judge Wilcock's office, they both burst out laughing.

"If I ever become like that old geyser, you have my permission to shoot me!" exclaimed Paul.

"Hey, I don't need your permission," said Georgina. "I'll probably shoot you anyway." Paul rolled his eyes.

"Right. Let's get to the MTA. It's going to be a long haul looking through all the recordings. And let's hope there's a pot of gold at the end of this rainbow."

Director Len Wyatt was meeting with three key officers of the witness protection programme. His wife's family had a hunting lodge in the mountains, and he had told Helen that he needed some quiet time to de-stress and that he would be going up there alone for a few days. Helen immediately suspected that he was going there to liaise with yet another woman but now she no longer cared. She was having a delicious affair with her tennis coach so in fact, it suited her perfectly that her husband would be away. Both kids had study sleep overs so she and her beau could bang away to their hearts' content.

Wyatt knew all three officers very well as they had been involved in many a clandestine operation together. As far as they were concerned, witness protection was there to serve their purposes and only protect the witnesses they wanted protecting. Anyone else who was perceived to be an enemy or whose views did not match theirs, was easily dispensed with. Once someone disappeared under the cloak of protection, only the officers involved would know whether they emerged the other side as someone else with a new identity or didn't emerge at all. Of course, it never occurred to them that their self-interested approach was literally breaking the law. Nor did they care. Small wonder that there was some measure of distrust in the programme.

Wyatt outlined his plans. Agent Stonehouse's court case was due to start the following week. He needed them to find out where he was being held. There were multiple safe houses and Stonehouse had to be in one of them. Once they found him, he was to be eliminated. Wyatt was unconcerned about any public outcry since he had the solution to soothe the American public's indignation. Once Stonehouse was gone, he would offer up Ryder Mullens, not only as the killer of Dr. Chevalier but the killer of Agent Stonehouse too. It would be a totally feasible explanation since Mullens would have wanted to silence Stonehouse to save his own skin. Once Mullen's mug shot was out there for the world to see, it would only be a matter of time before he would be found and charged. A perfect plan. And he, Director Len Wyatt of the FBI would take all the credit.

"Gentlemen…you have three days to find that safe house and set up an ambush," said Wyatt looking from one to the other. The three men exchanged looks.

"Shouldn't be a problem. We know how to access all the witness protection records. Leave it to us. It will be done."

"Well make sure it is! This Stonehouse character seems to have a whole host of guardian angels watching over him. He's escaped the bullet every time!" said Wyatt clearly annoyed.

"The difference is that we are professionals. We simply don't fuck up," said one of the officers.

"Okay, then that's it," said Wyatt standing up. "Coffee anyone?"

They all declined and said that they would be on their way. Wyatt saw them out. They chatted outside for a while, shook hands and the officers then drove off down the long and windy dust track.

The place seemed eerily quiet after they had left. Wyatt had never been up there in the mountains alone before. It felt quite unsettling. The morning sun was streaming in through the massive glass windows. The entire house was made up of a glass outer shell with timber inner walls, and whilst it was a masterpiece of contemporary architecture, it did make Wyatt feel somewhat exposed. And a bit lonely. Well, he thought to himself, he could always summons any one of the women he was having an affair with. Or…he could simply enjoy some pleasurable time on the dark web. Yes, he thought. He would go with the latter. He had another child virgin on order, so he had much to fantasize about and much to anticipate.

High up from a hidden vantage point, Mullens had watched the three men leave and saw Wyatt go back into the house. He watched him walk to the kitchen and put the coffee machine on. Mullens knew exactly who the three men were. Senior officers in the witness protection programme. He also knew why they were meeting. They were going to go after Stonehouse…and then him. Mullens was no fool. He could read Wyatt like a book.

He had captured a series of hi-res photos and video footage of all four of them outside. There could be no official reason for the director of the FBI to be meeting senior officials of the witness protection programme in the middle of nowhere. Wyatt would be hard pressed to convince any judge or jury otherwise. Mullens stood up carefully and went back to his makeshift camp. It had been a hard circuitous slog up the mountain, and he had to ensure that he remained undetected.

Georgina and Paul were exhausted. They had viewed recording after recording. Nothing yet. It was a hit and miss endeavour especially since there was sometimes up to five minutes in-between buses and the action of Levenstein throwing his Starbucks cup into the trash bin could well have taken place in any of those windows. After five hours they had nothing. Paul sighed.

"Well, it looks like the dashcam gods prefer limos to buses. Perhaps we should call it a day Georgie," suggested Paul. "I'd say that we're simply not going to be able to identify Levenstein."

Georgina did not answer right away. She was staring at a frozen image of a woman looking over her shoulder. "Not necessarily…" and she turned to Paul and continued.

"Paul, we have been looking only from one direction hoping to get a frontal image of his face. What about from the other direction?"

"But how will the back view of him help identify him?" Paul asked.

"It wouldn't…but that would only be if he wasn't looking around. People look around all the time," and she pointed to the image on the screen of the woman looking over her shoulder. "I don't think we should assume anything."

Paul rubbed his chin contemplating her words.

"I get your point Georgie…you're right. Okay, so let's start going through the dash cam footage of the buses going the other way. But first I am starving. We can go to the diner around the corner."

"No, you go Paul. Perhaps bring back a bagel or something for me," said Georgina. "I'm going to push on."

"Okay, see you in twenty," said Paul standing up. "And you had better have something for me when I return or I'm dumping you as my partner," he joked.

"Promise?" Georgina laughed and she turned back to the screen and started sorting out the reverse bus route recordings.

Half an hour later Paul arrived back with a takeout bagel and soda for Georgina. He looked around. She was nowhere to be seen. He sat down and scooted his chair closer to the screen. He froze. The recording was paused and there was an image of a man with a Starbucks coffee in his hand. Paul toggled the screen back a couple of minutes and then pressed play and watched the recording.

The dashcam was stationary. Possibly there were several people getting on and off a bus. A man came into view walking down the sidewalk, his back to camera. He then paused and the back of his head tilted backwards as he drained the last contents of his coffee. Suddenly his head turned to the left, and then he turned around fully and was looking in the direction of the dashcam. He was only about ten or twelve feet away, so the image was very clear. Other people on the sidewalk did the same thing so it could have been the case of a horn honking, or squealing brakes or some other stimulus that had caught their attention. Then the source of the distraction was revealed as flaying arms momentarily came into view. It seemed that there was a punch up between two people on the sidewalk and it had spilt onto the road in front of the bus for a few seconds. Just as quickly, the arms disappeared from view. The man stood still and watched whatever was happening for a few more seconds, still holding the cup in his right hand. Eventually he turned away and pushed the cup through the opening of the same trash receptable that Georgina had recovered the evidence from. He then continued down the sidewalk. The dashcam visual started to move sideways indicating that the bus was pulling out. It swung left, then right and then continued on a straight trajectory. It passed by the man walking and continued down the road.

Paul toggled back again and paused the recording on the man looking straight at the camera.

"I think it's him," said Georgina behind him.

He swung around. "Georgie! You're as bad as Murphey! Stop creeping up on me!"

Ignoring him, she leant forward pointing at the image.

"Same height, same build…I've been talking to Brad where the signal was better and I've sent him screen shots so that he can start an initial analysis on height etcetera. He has the necessary software, but he will need the original recording too."

She then expanded the image homing in specifically on his hand. She took a screen shot. She then clicked on Google and typed in a specific command. Up came a photo of Chad Levenstein holding a glass of wine at some fund-raising event. She expanded the shot and took a similar size screen shot of his hand. She then dragged the two screenshots side by side and there it was. An identical ring on the third finger of both images. Paul was rivetted.

"Well Georgie! You have indeed earned your lunch and a gold star!" exclaimed Paul.

She gave him a disdainful look.

"I only do platinum you cheapskate," she retorted and then continued.

"It gets better. Two buses later there's a clear shot of

Salome throwing his cup into the same trash bin," she said. She pulled up the recording and there was John Salome doing exactly that. A few seconds later, Georgina came into frame and they watched how she twisted sideways, extracting the cup through the awkward aperture of the trash bin, then depositing it into an evidence bag. The bus started to move, and the dashcam swung out to the left and Georgina disappeared from view.

"Was there anyone else doing the same thing? More Starbucks cups being thrown away?" asked Paul.

"No, not from any of the other recordings. I looked…but we are talking about one specific day, so although it's not likely it's not entirely impossible," said Georgina. "None the less I am pretty sure it's him."

Paul looked heavenwards with his palms pressed together. "Okay dashcam gods…I take it all back," he implored. "I beg for your forgiveness!"

"Hey! What about this goddess?" she said indignantly, pointing at herself.

Paul sighed, and getting down on his knees he started the arms-raised-up-and-down worshipping routine. Georgina laughed and looked around at the other people who worked on that floor. They were all staring open-mouthed at the two of them. What was going through their minds was probably best not to even consider.

They packed up their things and then went through the procedure of signing out and taking possession of the original time-stamped recordings as evidence from the MTA. They thanked the supervisor and Mrs. Alcott and left to go back to the precinct.

"Should we swing by the NYPD headquarters?" suggested Paul. "The commissioner will be dead pleased."

"Hmmm…I don't think so. Not yet. Let's wait for Brad's analysis," said Georgina.

"Yep, you're right. We need further confirmation," agreed Paul. "This may just be the best thing that has happened on this investigation other than identifying Simon's killer."

He immediately glanced sideways at Georgina, worried that his comment may have been inappropriate, but her mind was elsewhere and focused on Levenstein.

"Something about his demeanor reminds me of previous images I have seen of Chad Levenstein over time," mused Georgina.

Paul suddenly stopped and turned to her.

"Georgie…I have just had a thought," he said, his eyes wide. "There was a British professor I read about…I forget her name, but she developed a forensic technique which secured the conviction of a pedophile purely from the evidence of his hands. Apparently the veins on the back of each person's hands is as distinctive as a finger print. It may be an idea to find out who she is and have her analyze Levenstein's hand in comparison to previous photos."

Georgina looked at Paul fascinated by this revelation.

"That is a really good idea. The more confirmation the better for our case. Believe me, there is going to be massive resistance. People will battle to comprehend that such evilness and deception could possibly have taken place. The entire American public…and the world for that matter, were hoodwinked."

They arrived at the car and set off for the Midtown North Precinct.

"I'll get the dashcam recording to Brad this evening." volunteered Georgina. "Perhaps you can research that British professor?"

"Sure Georgie…and well-done girl. You have been a major contributor to this investigation. Your epiphany on the bus dashcams was nothing short of genius."

Georgina looked across at Paul and play punched his arm.

"Hey, I've had a good mentor. Pity about the monumental age difference though not to mention that my partner is dead ugly," she added grinning.

Paul laughed. "The abuse I put up with!"

CHAPTER THIRTY-FIVE

That evening, Mullens crept down towards the house, moving slowly and carefully. It was a dark night, so he was extra cautious. He skirted around the back of the house, down the side towards the front and positioned himself where he could see the interior clearly. Wyatt was sitting at a desk off to the side of the lounge area. Mullens crept closer until he was crouched behind one of the patio sofas and he saw Wyatt scrolling through various child pornography websites. Even Mullens, who was a hardened assassin was appalled by the images. He raised his mobile phone which was muted and took a series of photos. It was too risky to use his standard camera. The shutter on such a quiet night would have sounded like a Guy Fawkes display. He then swapped to video mode and did the same thing, zooming in and out so that it was totally evident as to what Wyatt was watching.

A Coyote yipped in the distance and Wyatt turned his head. Mullens ducked down and waited. After a while he slowly looked up, but Wyatt was gone. He then heard one of the sliding doors slowly open. Without hesitating he silently rolled off the patio and lay dead still in a clump of bushes, hardly breathing. He heard footsteps walking cautiously towards where he was lying and through the foliage, he could see Wyatt peering out into the darkness, a shotgun in his hands.

"Scat!" he yelled.

A Cayote yipped again much closer and Wyatt jumped. He fired off a shot which reverberated through the hills and valley. After the last echoes had died, there was total silence. Mullens kept dead still.

"Godamned Cayotes," Wyatt mumbled. "I'll shoot the lot of you."

He stood motionless for a while and then slowly he turned back towards the house. Mullens heard the door sliding shut again and click as the lock was pushed down. He waited a few minutes before he looked over the edge of the patio and saw that Wyatt was now in the kitchen making dinner. Slowly he stood up and turning, slipped away quietly into the night.

As soon as Georgina had left Brad's apartment, he got straight down to analyzing the dashcam recordings she had given him. He was using Photogrammetry software to analyze the image of the man looking in the direction of the dashcam and he created a computerized 3D mesh from the image. He then did the same from various photos from the internet of Levenstein standing in a similar pose. He then superimposed them one at a time to compare the build, height, and dimensions of the man in the street and that of Levenstein. They were startingly similar. He then started to work on the face with 2D geometric mapping, using the distinguishing characteristics of individual landmarks such as the nose, mouth, eyes, and the distance between them to create a numerical code called a faceprint. So, whilst facial aspects of an individual can be changed through cosmetic surgery, the overall structure and dimensions of the head and face stay the same. When Brad had finished his facial comparisons, the results were the same as the body images. Overwhelmingly similar.

Brad then homed in on the hand. On very close scrutiny, he ascertained that the ring was identical in the dashcam photo to the various internet images of Levenstein that Georgina had sent to him. However, there may be other rings in the world like this particular one so it wouldn't represent any conclusivity. He then created a numerical code for the hands in the two images, including distances between the knuckles, the breadth of the hand and the length of the parts of the digits that were visible. Unlike the face and body analysis, they were not startingly similar; they were identical. In his opinion, the man in the image and the photo of Chad Levenstein were one and the same. He was satisfied that the dashcam photo could be used to identify him.

Lastly, he analyzed the resolution of the image and considered it to be of a high enough resolution for surveillance facial recognition. Clearly the MTA had installed high quality cameras in their buses which may well have been with criminal surveillance in mind. New York had a plethora of cameras that were used every day for the exact purpose of monitoring behaviour and tracking criminals.

Of course, they could put the photo on the eight o' clock news and no doubt thousands of people would claim to know who this person was, but it wouldn't work for three reasons. Firstly, too many people would be looking for fifteen minutes of fame. Secondly, mainstream media had become entirely controlled. Hell would freeze over long before any TV station or newspaper would run the story. Thirdly, Levenstein would go to ground in a heartbeat and that would scupper any chance of detaining him. In conclusion, Brad decided that standard street camera surveillance facial recognition was going to be their only option at finding Levenstein and that would depend on him still being in the US. Once they had him in custody, a DNA check would confirm conclusively whether it was him or some other random individual.

Brad stood up and stretched. He had been working for hours and it was well past midnight. He decided to make a strong coffee and then he would start writing his report plus his recommendation that the facial recognition route be the most likely to produce results. Fortunately, this was neither Illinois nor Texas, so facial recognition surveillance of an individual was legal without their consent. However, there was absolutely no guarantee that Levenstein was still in New York, a vast city with 8,4 million people in it. But…it was a good start.

Stay positive, he said to himself. Something's gotta give!

A few days later, the report from the forensic hand specialist from Lancaster University in the United Kingdom came in. The professor firstly gave a full grounding on the technology she used, cited various cases which had resulted in convictions based solely on hand identification, and then finished off with her detailed report on the case sent to her. In her opinion, the hand featured in the photo of the man taken by the dashcam compared to twenty random photos in similar poses sent to her by the investigative team in New York, was without any shadow of a doubt the hand of Chad Levenstein.

The team were ecstatic. One more nail in the coffin.

Baker looked around the boardroom table at the team gathered around him with a broad smile on his face.

"Well, well, well…quite the team we have here! Congratulations!"

His delight was evident that Levenstein appeared to have been identified. He continued.

"I know we're not out of the woods yet and that we still need to find him and obtain a DNA test. But we are well on our way."

"Sir, we really have Detective Harris to thank for this," said Paul. Everyone looked at Georgina nodding.

"No…," said Georgina quickly. "It's been a team effort sir, and I am mighty proud to serve with everyone here."

"We get that, but you have been pivotal in terms of identifying Levenstein and for that we are all grateful." Baker went on. "You have been dealt a terrible blow recently Detective Harris and yet your tenacity and commitment has shone through. Well done."

"Thank you, sir," said Georgina and she looked down

slightly embarrassed.

There was a soft knock on the door and Hillary entered with a large tray of coffees…and cookies.

"I see that we are celebrating!" said Baker "Coffee *and* cookies! Wow!"

"Well, I could hardly serve scotch could I sir!" said Hillary smiling cryptically.

Baker and Paul exchanged looks but said nothing. No doubt she had seen the glasses and the somewhat depleted scotch bottle after their evening meeting which had gone on late into the night a couple of months before.

"Thank you, Hillary," said Baker. He then turned to Brad. "Where do we stand on the initiation of street facial recognition?"

"It's all been done sir," answered Brad. "Now we wait and hope that Levenstein is still somewhere in New York. If we get nothing, we will extend the surveillance further afield."

"Okay great. We will rely on you to advise us immediately if we strike gold," said Baker.

He looked around at the team and said.

"And now about Agent Stonehouse. He is due in court on Monday morning. I would like to ask you four detectives to accompany the escort to the courthouse. I would prefer not to solely rely on the witness protection officers. A show of force is not a bad thing anyhow. It's highly unlikely that Stonehouse's location has been compromised but I'm not taking any chances. My question to you is, are you able and willing to do this?"

"Yes, if course sir," volunteered Les. The rest of them nodded their affirmation.

"Okay, thank you. I will notify the relevant officers and I will ask Hillary to write down the address for all of you. Memorize it please and then destroy it. You too Agent Townsend in case we need back up. We cannot have the location compromised in any form or manner, so I don't want anything communicated via email or text or even written into a notebook," he added.

"Yes sir, we understand," said Les.

"Well officers…" and then looking at Brad he added, "…and agents, we are getting closer to our goal. Please be careful out there."

He stood up and they all stood to attention.

"As you were. Stay and enjoy the coffee…and cookies," said Baker pointing to the tray. "And you had better finish them all. I have learnt the hard way. Never annoy Hillary!" They all laughed and thanked him and sat down again after he had left the room, smiles all round.

CHAPTER THIRTY-SIX

"I want to take the stand!" demanded Stonehouse.

"Absolutely not!" yelled Radcliffe.

"It's my choice!" yelled Stonehouse right back.

Radcliffe looked at him incredulously.

"How badly do you want to see the outside of prison? Or are you very attached to prison bars and crappy food not to mention really unpleasant anal sex once you're convicted, and your ass is put back into Rikers, eh?"

Stonehouse winced. Radcliffe was pretty sure he heard the clap of a sphincter muscle. He continued.

"Because that is what's going to happen to you if you don't follow my lead and do what I tell you to do. You are an agent, not a godamned defense attorney!"

Stonehouse looked like a sulky child.

"I just want to clear my name," he mumbled looking defensive.

"Well then shut up and do as I say!" said Radcliffe, his tone exasperated.

"Okay! Okay!" said Stonehouse, putting his hands up. "I get it." And he zipped his mouth with his fingers.

"Yes, best you zip it or else we're going back to the nodding routine," said Radcliffe with a hint of a smile.

Stonehouse nodded. Radcliffe continued.

"Now, when we are in court, you're going to hear all manner of vile things being said about you. The prosecutor has a job to do and that is to convict you. The jury will be watching your every move. Keep your facial expressions and body language neutral. No indignation, no emotion, no nothing. *I am your voice*. Period."

Stonehouse nodded again.

"Good. The prosecution will get to present their case first. That will give us the opportunity to add to our defense if necessary, providing there are no additional discovery documents that could delay proceedings. I want to get this case dismissed as soon as possible. So…I will be paying close attention to everything the prosecution says plus *their* expressions and body language."

Radcliffe looked at Stonehouse to ascertain if he was taking everything in.

"I have been in court many times you know…" whined Stonehouse.

Radcliffe ignored him and continued.

"Their key witness is the concierge. He saw you enter the building and you flashed a badge and impersonated a detective. That is not going to put you in a very good light. He saw you leave too. The only other people who entered the building was a gas technician whose identity badge checked out, and detectives Harris and Damote.”

“But it was the gas guy who did it!” declared Stonehouse.

“As you have told me multiple times! Go back to nodding please.” Radcliffe continued.

“We know it had to have been the gas guy, but I have no proof. Yet. All I have to do is create reasonable doubt and they won’t be able to return a guilty verdict. Just let me do my job and you will benefit from the results.”

“When do I get to tell the people that Director Wyatt instructed me to impersonate Detective Damote?”

“You don’t. I do that. When it is the right time. And they’re not people. They are jurors. They are much, much worse than people.”

Radcliffe stood up.

“Now…get some rest. Next week is a big week for you. For both of us. *Do not* talk to anyone here even if they are witness protection officers. Keep your head down and your mouth firmly shut. Got that?”

Stonehouse nodded. Radcliffe stood up, packed his files into his briefcase and left.

Georgina reached up and hugged her father.

“How are you doing kiddo?” he asked her as he took her jacket and closed the front door.

“Okay Dad, all things considered. I think it’s because I am

busy. Work is a good distraction." Georgina replied.

"It always is. I threw myself into my work when your mother passed. Almost worked myself into a stupor. But it helped and here we are…both of us still kicking."

He smiled at Georgina and then asked. "So how is the investigation going?"

"Well, we are making really good progress Dad. The Stonehouse trial starts on Monday. There are going to be quite a few surprises!"

"No doubt," he said. "Especially if you've had anything to do with it!"

Georgina smiled at her father, leaning into him.

"Right kiddo…let's rustle up some food. I'm starving!" he declared.

"Ditto," said Georgina and they headed arm in arm to the kitchen. As they walked, he said.

"Any more evidence you may have brought with you for my freezer or my safe? Any body parts…just wondering you know…"

Georgina laughed. "Nope. They are both bursting to capacity! Can't fit another thing in Dad!"

"Glad to hear it!" He shook his head and chuckled.

Brad ladled the French Onion soup into two bowls for Sophie and himself. She watched him flourish an Italian parsley garnish on top before he handed her a bowl.

"You do realize that the best way to a woman's heart is to take over kitchen duties?" she said smiling at Brad.

"Yep, I know," he replied. "Consider yourself lucky that I enjoy cooking so much."

"Oh, but I do," said Sophie as she leaned across and kissed him. She than dipped her spoon into the soup.

"Hmmm…this is amazing! Thank you, Brad."

He smiled, pleased that she was enjoying it. After a few minutes she said.

"So, are you pretty confident that the dashcam guy and Levenstein are one and the same?"

"Yes, I am. However, only a DNA test will confirm it for sure. Even if we capture him on facial recognition, it is going to be mighty difficult to get a DNA test done. He wouldn't consent to that in a million years, and I doubt too many judges would believe this whole story and issue a warrant for us to action."

"What about Detective Harris's father? He's a judge."

"No that won't work. It would be perceived as nepotism. If he was ever appointed as the judge over any proceedings associated with his daughter, he would have to recuse himself."

"Yes, I get that, but would random facial recognition not constitute an exception?

"No. It would come out sooner or later and then all the evidence will be negated. We can't run that risk. We are literally going to have to wait and see what opportunity presents itself."

Sophie was quiet for a while. And then she said.

"That club…the one that the police commissioner has been monitoring. Is there any chance that Levenstein could possibly be a member? If his face was altered enough through cosmetic surgery, could he not pass as a member unrecognizable as Chad Levenstein?"

Brad thought about it, his brow furrowed.

"Well, one can only be nominated by other members. But it's not entirely impossible. I imagine that there would have only been a handful of people who were in on Levenstein's bogus suicide, so they may well be members themselves. And other members probably wouldn't know Levenstein's voice if they hadn't been associated with him previously. Let me convey your thoughts to the others and see what they think."

Brad remained lost in thought for some time until Sophie waved her hand in front of his eyes.

"What must a girl do to get dessert around here?"

Brad snapped out of his reverie and looking at Sophie shook his head in despair.

"Why do women never get it. They *are* dessert!!"

The electronic clock started to beep and flash for the fourth time. Eventually, after doing his best to ignore it by pulling the pillow over his head, Brad felt around on the nightstand until he found the damn thing and silenced it. He groaned as he peeked out from under the pillow and looked at the time. Monday morning and Stonehouse was due in court in two hours. He propped himself up onto his elbow and looked over his shoulder at Sophie. She was sound asleep. He rolled over and reached for his mobile, running his hand through his hair whilst yawning. He screwed up his eyes as he tried to focus on a text message that had been sent to him just after midnight. He opened it, rubbing his eyes to help him focus. Suddenly he sat up, swinging his feet onto the floor. The message was from one of the facial recognition surveillance rooms.

Levenstein had been spotted!

He jumped out of bed and as he made his way through to the kitchen, he dialed Georgina. This was amazing news! Sophie appeared behind him, her hair all tousled, wearing one of his T-shirts she had slept in.

"What's up Brad?" she asked sleepily. He spun around.

"They've spotted him Sophie!" he said excitedly. "I just can't believe it! They've spotted Levenstein!"

Thirty miles away, there was a flurry of activity in the basement of an apartment building. There were five vehicles in total that would be escorting Stonehouse to the New York Supreme Court. Georgina, Paul, Les, and Jordan were waiting for Stonehouse to be brought down from one of the apartments. There were five other witness protection officers waiting with them. One of the officer's radios crackled and they all heard that Stonehouse was on his way down with the other four officers. The officer turned and signaled to the drivers of the vehicles who then fired up the engines.

At that moment Georgina's mobile rang. She took it out of her pocket, looked down and recognizing Brad's number, pressed answer. She could hear that it was Brad but couldn't make out what he was saying against the sound of all the car engines echoing in the basement. She blocked her one ear and walked away from the noise.

"Hang on Brad...I can't hear you..." said Georgina moving further away. She looked back at Paul who was waiting next to one of the vehicles. She mouthed that it was Brad. Paul shrugged indicating that he didn't understand what she was saying. Georgina turned away and pressed the mobile closer to her ear.

"You'll have to shout Brad!" she yelled into the phone.

"What…? Say that again…"

Finally, she caught Brad's words, her eyes widening, and she spun around gesturing to Paul.

"My God Brad! That is amazing!" she shouted down into her mobile.

Paul looked at her and mouthed *What?* as he started to walk towards her. At that moment Stonehouse emerged from the basement elevator flanked by four officers. They made straight for the nearest vehicle as Les and Jordan opened the doors. Paul glanced over his shoulder, then started walking backwards towards the cars, gesturing to Georgina to join him. As she moved forward, she yelled across to him.

"They've spotted him!"

Suddenly she seemed to lift straight up into the air and was thrown forward. A bloom of red appeared instantly on the front of her white shirt and Paul watched in absolute horror as the mobile flew out of her hand and she sailed through the air in slow motion, her arms flaying as she landed face down on the hard concrete of the garage floor. There was a deafening barrage of gunfire and two of the officers threw themselves on top of Stonehouse. Paul started running towards Georgina as the remaining officers and Les and Jordan opened fire in the direction of the attackers. He dived onto his stomach and crawled the last few feet to Georgina. The bullets whizzed over his head and in his peripheral vision he saw staccato bursts of light emanating from behind the columns in front of them.

It was utter chaos. The gunfire was deafening and then suddenly it was replaced by a faint high-pitched whine in Paul's ears. He was watching a silent scene of mayhem unfold. He glanced over his shoulder and saw two officers dragging Stonehouse into the elevator. As the doors started to close, Paul saw one of the officer's neck explode in a plume of red, his legs buckling under him as he collapsed, and he caught a glimpse of Stonehouse curled into a fetal ball as the doors closed.

Georgina was motionless and Paul dragged himself on top of her to shield her from further fire, his hands covering her head. He glanced sideways and saw boots moving rapidly past him as the other officers advanced on the attackers. He heard the squeal of tyres and a van from fifty feet away screamed towards them and streaked right past them within inches of where they were lying. Paul saw at least five assailants dressed in black emerge from behind the pillars and run for the vehicle, piling in through the open door on the side as it slowed down momentarily. It then accelerated, the engine roaring as they slammed the sliding door shut and Paul saw sparks of gunfire ping off the side of the van as it headed for the exit. And then it was gone, the sound of the screaming engine fading up the ramp out onto the street.

Silence descended on the basement. One officer was lying dead a few feet away from Paul, and Jordan was propped up against one of the vehicles, groaning as he clutched his leg, blood seeping through his hands. Les was kneeling next to him and then he quickly stood up, touched Jordan's shoulder, and ran towards Paul. For the rest of the officers, the bullet proof vests and helmets had protected them. None of the assailants had been killed but there may have been injuries.

Brad stood frozen in horror holding the mobile in his hand staring at Sophie. He had heard the entire attack and was rooted to spot in total shock. He looked down and activated the speaker but there was silence for a good three seconds. Then suddenly there was shouting, and they heard Paul screaming for someone to call an ambulance. Brad was galvanized into action, and he shoved the mobile into Sophie's hands. He ran to his bedroom and as he was pulling on his trousers, he snatched up the receiver of the phone next to his bed and punched in 911, his hands shaking as he yelled the address of where Georgina and Paul were as soon as an operator answered.

"Officers down! Assistance needed urgently!" he shouted into the phone. He hurriedly pulled on a T-shirt, grabbed his jacket and car keys, and ran out of the room.

"Don't answer the door Sophie! Lock yourself in!" he yelled as he pulled open the front door of his apartment. "I'll call you. I love you!"

And with that he slammed the door shut and was gone. Sophie stood there open mouthed in a daze holding the mobile, listening to Paul's voice, calling Georgina's name over and over again.

CHAPTER THIRTY-SEVEN

Police Commissioner Ed Baker was in his office in a meeting with the mayor of New York, when Hillary knocked on the door, apologized and walked behind Baker's desk and whispered in his ear. His eyebrows shot up and he immediately looked at the mayor and said.

"I do apologize but we will have to cut this meeting short Mr. Mayor. There's been an attack on the Stonehouse escort team." He stood up.

"Oh my God!" exclaimed the mayor. "Of course…" he said, immediately standing up too. "Please keep me posted if you can."

"Yes, I shall do that," said Baker as he hurriedly put his jacket on. "Hillary, please ask the driver to meet me at the front."

"Yes sir," she replied running out of the room.

"And I would like Fredman and Stiller to come with me," he shouted after her.

"I'll accompany you down," said the mayor.

Baker nodded and they both headed for the elevators.

Brad Townsend arrived at the White Plains hospital where they had taken Georgina and Jordan. Given Georgina's condition, she needed immediate medical attention, and this hospital was the closest to the safehouse apartment where they had been keeping Stonehouse. As the elevator doors opened, he saw Les and Paul sitting on some chairs at the end of the corridor. They both looked ashen. Somebody had given Paul a surgical gown to wear as his shirt and jacket had been covered in Georgina's blood. They both looked around as Brad got to them.

"Christ almighty!" he said. "What happened?"

They both stood up, their expressions grim.

"How are they?" asked Brad looking from one to the other.

"Jordan is okay…they are removing a bullet from his thigh. No arterial damage. Georgina…" Paul's voice trailed off.

"What?" asked Brad his eyes wide.

Les shrugged. "We simply don't know. They are prepping her for surgery now. She hasn't regained consciousness."

Paul looked away, his eyes brimming. Brad reached out and touched his shoulder.

"I heard it all buddy. I am so sorry…so very sorry," he said looking intently at Paul.

Paul looked back at him and shaking his head said bitterly.

"Looks like I'm bad luck to have as a partner. The bastards…"

Les looked towards the elevator and Brad and Paul

followed his gaze. The police commissioner with two accompanying officers emerged and walked briskly towards them. They all stood to attention.

"As you were please," said Baker when he got to them. He indicated for them to go into one of the grieving rooms where they could talk privately. They all filed in.

"What is the status of detectives Harris and Brown?" he asked, his face grave.

"Detective Brown will recover sir. It's a manageable leg wound." said Les. "But we are not sure about Detective Harris. It's too early to tell. She suffered a major bullet wound from close range. Two other officers were killed in the attack."

Baker looked down, his brow furrowed, his jaw working.

"Any idea who did this?" he asked looking again.

"Not yet sir," said Les. "However, we suspect that it must have been someone from witness protection. Someone from the inside who had the location information. These guys were pro sir."

"Yes, so it would appear," said Baker as he rocked back and forth on his heels. They were all silent for a while and he scanned their shocked faces and noted how pale they all looked, particularly Paul.

"C'mon. You all need something in your stomachs. You've gone through a shocking ordeal. We're going to the cafeteria," said Baker.

"I can't say that I have any kind of an appetite sir," said Paul.

Baker looked at him and said kindly.

"Let's go Detective Damote. You are going to have a coffee at least."

Paul nodded and they all followed the commissioner to the elevator. As they walked Baker introduced them to his accompanying officers. They all shook hands and then took the elevator down to cafeteria.

When they returned, Georgina's father had arrived, and he was standing staring out of one of the windows. Baker indicated to the others that he needed to speak alone with Judge Harris. They all nodded and moved away down the corridor and sat down. Ed Baker approached Georgina's father.

"Judge Harris?" said Baker quietly.

Georgina's father looked around, his expression dazed.

"Commissioner…" he extended his hand, and they shook hands.

There was an awkward silence between them. Eventually Georgina's father shrugged and said.

"I suppose no news is good news."

Baker nodded. He paused and then said.

"I am truly sorry Judge Harris…this has been a most shocking event. We will catch the perpetrators in time but all that matters now is your daughter's recovery. This is a good hospital. She's in good hands."

Georgina's father glanced past Baker towards the door that led to the operating theatres and then looked at back at Baker, his gaze unwavering. Eventually he said.

"Commissioner, I have to ask you…" he paused.

Baker waited, saying nothing.

"Did you put my daughter's life in danger today?"

Baker was taken aback by the question, but he concealed his surprise. He looked down and gave it due consideration. Finally, he looked up at him and said.

"Yes sir…I did." He held Georgina's father's gaze and then continued. "I put the lives of each and every officer who serves under me in danger every day. Every single one of them."

Georgina's father nodded slowly, his expression unfathomable. Then he turned away and looked out of the window again. Baker stepped forward and the two of them stood there, shoulder to shoulder, watching the world outside continue, oblivious to the pain in Georgina's father's heart and the anger in Baker's. Two good men, powerful in their own rights, standing side by side, praying silently for Georgina's life.

CHAPTER THIRTY-EIGHT

"You had just one job to do! One job…and you fucked it up!" Wyatt yelled at the three men standing in front of him. "Have you seen the news? It's one big shit show!" He stabbed his finger in the direction of TV in his home office and their eyes swiveled to the news anchor, her face a picture of drama as the news unfolded on the attempt on Agent Stonehouse's life.

"Two dead officers, two injured, one critically! Not to mention that the goddamned target is still alive! He's probably in a safe house on Mars now!" bellowed Wyatt. "There's no chance we will get anywhere near him now. Do you have any idea what is going to happen now? The police commissioner will not rest until he finds out who did this. He is not a man you want to mess with. And yet, here we are right in the boxing ring with him. Mark my words, he will find you."

They all exchanged looks of alarm, unsure of what to say or do. Wyatt glared at them. He continued.

"You had better all get down on your knees and pray that what I am about to do will save your skins. If it doesn't work, you are all toast!"

He was breathing heavily, his hands on his hips.

"Now get out!" he shouted.

They all scuttled out, relieved to be able to escape. They knew he was right. They had messed up. But they also knew that Wyatt would hand them on a platter to the commissioner in an instant if he could be absolutely sure that it wouldn't lead back to him.

However, it was Mullens that Wyatt was going to throw under the bus. The time had come to be the hero again. All other plans had failed, and this was going to be the only way now to make sure that Stonehouse's trial would not take place. Stonehouse knew about Levenstein. This simply could never come out. Once Wyatt made an announcement that Mullens had killed Dr. Chevalier, then Stonehouse's case would hopefully be struck off the roll. Then once Stonehouse was released, he would no longer have protection and that would make him a sitting duck. Wyatt would waste no time in eliminating him. He would do it himself if necessary.

Wyatt shook his head. It used to be so easy to eliminate witnesses and to manipulate trials. Gone were the days when the director of the FBI could wield unquestionable power. Now he had to contend with all these damn do-gooder cops who took their oaths seriously. That's not how the world works. When would they get it into their thick skulls that they were there serve the elite. Not the godamned American people who were mostly halfwits and useless eaters. He walked over to the drinks tray and poured himself a double. On top of all of this, he had to contend with being made a fool of by his own wife and her limp-wristed tennis coach, doing nothing to conceal their indiscreet affair. He threw back the scotch and poured another double. The world be damned!

Through the glass window of the door leading from the operating theatres, the surgeon momentarily observed the group standing in the corridor waiting for news on Detective Harris. He recognized the police commissioner and presumed that the other older man was her father. The rest certainly all looked like law enforcement. Seven men in total, all deeply concerned for her well-being. He pushed the door open and walked towards them. All conversation ceased as they turned towards him, their expressions a mix of hope, expectation, and dread.

"Good day gentlemen. I am Dr. Bruce Barrett, head of the surgical unit." He paused and took a deep breath. "I think it's safe to say that Detective Harris probably has as much tenacity in how she lives her life, as in how she fights for it. She is still with us and believe me… it is a miracle."

He continued. "She's in critical condition, but I am hopeful. She survived five hours of surgery and for the moment she appears stable."

Everyone exchanged looks, daring to smile. There was hope and that was something to be grateful for. The surgeon went on.

"Detective Harris suffered a myocardial rupture and damage to the interventricular septum from a bullet which entered through her back and exited through her chest. We think the fact that the bullet exited her as opposed to circulating within the chest cavity is why she has survived this injury thus far. The surgery was successful, but our overriding concern now is minimizing infection and internal bleeding."

The surgeon then looked at Georgina's father.

"I assume you are Detective Harris's father?" the surgeon asked.

Judge Harris nodded. "Yes doctor, I am."

"May I have a word with you please?" he said, moving away.

"Of course," replied Georgina's father as he followed the surgeon.

All the other men turned to each other and started discussing the news about Georgina, hopeful that she now had a chance of survival.

"Well, he certainly summed up Detective Harris, sir," said Les to the police commissioner.

"I would agree with that. It's only about year ago I pinned a medal for bravery to her chest," replied Baker.

He noticed Paul looking away from the group and he knew that he was thinking about the partner he had lost not so long ago. Baker reached out and squeezed his shoulder and nodded. That was all he had to do. Paul understood that the police commissioner knew exactly what he was feeling, and he was offering him comfort discreetly.

"Sir…," said Brad. "May I have a word please?"

He didn't want to say anything in front of the other two officers from Baker's office.

"Yes of course," said Baker and they walked away from the group.

"I was talking to Detective Harris on the phone when the attack happened sir," said Brad when they were out of earshot.

"Go on…," said Baker.

"I was in the process of telling her sir, that one of the facial recognition surveillance rooms has picked up Levenstein." Baker looked surprised. "Wow! That is amazing news. Where?"

"Well firstly sir, Sophie de la Motte who did the forensic work on the syringe cap suggested to me that it was possible that Levenstein may be a member of the club in the Wagstaff building. He would be unrecognizable as Levenstein if he had had cosmetic surgery."

"Yes…go on?" said Baker frowning.

"Well, the facial recognition occurred one block from the Wagstaff building sir," said Brad.

"Well, that is very interesting Agent Townsend. I don't believe in co-incidences, do you?" said Baker.

"No sir, I don't. I think Miss de la Motte may be right." Baker nodded, deep in thought.

"If she is right, then I need to get the image of Levenstein from the dashcam to my undercover agent in the club. She will be able to confirm very quickly if Levenstein has been there at any time in the last six months since she has been working undercover."

"Just what I was thinking sir," said Brad.

"Okay, I will get onto it immediately and will let you all know," said Baker.

"Thank you, sir. One more thing…do you have any theories on who the perpetrators were who attacked the escort this morning?" asked Brad.

"I have my suspicions, Agent Townsend. I think the whole house of cards is going to come tumbling down very soon," said Baker cryptically. "But first, I need to get in touch with my operative. Please call me later and update me on Detective Harris. And please tell Judge Harris that I will be in touch in the next couple of days."

"Yes sir, will do," said Brad and he stood to attention.

The police commissioner indicated to his two officers that he was leaving, and the rest of the group stood to attention. Baker nodded, thanked everyone, and headed for the elevator with his two officers in tow. A few minutes later Georgina's father returned, and Brad conveyed the commissioner's message. Georgina's father then told the group that the surgeon had taken him to see her.

"They are keeping her in an induced coma as it is important that she remains motionless and exhibits no stress from the memory of the attack. If they can prevent an infection from occurring, then he feels that she will pull through and will make a full recovery without any long-term issues. However, she is not out of the woods yet. She is still in critical condition and there is still a chance of internal bleeding. We just have to hope and pray for her."

He looked at Paul, Les and Brad and continued.

"Thank you to all of you for your support and caring."

They all nodded solemnly. Then Paul said.

"I'll stay here with you Judge Harris."

"Thank you," he replied.

"I'm going to pop in and see Jordan," said Les. "He's

anxious to know about Georgina. Then I'll go back to the precinct. The forensics team are going to need information to piece together the attack. I will be back first thing in the morning."

Brad wanted to tell Paul about the facial recognition but obviously he couldn't say anything in front of Judge Harris. But Paul knew anyhow. He had heard what Georgina had shouted moments before she was shot.

"Please tell Jordan I'll visit him shortly," said Paul.

"Will do. I'll call you later," replied Les and Paul nodded. Les and Brad said goodbye to Judge Harris and as they walked to the elevators, Brad used the opportunity to tell Les about Levenstein. Paul watched them go and saw Les high five Brad and knew exactly what Brad had told him. He then turned to Georgina's father.

"Judge Harris…may I get you something from the cafeteria? A coffee perhaps?

"Let's go there together Paul. And as I said before, please call me William."

Paul smiled. "Thank you, William."

An hour later, Stiller, one of Baker's officers returned with a package for Paul.

"From the commissioner," he said as he handed it to Paul. Paul opened it and inside was a fresh change of clothes.

"Ah great! Please can you thank the commissioner for me. That was very kind and thoughtful of him," said Paul smiling. "I was starting to feel like a cross dresser in this gown!" He looked down and laughed.

"I'll do that detective," said Stiller.

He then looked at Judge Harris, nodded his head courteously and left.

"Police Commissioner! What a surprise!" purred Lela Hinton. "We are only accustomed to seeing you on Friday evenings."

"Well…as the police commissioner I shouldn't be that predictable now, should I?" Baker said smiling.

He saw Tanya pass behind Lela so at least he knew she was on duty. During work hours they had no way of communicating because the *Nymphs* were banned from having their mobiles anywhere near the premises for obvious reasons and during their shifts their clothes and bags were locked away and only Lela had the key. Lela caught a glimpse of Tanya in the corner of her eye.

"Tanya…please come here," said Lela. She turned back to Baker and asked.

"What can we get you Commissioner?"

"My usual please," said Baker.

"Right away," she said and nodded at Tanya

"Thank you Lela," said Baker inclining his head.

And with that she glided away to the other members. Baker looked around and wondered if Levenstein was here right now. Nobody would know it was him unless they had been part of the whole plan.

Five minutes later, Tanya placed the commissioner's scotch on the coaster in front of him. She said nothing. The *Nymphs* were not allowed to converse other than asking a member what he wanted or replying to a question. Baker leant forward, picked up the scotch and discreetly moved the coaster to one side. Underneath was a close up of the dashcam photo of Levenstein as he looked now. He asked her very quietly but with urgency in his voice.

"Have you seen this person here at any time?"

Tanya pretended to be arranging the coaster and looked at it closely. She then straightened up, aware than Lela was watching her from across the room.

"Yes of course Commissioner," she said sweetly, then she turned and left the room.

When Baker had finished his scotch, he got up to leave.

"Going so soon?" asked Lela silkily.

"Duty calls I'm afraid. Not what I planned, but I must leave. Thank you, Lela," he said and turned to go.

"Commissioner…," said Lela.

He turned back to her and waited for her to continue.

"I may be letting Tanya go. Would that be an issue for you?" she asked tilting her head.

Baker frowned and then said.

"No, not at all. Why should it? *Nymphs* come and go," he said spreading his hands. He smiled at Lela and then headed for the elevator.

Lela watched him go, her eyes narrowed. Something was not quite right with his relationship with Tanya. Then she laughed inwardly. Of course, it wasn't right! He was a married man. But there was something else worrying her, but she couldn't quite put her finger on it. Tanya was a great asset but not indispensable. She would let her go once she had a replacement.

CHAPTER THIRTY-NINE

Wyatt loved press briefings. He enjoyed the rush of having everyone hang on his every word. He walked to the lectern, confident and in control. He scanned his eyes over the press and was pleased to see that the usual sycophants were there to do his bidding. He cleared his throat.

Ladies and gentlemen of the press...I have a somewhat surprising announcement to make. We, the FBI have been working around the clock, not only to do our very best to protect Special Agent Stonehouse...and to that end, we have been successful given that no attempts on his life have succeeded, but also to re-examine our original conviction that he was the killer of Dr. Simon Chevalier. After hundreds and hundreds of man hours...
And he paused for a few moments for dramatic effect...
...we are indeed humbled to say that we were wrong.

There was an immediate swell of chatter in the room as the reporters looked at one another, taken aback by this revelation. Wyatt raised his hand and the chatter died down and everyone refocused their attention on Wyatt. Once he had their full attention, he continued.

At the same time…we are indeed proud to announce that we have identified the true killer. His name, ladies and gentlemen of the press, is Ryder Mullens.

 With that he turned and pointed to the screen behind him, and an image of Ryder Mullens appeared. The room erupted and cameras flashed as the reporters captured the image on the screen.

*Director Wyatt…*said one of the journalists raising his hand. Wyatt looked back.

*Yes Gregory…*he said pleasantly. The press loved it when you knew their names. It made them feel on top of the pile.

At your last press briefing, you used the words…beyond reasonable doubt. Will you be using those same words again?

Wyatt bristled but did not show it. Stupid prick he thought. He made a note to himself to call Gregory's editor and arrange to have him reprimanded. Or fired, even better. Wyatt continued smoothly.

You have a point, Gregory, although at the time, there was overwhelming evidence that supported it. However, we now have damning evidence against Ryder Mullens, but we will wait for the appropriate time to present it.

Gregory pushed on.

 Has Ryder Mullens been arrested yet? And could Agent Stonehouse and Mullens have been working together?

Wyatt was getting annoyed. This reporter was asking way too many questions. Idiot. His job was to listen. However, he maintained his composure.

Not as yet. However, with his identity now being made public, it will only be a matter of time before he is detained. Regarding them working together? I very much doubt it. It appears that Ryder Mullens had a vendetta against Dr. Chevalier and Agent Stonehouse relating to a previous conviction. This was purely a revenge crime, and the new evidence indicates that he planned it so that it would look like Agent Stonehouse was the perpetrator.

Wyatt was starting to feel the heat. He was having to lie on the trot, and he never liked doing that. That was how one got caught out. But the last thing he needed was for Stonehouse's case to go ahead. Another reporter put up her hand.

Director…does this mean that Agent Stonehouse's case will be struck off the roll and he will be released?

Wyatt paused for a few moments. This was tricky. The truth was that the only evidence he had on Mullens was that Mullens was acting on his orders, the revelation of which would translate to both of them going to jail for a very long time. He had to create a distraction and ensure that Mullens was eliminated within hours of being detained. Neither did he have the power to alter the present status of Stonehouse's charges. His biggest worry was that Stonehouse would blab to the whole world about the original cause of this whole sorry mess which was the DNA match to the most notorious sex offender who was supposed to be dead, buried and forgotten. He needed Stonehouse's swift release so that he could finally eliminate him. He would have done it already if he knew where the godamned idiot was being kept. But for the moment, he had to be careful not to look like he was speaking for the courts. Wyatt was the master of innuendos. He continued.

That is not for me to say although I expect that will ultimately be the case. We shall have to wait and see what the courts decide. Thank you, ladies, and gentlemen.

There was a flurry of questions, but Wyatt ignored them as he left the podium and exited the briefing room as fast as he could, without it being obvious that he wanted to get the hell out of dodge.

"Is there anything else I can get for you Mr. Brooks?" asked the hostess in the first-class lounge of the Atlanta Airport.

Ryder Mullens looked up, smiled, and shook his head as she placed the Martini in front of him, accompanied by a small platter of salmon blinis topped with caviar.

"Thank you," he said, and he turned back to the TV screen. It had been highly entertaining watching Wyatt pontificate and posture in front of the press, and he had chuckled out loud when he had seen his own face for the whole world to see. On reflection, he did look a bit dodgy with his beard and longer hair. To be honest he preferred his present look, which was clean shaven with a buzz cut, complemented by his crisp white shirt, casual blazer, and chinos. Of course, the tortoiseshell glasses added the finishing touch. He looked at his watch and noted the time. No rush. His flight to Milan was not leaving for another two hours. Plenty of time to enjoy the luxuries of first-class travel.

Paul shook his head after watching Wyatt's briefing. What an absolute jerk he thought to himself. He was none the less very curious as to why Wyatt had chosen to expose Mullens now, especially because he was certain that Wyatt had no knowledge of the camera footage of Mullens actually committing the crime. Could he have found out about it or was he merely creating a diversion? And how would he secure a conviction? His thoughts immediately turned to Murphey. Then he rejected the idea. They had all been vigilant with the evidence which was safely secreted away in Judge Harris's safe. Besides, Murphey was keeping a low profile after the showdown at the precinct a few weeks before. Since it was now obvious that Wyatt was behind Simon's murder, why would he risk exposing Mullens who he himself engaged? Did he have unequivocal proof or was he running scared? Especially given the failed attempts on Stonehouse's life. With those thoughts circling in his mind, Paul walked back to the private ward where Georgina was lying, still in an induced coma. He handed a bottle of soda to her father.

"Thank you, Paul," said Judge Harris.

"Jordan sends his best to you. He is doing well and should be discharged in the next couple of days," said Paul.

"I am glad to hear it," said Judge Harris.

They both looked at Georgina, her chest rising and falling with the respirator. No change. Her complexion was deathly pale, and her eyes were bruised a deep purple colour and swollen closed from the fall. She had a cut across her cheek and a fractured shoulder. But the worst of the injuries were the invisible ones. The surgeon had done what he could and now it was a matter of her internal tissues healing. Paul could feel the life force within her. She was going to make it; he was sure of it. No ways was he going to lose another partner.

Mullens thanked the hostess and left the lounge for his departure gate carrying a briefcase in his left hand and a package in his right. He approached the UPS box and cast his eye over the pre-paid package addressed to Detective P. Damote of the Midtown North Precinct of the NYPD. He tipped it through the flap and heard the thump as it landed. By the time it reached Detective Damote's desk, he would be long gone, beyond the reach of any of them. Always the elusive ghost. Smiling to himself, Mr. Stanley Brooks walked away with a new name and a new life.

Two days later, Paul was at his desk when someone from the front counter brought through a package that had just arrived for him.

"Another package!" he exclaimed. "This is like Christmas." he said chuckling as he glanced across at Les who was temporarily using Georgina's desk.

He turned it over, looked at the sender and frowned. Sitting back in his chair, he whistled, shaking his head.

"What is it?" asked Les, now curious.

"It's from Ryder Mullens," replied Paul looking up at Les, his eyes wide. They were both silent for a few seconds.

"Don't open it here," warned Les looking around.

"Of course. I'll call Brad. Let him process it all very carefully, perhaps with Sophie's help. But I'll let the commissioner know in the interim. I have a pretty good feeling there's going to be a lot of damning evidence in this package," Paul said tapping it with his finger.

Les nodded in agreement.

"Let's get to Brad asap," he said. They both stood up and as they headed to the elevators, Paul was already dialing Brad's number.

It turned out to be the proverbial Pandora's box. Mullens had recorded every conversation that had taken place with Len Wyatt. There were both audio and video recordings, recorded with secret microphones and cameras. There was even video footage of Wyatt watching child pornography. A bigger surprise was the recording from the cabin when Brad and Simon had met in the Catskill mountains. That had solved a lot of unanswered questions as to how Wyatt had known so much. As they all listened to the cabin recording, it was bittersweet moment to hear Simon's voice and the laugh that they all knew and loved so much.

In his covering letter, Mullens never admitted to actually killing Simon. Nobody would be that stupid. But it was a moot point anyhow since they had the video evidence. Clearly Mullens was now long gone. They had no idea where he had gone to, but they were pretty sure that it was very far away. They would focus on finding him at a later point in time. But for now, they had other big fish to fry.

Paul, Les, and Brad headed for the NYPD headquarters, calling ahead to give the commissioner the head's up that they had some new and critical evidence.

Commissioner Ed Baker was delighted. Coupled with the video footage of Wyatt's pedophile goings on in the club, and the audio and video footage from Mullens's package, Wyatt would be going away for life, along with the rest of his perverted buddies. And they were closing in on Levenstein and the proof of his fake suicide would rock the world, never mind just America. By the end of the entire operation, Baker estimated that at least thirty or more very high-profile people from government, big tech, and top corporations, would be serving lengthy sentences. It would be a clean-up operation never witnessed before in the history of America. Only Watergate would be comparable. Other scandals like Enron, the Lewinsky affair and many more, would look like dolls' tea parties by comparison. And then there were all the global arrests to look forward to. Interpol had their work cut out for the next two to three years. The international courts would be bursting at the proverbial seams. However, the most important result would be the massive exposé on child trafficking. It would shine a light on the most heinous of crimes and hopefully it would break the back of the pedophile ring that went all the way to the top of American politics and industry. With the key players incarcerated, child trafficking would be substantially reduced. Unfortunately, there would be some invisible members of the elite who would escape the noose but as they say…*never say never*. Perhaps their day would come too.

Georgina's father opened the safe in his apartment and lifted out the box with Georgina's papers. He placed it on his desk deliberating whether he should open it or not. It was a conundrum. He was a judge, and the evidence was confidential. However, Georgina had said that if anything happened to her, what she had secreted in his home would lead the way. He opened the box and within a minute he had found the printout report of Chad Levenstein's DNA. He sat back stunned and shocked, battling to process the information that clearly indicated that Levenstein was still alive. How was it possible? He then found another report and a small memory card in an envelope marked Dr. Chevalier's murder. He opened the folded sheet of paper and read the report on the chemicals that had been injected into Simon. He felt his heart squeeze. He had been involved in a case many years ago where a Russian spy had used the exact same chemicals. He knew that they were fatal. He took the memory card and slotted it into his laptop, pressing play. Nothing could have prepared him for what it contained. The footage of Simon's murder was utterly brutal and the fact that the killer tried to make it look like a suicide took on an evilness that was indescribable. Watching his own daughter being witness to such violence caused a rage to well up inside of him, as intense as he had felt when the reckless driver who had killed his wife had been let off with a simple warning. And now his daughter was lying in a hospital bed, holding onto life by a thread…yet another victim to people whose viciousness knew no bounds. He carefully replaced everything back into the box and locked it in his safe. He then headed to the kitchen. Opening the freezer, he slowly pulled open the bottom draw and examined the contents. Through the plastic he could make out a Starbucks coffee cup and in another plastic bag was what looked like a syringe cap. He stared at them both and then carefully replaced them. He went back to his study and called the police commissioner.

CHAPTER FORTY

In front of each person gathered around the police commissioner's boardroom table, was a copy of a dossier named Operation Pincer. The plan was simple. Once the last piece of the puzzle was slotted into place, simultaneous arrests and indictments would be initiated. Judge Harris had met with Judge Wilcock who had agreed to sign off on all the warrants of arrest. Even with his daughter out of the picture temporarily, Judge Harris was not going to risk being the judge signing off on the warrants and thus possibly inviting in an opportunity for the defendants to claim a conflict of interests. The public outrage in response to the revelations that would take place would be so enormous that he doubted anyone would be focusing on semantics, but none the less, he was doing everything by the book. No chinks in the armor. So, he had recommended Judge Wilcock to the commissioner and had facilitated the introduction.

The last piece of the puzzle was Levenstein's DNA. The police commissioners undercover operative Officer Tanya Davidson would attempt to obtain evidence of his DNA as soon as he appeared at the club again. If she was successful and once it was processed and hopefully confirmed to match the DNA from the original Starbucks evidence, Operation Pincer would receive the green light from Police Commissioner Ed Baker. Multiple teams would close in from different directions so swiftly and efficiently, that the offenders would have no time whatsoever to warn each other. Everything hinged on the DNA match.

"Firstly, welcome back Detective Brown," said Baker, taking his seat at the head of the boardroom table.

"Thank you, sir," replied Jordan smiling.

"How long do you expect to be on crutches?" asked Baker.

"No more than two weeks, I think. I'm making good progress sir," replied Jordan.

"Glad to hear it," said Baker nodding. He indicated for everyone to sit down. He looked around at the team and then opened the file in front of him.

"Okay, so here is the list of the people who will initially be arrested," he said. "Chad Levenstein, Len Wyatt, Alan Turner, Roy Sedgefield, Lela Hinton, and Ryder Mullens, if we can find him. Whilst all the arrests are in progress, a team will be raiding the Ohio storage unit and will confiscate all the original historical evidence on Chad Levenstein and the DNA evidence he had on all his pedophile mates. We have no idea how many people are going to be revealed at this point in time. Suffice to say that we are prepared none the less. Once all that information has been processed and analyzed, that is when the second wave of arrests will take place. And there will be many, not only here but all over the world. Interpol is standing by. There will be nowhere these criminals will be able to run to." Baker looked up and observed his team. "Any questions?"

They were all silent. It had finally dawned on them that they were part of what in years to come, would be one of the most significant take downs in America's history. The enormity of it was suddenly quite sobering. Baker continued.

"We have no idea how high up the food chain in government and industry the DNA evidence that Chad Levenstein collected will lead to. Be as it may, no matter what position any individual holds, they will not be protected from prosecution. And that includes the President of the United States. I do hope it does not come to that."

Baker looked around the conference table and noted how tense the atmosphere was.

"Right team, now we wait for the last piece to fall in place. Take a few days off while you can. Once this breaks, it will be all hands-on deck and we'll be working 24/7."

He smiled and then stood up. They all immediately stood to attention. Before walking out the door, Baker turned and looked at all of them again.

"I don't think I have ever worked with such an exceptional group of people before now." He nodded, turned, and went back to his office.

They all looked at each other, surprised and moved by the words of the commissioner. All that was missing was Detective Georgina Harris. They missed her. She was such a vital part of the team and they truly looked forward to the day when they would welcome her back into the fold.

Two hundred miles away, there were raised voices in the Wyatt household. Len Wyatt had been nominated as one of the finalists for the coveted Distinguished Honour Award and Helen was clearly not interested in attending the event with him.

"You enjoy all the trappings that I provide!" yelled Wyatt. "You had better make sure your pretty little ass is at that function or else!"

"Or else what?" fumed Helen, her eyes glittering. "You think you can threaten me? Why not take one of your many lovers or even better, perhaps one of your little underage playthings…"

Wyatt's face turned as white as a sheet. He slowly walked towards her.

"What did you say…?" his voice quiet and threatening.

Helen backed away but kept her indignation on the boil.

"You think I don't know what you are Len? Hmmm? You think I don't know about your perverted little websites and your secret little clubs? What do you think your own daughter would think if she knew her Daddy likes to fuck girls her age and younger!"

Wyatt grabbed her and slapped her hard across the face and she fell back onto the bed. He lunged forward and grabbed her, jerking her up onto her feet and slapped her again with even greater force. She cried out and struggled to free herself from his grip. He held her inches away from his face.

"You mention one word of what you have just said, and you will *never* see the outside of a mental asylum in your pathetic little Gucci filled life! Do you understand?" Wyatt tightened his grip and shook her.

"You're hurting me!" she cried.

"You have no idea what real pain is. Don't push me Helen or I'll show you."

For the first time in their marriage, Helen was truly frightened. Her husband was a monster, that she knew. But only to others, never to her. He finally released his grip and pushed her back onto the bed.

"And one more thing…" he said pointing at her. "That pathetic little excuse of a man who thinks batting about a tennis ball is rocket science, if I see him or even hear that he has been near you, I will fuck you up so hard that no man will ever find you attractive again. Ever!"

He walked out the room slamming the door and Helen began to sob. Loud uncontrollable sobs. All the pain of her marriage came to the fore, and she realized that she was utterly trapped. No one could help her. Not now, not ever. She turned, curling up into a ball, feeling utterly helpless and frightened as the horrible realization dawned on her. She was outsmarted, outpowered and out of options.

Tanya discreetly watched the man from the dashcam photo who now went by the name of Ashley Wakefield. He was sitting in the club lounge enjoying a drink and conversing with two other members who she knew to be Roy Sedgefield and Alan Turner, the most high-profile men in social media and Silicon Valley respectively. Her stomach turned. As she quietly observed them, she did a comparison in terms of Levenstein's facial features now and what he had looked like previously. Clearly, the surgeon had done a good job. It was hard to associate the two except for perhaps those predatory close-set eyes and his build. He was an arrogant and dismissive man and her skin crawled anytime she was near him. She kept a close watch on his drink. It was critical that there be no mix up between Levenstein's glass and the others. Lela glided over to the group to engage in the usual inane conversation. These men were bad enough but in Tanya's mind, Lela Hinton was a whole lot worse. What kind of woman would be part of trafficking young girls who in fact were still children, to be sexually abused by these monsters. She hoped that there would be a special place in hell for a woman like Lela Hinton, alongside Levenstein's partner who clearly was no longer enjoying a life of luxury. Her reverie was interrupted as she realized that Lela was summonsing her, and she walked over to the group adopting her usual graceful catwalk.

"Tanya, get these gentlemen fresh drinks," said Lela in her usual nauseating, sugary voice.

Tanya smiled sweetly and bending down, she gathered the glasses and put them onto the tray, discreetly separating Levenstein's glass from the others. She could feel Levenstein's eyes burn into her, and it took all her resolve not to reach out and slap the supercilious smile off his face and to blurt out to everyone that she knew exactly who he really was. He reached out and ran his hand up the inside of her thigh and brushed his fingers between her legs. Turning away, she felt the bile rise in her throat. Sedgefield and Turner stared wide-eyed at Levenstein. He was violating the club's rule, and it was not a good idea for him to attract any attention to himself. Tanya was private property; they all knew that. But Levenstein couldn't care less. He may look different now but the arrogance he had been well known for, was fully evident.

It was almost midnight when she was dressed and ready to leave for home. After looking around, she carefully took an evidence bag out of her pocket, reached into one of the vases in the passage and deposited Levenstein's glass into the bag, carefully sealing it. She then placed it gently in a small box in her shoulder bag, careful that nothing could damage Levenstein's DNA on the glass. Lela was in the kitchen discussing the menu with the chef for the following day so she would not have seen Tanya's actions on any of the cameras. If she reviewed any recordings, then perhaps in time she would see what Tanya had done. But for now, she was safe.

As she headed for the elevators, she heard Lela call out her name. Tanya froze. Turning slowly, she looked directly at Lela standing a few feet away from her and said sweetly.

"Yes Miss Hinton?"

"Come to my office Tanya…now," commanded Lela, her expression hostile.

Tanya dutifully followed, her heart thumping in her chest. Had Lela seen what she had done? Lela sat down in her chair but did not offer Tanya to sit. She looked at Tanya, her expression hard.

"I have been observing you for some time now Tanya and I am not comfortable with your relationship with the police commissioner."

Tanya said nothing. Lela went on.

"I am letting you go. Discretion in this club is key and I feel that you may have crossed that line."

Still Tanya said nothing. This unnerved Lela slightly. Usually, the *Nymphs* would plead to retain their very lucrative jobs, but Tanya was saying nothing, her expression unfathomable. Eventually Tanya spoke.

"As you wish Miss Hinton," she said evenly, holding Lela's gaze.

Lela opened her draw and removed an envelope.

"Here is your paycheck. I am sure you understand the consequences if you are to ever reveal anything about this club to anyone at any time…" Lela let the threat hang in the air. Tanya said nothing so Lela decided that a bit of emphasis would not go amiss.

"Only one *Nymph* ever made the mistake of opening her mouth. Let's say that she is now so disfigured, no one would want to even look at her let alone listen to anything she may have to say."

Tanya's lack of response was bordering on insolence Lela thought to herself. It was unnerving and annoying. She added.

"Do you understand Tanya?" and Lela held out the envelope, her red talons reminding Tanya of the bloodied sheets of the child virgins whose innocence had been ripped from their lives here within the walls of this obscene club.

"Perfectly," said Tanya her expression totally neutral.

She took the envelope from Lela and without a backward glance, she left the room and the club as a *Nymph* forever.

CHAPTER FORTY-ONE

"We're on the home run," said Paul to Georgina. He was sitting next to her hospital bed watching her steady breathing. The hiss of the respirator was almost deafening in the silence. She looked somewhat serene today and he wondered if she perhaps could hear him. Not likely but then again, it was not that important. In the not-too-distant future, they would bring her out of the coma, and she would wake up to a world that would be changed forever. And many of those changes would be attributed to her.

The surgeon walked into the room and smiled at Paul.

"It's only a day or two now and we will slowly bring her back to us. It appears that she has healed well, her vitals are good and for all intense and purposes, once she has regained consciousness, she will probably be well enough to go home in about two weeks."

"That's wonderful to hear doctor. She will certainly have a lot of people waiting to welcome her home."

"Ah that she will," replied the doctor smiling as he examined her chart and checked her pulse. He looked up at Paul.

"She's quite the fighter," he said.

"Don't I know doc! I work with her!" said Paul and they both laughed. "In fact, the silence has been a welcome change," he said jokingly. Then he hastily added. "I'm only kidding."

"I know you are," said the surgeon gently. "She is indeed fortunate to have such caring colleagues."

He glanced back at Georgina, nodded to Paul, and left the room. A few minutes later, a nurse came in, acknowledged Paul, and adjusted Georgina's drip. She then gently rolled Georgina to the left and then to the right, repeating the sequence a few times, before settling her on her back. After straightening the sheets, she smiled at Paul, and left to attend to her other patients. After a few minutes, he squeezed Georgina's hand and stood up to leave for the police commissioner's office. He bent down and whispered to Georgina.

"This is it partner. The make or break. This is for you and Simon."

He squeezed her hand again and headed for the elevator. As the doors opened, Georgina's father stepped out. They chatted for a few minutes and then Paul took his leave. As the elevator descended, he became aware that he had the proverbial butterflies doing laps in his stomach, his anxiety levels rising with the knowledge that everything hinged on the DNA that Sophie would be processing.

Across town in Queens, Sophie waited until everyone from the lab had gone home for the night. Carefully she extracted the glass from the evidence bag that Office Tanya Davidson had delivered to her that morning. The analysis would take less time than usual since she had the comparative DNA from the original Starbucks cup, so it wouldn't be a matter of trawling through a massive data base looking for a match. But none the less, it would require the same exacting applications and concentration.

This is it, she said to herself. *The last piece of the puzzle.* And then she laughed. No pressure! She looked at the time. Six o' clock exactly.

Wyatt straightened his bow tie and looked at his reflection in the mirror. Not bad he thought to himself. His perfectly trimmed greying hair gave him a distinguished air whilst his steely blue eyes spoke of ruthlessness and sexual prowess. At sixty-two he was still a good-looking man, made all the more attractive to women by the power he wielded. His focus shifted to Helen who was zipping up her red sequined dress, her expression distant and neutral. They had hardly spoken a word since their last altercation. No matter he thought to himself. She was behaving herself and that was all he cared about. As they walked towards the elevators, Helen called the babysitter in Washington to check on the kids. Technically the kids no longer required a babysitter, but Helen felt more comfortable knowing that there was someone there keeping an eye on them. They were both silent as the chauffeur drove them to the Rockefeller Plaza. Helen looked out the window at the ordinary people on the New York streets, wondering what their lives were like, contemplating her own gilded cage. She thought about the years ahead with this monster sitting next to her and she just couldn't imagine that she would ever know happiness again.

"You had better start smiling," said Wyatt to Helen as they arrived at the Rockefeller Plaza. "You chose this life, so deal with it."

Helen chose to ignore her husband's comment and looked away steeling herself for the cameras. The limousine glided to a halt and two gloved attendants moved forward and opened the car doors. Wyatt and Helen got out and they paused at the end of the red carpet, hand in hand, both smiling for the press and spectators. The picture-perfect success couple. A news reporter was talking to camera about Len Wyatt, the esteemed director of the FBI and his beautiful wife Helen, speculating as to who of the four finalists would win the coveted award tonight. After half an hour of palm pressing and endless smiling, they finally took their seats in the sumptuous Rainbow Room. Wyatt looked around and saw Roy Sedgefield at a nearby table. Alan Turner was also there, and they both gave Wyatt the thumbs up, rooting for him to win. Helen glanced around and for the first time, she detested all the glitz and glamour. Previously she had thrived on it. Now she felt trapped, imprisoned and she prayed that the evening would pass quickly. She looked over at her husband and realized that she truly hated him. She realised that only once she could feel indifference towards him, would she then be finally free of him.

A five-course meal was then served with different entertainment acts taking place on the stage. It was a lavish affair with no expense spared for the proverbial who's who of corporate and political America. Helen picked at her food making polite conversation with the other guests, studiously avoiding eye contact with her husband. She wondered what the other guests would think if they knew what kind of a man he really was and what he did to girls probably the same age as their daughters.

Sophie had finished lifting and processing the DNA evidence from Levenstein's glass. She sat down at her desk and commenced entering all the information into the programme. While she waited for the machine to process the report, she very carefully packaged up all the evidence for storage, diligently labelling everything. There was no room for error. She had conducted the analysis of the DNA with the same diligence she applied to all forensic evidence, never deviating from the prerequisite protocols and procedures. The precision required from forensics technicians was critical. Sophie was one of the best.

Brad looked at everyone gathered in the commissioner's boardroom. Present were Paul, Les, Jordan, Tanya, the police commissioner, his personal assistant Hillary, and himself, all waiting for news of the results. He wished he could be with Sophie, but he would have just been a distraction. She needed to concentrate unhindered. Untouched pizzas were going cold. No one had an appetite and there was very little conversation, each of them preoccupied with their own thoughts. Word had come through from the surveillance teams that Levenstein had been seen entering the Wagstaff building twenty minutes earlier, so they knew his location for now. They presumed that Lela Hinton would also be there since she hardly ever took time off. The club was her life. Wyatt, Sedgefield, and Turner would all presently be at the Distinguished

Honour Awards ceremony taking place at the Rockefeller Plaza, so their whereabouts were accounted for too. The warrants of arrest were sitting on the boardroom table, ready to action. Downstairs in the basement, two SWAT teams were standing by for instructions whether to proceed or stand down. Likewise in Ohio, a team was waiting a few miles from the storage facility where all the Levenstein evidence had been secreted. Judge Wilcock had signed off the search warrant to carry out the raid.

Across town, Sophie looked over at the printer which had been whirring and clicking whilst printing the pages but had now stopped and was silent. She sat there and stared at it for a while. The lab was eerily quiet. Everyone had gone home some hours ago and other than the security personnel downstairs, she was alone in the building. Eventually, she stood up and walked across the room. This was it. This was the moment they had all been waiting for. Holding her breath, she picked up the report and read the results. Slowly a smile spread across her face, and she finally exhaled. She looked up, squeezed her eyes shut and said a prayer of thanks.

It was Levenstein. The last piece had fallen into place.

Brad's mobile rang and everyone jumped. He snatched it up, pressed answer and the speaker phone icon.

"Sophie…" he said expectantly.

"Brad! It's him! It's Levenstein!" Sophie exclaimed excitedly. The room erupted. They all jumped up congratulating each other. Even the police commissioner high-fived Paul. The noise was deafening, and Brad had to yell into the phone to be heard, shaking his head in disbelief that a handful of people could make such a din.

"Well done Sophie de la Motte! Well done my darling! This is what we have all been hoping for. Thank you!" Sophie could hear the commotion in the background, and she raised her voice.

"We'll chat later Brad. I'll send the report through right away. I love you! See you later tonight!" and with that she rang off.

Everyone looked at each other eyes wide at the double revelation. Levenstein *and* the love affair nobody had known about.

"Well, well, well…sounds like love is in the air!" exclaimed Paul.

Everyone ribbed Brad and he blushed bright red. Commissioner Baker came to his rescue.

"Okay everyone!" said Baker, his hands raised, and they all finally quietened down.

"Paul and Brad, you go for Wyatt, Turner, and Sedgefield. Les, Jordan, and Tanya, you get Levenstein and Hinton. You have all waited a long time for this moment. Here are the warrants of arrest. Operation Pincer is a go!"

And with that the team exited briskly out of the boardroom and headed for the elevators, donning their vests whilst speaking via their radios to the SWAT teams downstairs. Hillary snatched up the phone on the boardroom table and called the Ohio team, telling them that the commissioner had given the green light to proceed. As the elevators closed and after all the commotion had finally died down, the floor was suddenly deathly quiet. Baker and Hillary looked at each other, momentarily lost for words.

"Well, there we go. They're on their way. Time to go home Hillary," said Baker.

She shook her head.

"Not a chance sir!" said Hillary. "I'm staying right here with you until they return for the debriefing."

He smiled at her.

"I guess I shouldn't even try and argue with you?"

"No sir. It would be a pointless exercise," she said. "Coffee sir?"

Baker hesitated and his smile broadened.

"Nope. Make it a scotch Hillary. For both of us."

Sophie switched off the light in her lab and quietly closed the door. All the evidence was locked away in the code protected evidence lockers and she suddenly felt extraordinarily tired. She didn't want to be alone tonight so she texted Brad saying that she would wait for him at his apartment. Brad felt his mobile vibrate as they were travelling in the SWAT van towards the Rockefeller Plaza. He took it out and smiled when he read Sophie's message. Swaying and rocking with the motion of the van, he texted back.

Keep the bed warm my love. I'll be back late. And well done! You are wonderful.

Ten minutes later, the van drove down into the basement of the Rockefeller Plaza and the SWAT team, Paul and Brad jumped out and headed for the elevators. Paul showed the security personnel the warrants for arrest, and they immediately stood aside and allowed the team to enter the elevators unhindered.

CHAPTER FORTY-TWO

Upstairs in the Rainbow Room, the cheese platters had been cleared and liqueurs were being served. The master of ceremonies, Carl Seymour, ascended the stage with the wife of the mayor of New York on his arm. They took up their positions in front of the microphone. The room quietened down and he slowly surveyed the crowd. Quite the turn out. He began.

"Mrs. Mayor, honoured guests, ladies and gentlemen, welcome to one of the most glamorous events of the year, the Distinguished Honour Award ceremony."

He paused for effect and then with a twinkle in his eye, he pointedly surveyed a number of the beautifully attired women in the room.

"Move over Miss USA!" he exclaimed, and everyone laughed. "I don't think I have ever seen so many beautiful women gathered under one roof as we have here tonight," he added as his hand made a sweeping gesture across the glittering room.

All the women preened and smiled at the flashing cameras. Wyatt looked over at Helen. She held his gaze, her expression hostile and then she turned and smiled at the CEO of Bio-Intech who was complementing her on her beautiful dress, his eyes dwelling a little too long on her full creamy breasts. Inwardly, he was wondering what chance he would have of bedding this beauty. Word had spread of her affair with her tennis coach, so as far as he was concerned, she was game for being conquered. Helen's aloofness had made her all the more attractive to the many powerful men her husband associated with. It was only Wyatt's own position of power that had kept them all at bay…until now.

Carl Seymour then went on to expound upon the history of the award and what attributes were pivotal to any person qualifying or even being nominated, and how difficult it had been for the judges to whittle down a short list and then to finally arrive at the nominee they thought most fitting to receive this year's award. It had been a close race but they had finally arrived at a decision. The tension in the room was palpable.

"And now for the moment you have all been waiting for!" he announced as he made a show of putting his glasses on. He unfolded a sheet of paper and began slowly reading out the names of the four finalists, drawing it out for dramatic effect. A hush descended over the entire room as everyone waited with bated breath. Winning this award represented a lifetime accolade for any recipient. Seymour then took an envelope from the inside pocket of his jacket and with a ceremonious bow, handed it to the mayor's wife. With great deliberation, she carefully opened it. Taking out the card, she glanced at it, looked up smiling and announced the winner.

"Mr. Len Wyatt, director of the Federal Bureau of Investigation!"

The room burst into applause. Helen looked around, her eyes taking in all the people smiling and clapping as Len Wyatt stood up. Her ex best friend Stella was clapping way too enthusiastically. She caught Helen's eye and looked away embarrassed, slowing her applause to a more dignified level. Helen rolled her eyes.

Wyatt looked around overjoyed whilst noting out the corner of his eye that Helen wasn't even acknowledging his win. He couldn't care less. This was *his* moment of triumph, and he was going to savour every second of it. He slowly made his way to the stage, shaking hands with people as he went, smiling and inclining his head, acting the part of a man totally deserving of such recognition. He walked up the steps towards the mayor's wife and kissed her on both cheeks as she handed him the award trophy. He turned and shook the hand of the master of ceremonies who then handed Wyatt the microphone. The applause died down and everyone waited for Wyatt to begin his acceptance speech. He had wanted this award his whole career and now his moment had finally arrived.

Madam Mayor, Mr. Seymour…honoured guests, ladies and gentlemen. I am both honoured…and humbled to accept this award here tonight.

He paused for effect and then continued.

Holding the position of director of the Federal Bureau of Investigation has its many challenges and this award tells me that I have carried out my duties with the integrity and commitment that all of you present here tonight, and the American people out there, expect of me. And for this I would like to thank you.

A movement in the back of the room caught Wyatt's eye but he pressed on.

I also have my predecessors to thank as they provided me with both the inspiration and example of what it is to serve my country in the role that I have proudly held for the last five years.

Wyatt's eyes darted to the dark figures that were moving down the sides of the room and the guests turned to see what was happening. What in the world was going on he thought, a sense of panic starting to rise in him. He continued, forcing a smile.

It is my sincere hope that I will also provide such inspiration to those who will follow in my footsteps as I followed in the footsteps of great men like Edgar J. Hoover and...

His voice faltered as four officers walked up the steps of the stage and took up positions close to the podium.

"What in the hell is going on?" bellowed Wyatt looking around bewildered.

The master of ceremonies and the mayor's wife were equally perplexed. Total confusion had broken out and people were pointing and gesticulating. Four officers from each side of the room headed towards the table where Sedgefield and Turner were sitting. Paul and Brad were waiting at the back for all the officers to finally be in place. Paul then turned to Brad and said.

"Do you remember all those months ago when you said to me that you wanted to see your director shamed in front of the American people?"

Brad nodded slowly, his expression somber as he looked at Paul.

"Well Agent Townsend...go get him mate."

Paul handed Brad the warrant for Len Wyatt's arrest. They smiled at each other, nodded, and then then split up with Brad heading to the stage and Paul heading to Sedgefield's and Turner's table. The chatter of the guests died down and a shocked silence descended upon the room. The TV cameras were rolling, and history was about to be made.

As Agent Brad Townsend approached the podium, Wyatt stepped backwards and for a moment Brad thought he would make a run for it. But Wyatt knew better. There was no escaping what was about to unfold. Wyatt glanced at the document in Brad's hand and realized exactly what it was. In a very measured voice annunciating every word clearly, Brad proceeded to read from the warrant.

"Director Len Wyatt, I am Agent Brad Townsend of the FBI, and I am arresting you on the following charges. Count one…statutory rape of minors under the age of consent as per…"

There was a loud gasp from the crowd. Wyatt was as white as the sheet that Brad was reading from. Brad hesitated for a moment and then continued.

"…as per the statutory laws of New York State which is a felony offence. Count two…conspiracy to commit murder on four counts as per the New York Penal Law 105.17…and count three, perverting the course of justice as per Section 319 of the Crimes Act of 1900. You have the right to remain silent…."

At this point, his voice was drowned out by the sheer volume of the crowd. Two officers had moved behind

Wyatt and were busy handcuffing him. As Brad continued to read him his rights, Wyatt looked across and saw Detective Damote doing the same with Sedgefield and Turner. Their wives were hysterical and other guests were trying to calm them down. Amidst all the chaos, Helen Wyatt quietly stood up and looked up at where Wyatt was standing, his face ashen. Their eyes met and he mouthed her name, pleading for her support during the worst nightmare of his life. She held his gaze for a few seconds and then she turned away, threading her way through the crowds as she headed for the exit. Wyatt watched her go without so much as a backward glance.

Across town, Lela Hinton was being the gracious hostess as always. There were only three men in the drawing room. She hadn't been expecting too many members this evening as many of them would be at the Rockefeller Plaza. She decided that this would be a good time to catch up on her paperwork. She was expecting a vehicle to arrive at any minute with an order for Ashley Wakefield. Since he had joined the club a while back, there had always been something familiar about him, but she hadn't been able to work out quite what it was. No matter. The members fees were all that mattered to her. She walked to her office and glanced at the monitors. At that moment a van drove down into the basement. Perfect. They were a little early but that was better than being late.

The room had been prepared and the couriers would escort the merchandise via the goods lift directly to Room 10. This was to ensure that no other members ever saw the underage girls being delivered and Lela always ensured that she was there to receive the order and supervise the preparations. She unlocked Room 10 and waited for the couriers to arrive. A few minutes later the door opened, and two foreign men walked in with a child who clearly was no older than twelve. Lela commanded that they strip the girl and lay her on the bed after which she asked them to stand aside. The girl started to cry hysterically, and Lela warned her to stop or else she would be whipped. One of the men stepped forward touching his hand to his belt and the girl ceased immediately, her little chest convulsing with silent sobs. A few minutes later the physician arrived with his medical bag. He sat down on the edge of the bed and prized the girl's legs apart. He then carefully inserted an instrument, examining her closely and after a minute he sat back and confirmed that the hymen was intact and that she was a virgin. He snapped his bag shut and left the room. Lela would mail him a cheque as she always did. The whole thing took no more than five minutes. She instructed the girl to stay exactly where she was. They then all left the room, and Lela locked the door so that escape for the terrified girl was entirely out of the question. She returned to her office and sat down at her desk to check that the surveillance cameras of Room 10 were fully functional on her computer screen before she would advise Ashley Wakefield that his order was ready. Had she glanced up at the monitors, she would have seen another van drive down the ramp out of which emerged eight SWAT officers accompanied by Detectives Les Johnson and Jordan Brown and Officer Tanya Davidson. Lela Hinton had no idea to what extent her life was about to unravel in the next fifteen minutes.

They split up into two elevators and Tanya gave them the code for access to the top floor. Within two minutes they were in the club. Les and Jordan plus four of the SWAT team members made a bee line for Levenstein who was sitting comfortably in the drawing room area conversing with two other members. Tanya and the other four officers headed down the corridor and walked straight into Lela's office. She looked up shocked and indignant.

"Tanya…what the hell…" and then she looked at the four officers utterly confused. She started to get up but then sat back down slowly in her chair.

"Lela Hinton, my name is Officer Tanya Davidson, and I am arresting you on the following charges. Count 1…"

Les was doing the same thing with Levenstein who remained cool and detached and almost bored as he listened to the charges against him.

"There is only one problem sonny," drawled Levenstein.

"My name is Ashley Wakefield."

Les looked down at him contemptuously and said.

"It's Detective Johnson to you and we know exactly who you are Chad Levenstein. The DNA is conclusive. This time, you are not getting away."

Out of the corner of his eye, Les registered the shock on the faces of the other two men. They stared at Levenstein, stood up and started to edge away.

"Sit down!" Les commanded. "You may not move, you may not leave, and I strongly recommend that you remain silent."

He nodded to Jordan and the other officers who took up their positions on either side of the men as they slowly sat down again. Standing against the wall were two of the *Nymphs* visibly trembling, their hands and arms trying to cover their nudity. Les looked over at them.

"Go and put clothes on immediately and come straight back here. If you attempt to leave the premises, we will arrest you."

One of the *Nymphs* timidly raised her hand.

"Our clothes are locked away officer," she stammered.

Les stared at her in disbelief.

"What kind of a place is this!" He threw his hands up in disbelief. Then turning to one of the officers, he nodded his head towards the dining room. "Go and get some tablecloths for these poor women! Christ almighty!"

He turned back to Levenstein and commenced reading him his rights, but Levenstein interrupted him.

"Sonny, you are way out of your league. You have no idea who you are dealing with. Best you run along and go and play cops and robbers somewhere else."

"Stand up!" ordered Les and he nodded to the other officers to handcuff Levenstein. They hauled him up onto his feet and cuffed him. Levenstein smiled at Les, confident that he was as untouchable as he always had been. In his mind this was a minor hiccup, and these officers would pay dearly for the interruption to his evening. He had been looking forward to the child virgin waiting for him in Room 10.

At that moment, a handcuffed Lela Hinton was being frog marched to the entrance of the club. Les instructed Tanya and four of the officers to remain at the premises and check all the rooms whilst he and Jordan took Levenstein and Hinton to the precinct to be processed. He cautioned the other members not to leave town after confiscating their driver's licenses and social security cards. The *Nymphs* were told to stay where they were. Tanya would instruct them later. They were staring at her, utterly shocked that someone they had always known to be a *Nymph* was in fact a police officer. Les, Jordan and four of the officers then headed to the elevators with Levenstein and Hinton. Tanya and the remaining officers split up, going in different directions down the east and west wings, kitchen and change rooms. As Tanya progressed down the east wing corridor, she suddenly heard a strange sound. It was like a distressed cat. Then she realized that it was more human than animal. She stood dead still, pausing outside Room 10. She then felt herself go cold. There was a child in there. She pushed the door, but it was locked. She spoke into her radio requesting assistance. A minute later, two of the officers appeared.

"We need to force our way in," said Tanya standing back. Between the two officers, they eventually managed to kick the door in. There was a scream and Tanya glimpsed a tiny naked figure dive under the bed. The three of them approached slowly and knelt down, peering under the bed.

A little girl was curled into a ball, sobbing uncontrollably, her little body heaving. Tanya reached out and touched her but she screamed and scrabbled away, her eyes huge and wet with tears, sheer terror reflected in them.

"C'mon sweetheart. I am not going to hurt you. I am here to make you safe," said Tanya gently.

She looked up at the officers and indicated to them to step away. It took ten minutes of coaxing until the little girl emerged, shaking like a leaf, her little face red and puffy. Tanya swept her up into her arms and leaning sideways, tugged the bed throw towards her and wrapped it around the trembling little body. She looked over at the two officers. They were utterly shocked and devastated, their faces stricken. They had never seen anything as pitiful in their lives. Tanya asked one of the officers to call child protection services and ask for immediate assistance. They then went through to the front of the club to wait. Tanya held the girl in her arms, rocking her gently, telling her that she was safe and would be going home. She couldn't help but wonder, where would home be? Would it be an orphanage, a foster home or would she be reunited with her parents? She silently prayed that this little girl would not be sent down the path of betrayal that she herself had suffered as a child. God willing, she would be given the love and protection that every single child deserves.

CHAPTER FORTY-THREE

The following morning, Police Commissioner Ed Baker arrived at the Midtown North Precinct. Officer Tanya Davidson was waiting for him, and they entered the interrogation room together. Lela Hinton looked up at them and Baker noted wryly that she was looking far less worried than she should have been. She smiled at him. He did not return the smile. They sat down and Tanya pressed the interview record button, stating the date and time and those present. As planned, they then just sat there looking at Lela. She eventually filled the silence.

"I am going to turn state witness," she announced.

Baker studied her for a moment and then said quietly.

"It's for us to ask you Miss Hinton."

She shrugged. "I have valuable evidence that you are going to want. So, I am volunteering."

Baker sat back folding his arms. "Let's hear it...."

"I have camera recordings of the underage sex that went on in the club. I also have DNA evidence of the men involved. We agree on a deal, and I will tell you where it is. Simple."

She sat back, confident that she had presented them with something they could not refuse.

"And what kind of deal are we talking about?" asked Baker his eyes narrowing. She smiled at him.

"Immunity from prosecution. No jail time and no record," she stated.

"You drive a hard bargain Miss Hinton," said Baker.

Lela laughed and said. "I'm a successful businesswoman."

Baker studied her for a moment.

"So, to all intents and purposes, if we accept your deal, life goes pretty much back to normal for you, except for the club. That stops, right?" asked Baker.

"Well, I guess it does," drawled Lela with a smile, inclining her head.

Baker was silent for a long time as he stared at her. Lela held his gaze. Tanya seethed inside at the arrogance of this woman.

"No deal," he said and stood up abruptly and turned to go.

"What?" exclaimed Lela as the smile vanished off her face. "I am offering you hard evidence! Forget your pride Commissioner. You need what I have! You need me!" she said in a shrill voice.

Baker slowly turned back and looked at her long and hard with undisguised disgust. He then looked over at Tanya and said.

"Your prisoner," and he walked out.

Lela was speechless. She watched the commissioner leave

the room and then looked at Tanya open-mouthed.

"You're both not getting it! You have absolutely nothing without my cooperation! You need my evidence!"

Tanya raised her eyebrows and then opened the file in front of her and slowly took out some photos.

"Would this be the evidence you are referring to?" she said as she spread out the photos of the labelled memory cards, the lock up, the stained sheets etcetera. She watched Lela visibly pale.

"Where in the hell did you get those from?" demanded Lela, outraged.

"Exactly where you kept them," said Tanya coolly.

"You are nothing but a common little thief!" yelled Lela. "I will sue you for breaking and entering! How dare you take what is mine!"

Tanya smiled and said. "I dare because it's evidence Miss Hinton, evidence which now belongs to the state. But by all means…go ahead and sue me. Sue the godamned world if you must. Given the severity of your crimes, you may well find your protestations will fall on deaf ears."

Silence descended upon the room as Lela stared at the photos and evidence, her expression aghast.

After some time, Tanya stood up and looked down at Lela with total contempt.

"You know Miss Hinton, you are a whole lot more evil than those perverted pedophiles. You are a woman and women are supposed to nurture and protect their young and the young of others. Your greed is so immense that there is nothing you won't do for a buck. They are going to throw the proverbial book at you. And given your age…" she glanced down at the file, "let's see…fifty-five…" she looked up again at Lela and continued. "…you will *never* see the outside of a prison for as long as you live. And nor will you deserve to."

There was a long silence. She stared down at Lela Hinton and for the first time she saw abject fear in her eyes. It was finally dawning on her that there was no escape from her diabolical actions. The walls of her sick perverted club had come crashing down just as the police commissioner had hoped it would and Lela was sitting slap bang in the middle of the ruins. Tanya gathered her files together, nodded to the guard and left the interrogation room.

"Hey, sleeping beauty…" said Paul as he took Georgina's hand.
She had finally emerged out of the coma and her eyes were slowly moving side to side, totally confused. Then Paul saw the realization dawn on her where she was and why.

She tried to speak but her voice failed her. She was simply too weak. Paul smiled at her.

"Take it easy. There's no rush partner."

"Les…Jordan?" she managed to whisper.

"Les is fine. Jordan took a bullet in his leg, but he is fine too. He now has a war wound to impress the girls and has already been discharged. You took the worst of it."

She nodded imperceptibly.

"You've been missing all the fun partner! So much has happened but I'm not going to tell you…I'm going to let you watch it," said Paul and he picked up the remote and switched on the TV which was suspended from the ceiling.

The news was full of it. Levenstein, Wyatt, his high-profile pedophile friends, and the club's owner Lela Hinton. The whole scandal had sent shockwaves throughout the world and there was constant speculation as to who else would be arrested. Delicate negotiations were already underway with the United Kingdom, all designed to protect alleged royal perpetrators. Paul observed Georgina as she watched the images and all the commentary. A tear escaped one of her bruised eyes and slowly rolled down her cheek. He imagined that she was thinking about the terrible sacrifices that had been made to bring these utterly evil people to book and how it had cost

Simon, the man she loved so dearly, his life. Paul squeezed her hand gently saying nothing. They watched the news for another ten minutes and then he could see that she was tiring, so he powered off the TV and said gently to her.

"Hang in there Georgie. You have been to hell and back. The doc says you're going to be just fine."

He heard a movement behind him. Her father had arrived, his face lighting up when he saw that Georgina was conscious.

"Kiddo! My darling girl is back!" he said moving forward, gently kissing her on her forehead. Georgina looked up at her father, her eyes brimming. Paul decided that they needed time alone so he told them that he would be back in the morning. He whispered to Georgina's father that she was incredibly weak. He nodded, understanding that they had to be very careful not to tire her out. Paul watched them both for a few moments and then headed to the elevators.

The reporter stood on the steps of the New York Supreme Court reporting to camera that the courts had dismissed all charges against Special Agent Stonehouse and he was now a free man. At that moment there was a flurry of excitement as Stonehouse and Radcliffe emerged from the courthouse and started to make their way down the steps.

The reporters rushed towards them clamouring for a statement. Stonehouse was going to enjoy this moment. He raised his hands and indicated that he was prepared to speak to them. Radcliffe slowly edged away to watch and enjoy the inevitable circus. The press closed in around Stonehouse.

"Are you relieved to be a free man?" asked one of the reporters shoving a microphone under his nose. He pushed it away with a pained expression on his face and waited until they had all calmed down before he started to speak.

"Arresting a man who was merely serving his country is indeed a monumental miscarriage of justice. And yes, I am relieved to be a free man. However, I intend not to seek revenge on those who wronged me but to rather set an example of forgiveness and patriotism by returning to my position as special agent and to serve my country further. No doubt my continued contribution to law enforcement will not only be appreciated and valued by my superiors, but also by the American people."

Radcliffe rolled his eyes. The conceit of the man knew no bounds.

"Do you have any comments about Director Len Wyatt?" demanded another reporter.

"Oh, you mean the ex-director? There is very little to say about a man who has failed his country so miserably," said

Stonehouse sanctimoniously.

"What are your plans now? Do you intend to take some time off after your ordeal?" asked one of the female reporters.

"Oh no. It's straight back into the saddle for me. There will be numerous demands on me…"

His voice trailed off as he noticed that everyone had become distracted and were looking to the left of him. Standing there was Detective Paul Damote and two police officers. They started to move towards Stonehouse and the press edged away. The officers took up positions on either side of him and began handcuffing him.

"Get your fucking hands off me!" yelled Stonehouse turning on one of the officers pushing him backwards.

"Hey! Stonehouse!" barked Damote as he waved the warrant of arrest in his face. "You are in enough trouble as it is. Be very careful of assaulting a police officer too!"

Stonehouse opened his mouth but before he could say anything, Damote pressed on.

"Special Agent Stonehouse, I am arresting you on the following charges. Count one…tampering with, the removal and destruction of state evidence constituting a felony crime. Count two…falsifying medical records of a law enforcement forensics officer in violation of the Healthcare Medical Act. Count three…threatening multiple police officers with false charges of arrest and indictment, a Class D felony. Count four…impersonating a police officer, a Class 1 Misdemeanor. And finally count five…perverting the course of justice as per Section 319 of the Crimes Act of 1900."

Stonehouse was rooted to the spot, his face flushed with rage. He turned to Radcliffe who he discovered was no longer there. He then spotted him walking down the steps. "You have no fucking right to arrest me Damote! There's my attorney! Hey Radcliffe!" he yelled. "Radcliffe!" Damote continued undeterred.

"You have the right to remain silent. Anything you say can and will be used against you in a court of law. You have the right to an attorney…"

Stonehouse interjected. "There's my fucking attorney! Radcliffe! Come back you fucking arsehole!"

Damote finished off. "If you cannot afford an attorney, one will be provided for you."

He nodded at the police officers. They then started down the steps, having to almost carry Stonehouse who was struggling and swearing at Radcliffe's retreating back. The press were following them like a pack of wolves, not missing a single second of the drama, all of it captured for prime-time news.

"I'll sue the fucking pants off you weasel!" yelled Stonehouse, struggling against the grip of the officers.

Radcliffe just carried on walking, waving his hand dismissively over his shoulder. Stonehouse was bundled into a waiting cruiser and was still screaming obscenities through the window as the vehicle passed by Radcliffe.

Baker chuckled as he pressed pause, turning away from the special report on CNN. At least Stonehouse was providing some form of light entertainment amidst the vile and constant repetition of the Levenstein and Wyatt news. There was a knock on the door and Hillary showed Roland Radcliffe into his office.

"Ah…the esteemed Roland Radcliffe himself," exclaimed Baker as he stood up. "I have been just watching your earlier disappearing act."

Radcliffe glanced over at the frozen image on the TV of Stonehouse yelling at him, his fact plastered up against the cruiser window. He chuckled, shaking his head. Baker gestured to one of the visitors' chairs for Radcliffe to take a seat. This time he did take him up on his offer and sat down.

"Coffee?" asked Baker.

"No thank you. No offence but I doubt your coffee is comparable to the standards I am accustomed to," said

Radcliffe smoothly.

Baker laughed, shaking his head. At least the man was audacious with some measure of aplomb.

"So now for what reason am I granted the pleasure of your presence again counsellor?" asked Baker cocking his head to one side.

"Well…," said Radcliffe flashing those white teeth of his. "I thought I would congratulate you in person on what was probably the highest profile group of arrests that has ever taken place in this good land of ours…and all in under an hour at the time I might add," said Radcliffe in a smooth drawl.

Baker smiled and waited for Radcliff to continue.

"Let's see…" and he started to count off his fingers. "The most notorious sex offender who was supposed to be dead, the most famous face of Silicon Valley, the most famous face of social media, the godamned director of the FBI and the Madame of all Madames! And now to add to the rogue's gallery, that idiot Stonehouse who deserves everything he's going to get." He looked at Baker incredulously. "That has to be a global record."

"Oh, that's still coming," said Baker smiling. "This is just the warmup. There will be a second wave of arrests all over the world…and here too. Watch this space."

"Yes, I can believe that," murmured Radcliffe.

There was a moments silence.

"So, what now counsellor?" ventured Baker.

Radcliffe looked around contemplating his answer.

"Busy, busy, I guess. Important clients to represent," he replied looking back at Baker, with a cryptic smile and a twinkle in his eyes.

"What…Stonehouse?" asked Baker incredulously.

"No, no! Not that low life. Try a little higher up the food chain," suggested Radcliffe, his smile broadening.

Baker looked at him and sat back, his eyes widening.

"No…surely not!" said Baker shaking his head.

"Yep! The one and only ex director of the FBI, Mr. Len Wyatt," said Radcliffe now grinning with delight. "I guess that makes us enemies all over again."

"I guess it does," replied Baker nodding, somewhat taken aback.

They looked at each other for a few moments and then Radcliffe stood up. Baker did the same and they both reached across the desk and shook hands.

"Well one thing that's for sure, at least I'm going to get to see the great Roland Radcliffe finally lose a case," said Baker grinning.

"Watch this space Commissioner," said Radcliffe as he cocked his thumb and forefinger like a gun and with that, he turned and left the office. Baker watched him go and shaking his head he chuckled and sat down again. Oh, the intrigues of law enforcement.

As Radcliffe passed by Hillary's desk, he paused. Without missing a beat or even looking up she said.
"The answer is no Mr. Radcliffe. Goodbye."
He smiled weakly and headed for the elevators.

CHAPTER FORTY-FOUR

Georgina was going from strength to strength and after a few days she was able to sit up. The news kept her entertained and every day there were multiple arrests both in the US and globally. Child trafficking cartels were collapsing by the day, and it was almost comical to watch high level politicians, judges, congressmen, bankers, CEO's, executives, immigration officers, police officers …you name it, being frog marched to waiting police cruisers, either protesting their innocence to the cameras or hanging their heads in shame. And then there was Hollywood. There were so many arrests of actors, producers, directors etcetera one couldn't help but wonder who in the hell was left to make movies!

What shocked Georgina the most was the extent of Levenstein's reach in terms of the global network he had created. He truly had been the spider in the centre of a vast web of deceit, not only regarding pedophilia but also massive financial fraud and money laundering. The investigative team, which had expanded to two hundred and thirty-five members, had uncovered a global money laundering operation of phenomenal proportions that all ultimately led back to a company called Pomona Incorporated registered in the United States of America.

As predicted, not only the public in the US but globally too, found it difficult to comprehend and believe that the photos they were seeing of Chad Levenstein, were the one and same Chad Levenstein who has been splashed across the news media over four years previously as the most notorious pedophile in the world. In the words of Mark Twain…*it is easier to fool people than to convince them that they have been fooled.* Chad Levenstein who was still protesting that his name was Ashley Wakefield (despite being unable to produce a smidgen of any personal history), was claiming that the charges were a major miscarriage of justice. He used the difficulty of ordinary folk to comprehend such deception to further promote his arrogant defense, but it was short lived. People have come to trust DNA and ultimately it dawned on the American people that there had been a high-level conspiracy to not only protect Chad Levenstein, but to protect all his associated pedophiles and financial criminals.

His time was up. The jury was back, and the proverbial chickens had come home to roost. Chad Levenstein was handed four hundred and sixteen life sentences, a record in the history of the American justice system. Even hardened criminals despise people who hurt children and Chad Levenstein and his cabal were headed for a very rough time.

During Len Wyatt's trial, Helen Wyatt filed for divorce and was granted it within weeks. His attempts to turn state witness were summarily rejected but he still sang like a canary. And those notes found their way to presidents, prime ministers, and princes…all over the world. He was handed three life sentences with no chance of parole, a strong message to global law enforcement. Sedgefield and Turner did not fare well either. Their sins were inescapable, and they would never see the outside of a prison again. It was only Mullens who had vanished into thin air without a trace. All leads petered off to nothing. The proverbial ghost eluded capture and was no doubt firmly ensconced in some exotic location watching all the trials and media hype with a smirk on his ghostly face.

Adrenochrome was the new word on everyone's lips. The TV stations were buzzing with it. The team had uncovered the most sick and sinister operation involving the torture of children with the sole purpose of sourcing a so-called elixir of youth in the form of adrenalin charged blood. This adrenochrome was used by movie stars and anyone pathological enough to engage in such a practice so that they could feel good about looking at themselves in the mirror. What was revealed was so horrific that members of the investigative team were routinely sent for counselling to be able to cope with the revelation of thousands of totally traumatized children kept in the most shocking conditions in locations all over the world. And those were the ones who that had lived to see another day. The murder count of children was something out of the worst possible horror movie.

Pedophilia, human trafficking, money laundering and Adrenochrome had attracted a plethora of colluders and hangers-on who were facilitators and middlemen, and who had benefited financially from all the spin off deals that lead back to the core perpetrators. They found themselves at the very sharp end of a very big law enforcement stick. A few managed to dodge scrutiny but it was only a matter of time before the spotlight would swivel and capture the scrambling cockroaches. Congress was engaged in addressing and changing the law that prohibited charging a serving president who turned out to be the biggest whinger of them all, protesting his innocence in front of any camera that would point in his direction. Time would tell but the evidence was not looking good for him. But the most enthralling aspect was the veritable shaking of the foundations of the Vatican. It started as insignificant and deniable tremors but ended with a devastating earthquake of evidence and convictions. The seat of the Catholic Church would never be the same again. And it was no different for many other faiths.

God's hand was unstoppable. What had started as a narrow path of guilt had turned into a national highway of convictions.

There were a couple of nice little bonuses closer to home. Captain Murphey had been given a dishonorable discharge with no pension. Couldn't happen to a nicer guy. Lela Hinton was sentenced to twenty-five years imprisonment with no parole. Special Agent Stonehouse was sentenced to six years for his various misdemeanors and this time, there would be no one looking out for his safety and well-being. Let alone his wobbly arse.

CHAPTER FORTY-FIVE

It was six months later, and they were all standing together with champagne glasses in their hands watching the happy couple. Brad and Sophie were laughing as they cut the wedding cake together. The little groom doll perched on the top tier of the cake had fallen over and was lying prostrate in front of the bride doll.

"Well that pretty much sums things up!" said Paul and they all laughed. "Brad literally worships the ground Sophie walks on!"

Police Commissioner Ed Baker was standing with his wife at his side and was watching all of them, his heart filled with pride. Georgina had recovered fully and was laughing at Brad whose cheeks were bulging with wedding cake. Paul was standing with his arm around his wife smiling down at her and he leant in close to her and whispered something in her ear. She looked up at him, feigning shock and they both laughed. Jordan was chatting up one of the gorgeous bridesmaids, pointing to where the bullet had entered his leg and she was listening totally enthralled, her eyes wide. Les and Hillary were standing off to one side watching Jordan, laughing, and shaking their heads.

This small group of people had brought down an entire cabal. Their tenacity and resolve had played out in the global arena and now thousands of people across the world were facing justice for their crimes. The sheer number of court cases would go on for years. They had shone a relentless spotlight on the extremes of perversion, greed, avarice and corruption and the success of their actions would be felt for years to come, maybe even centuries. And right there alongside them were the people who had paid the ultimate price and who would never know what their sacrifices had achieved.

As Ed Baker stood there, glass in hand, his thoughts turned to Dr. Simon Chevalier, a bust of whom now took pride of place in the entrance of the NYPD Forensic Laboratory. His legacy would not only inspire those who sought out the exacting science of forensics but would remind them of their duty to stand up to those who abuse their positions of power and to never lose sight of the oath of office they had taken. Baker then thought about Inmate 14677011, undercover Officer Lee Reynolds who had lain down his life to protect Special Agent Stonehouse, one of the most ungrateful and undeserving people on the planet and someone who fully embodied the arrogance that unchecked power spawns. He thought about officers

Lopes and Garcia of the witness protection programme, who knowingly took the risks associated with protecting those who were prepared to stand up to the evil of the world. All these people had not only believed in the rule of law but had upheld it fiercely, without question or deviation from their principles. And they had lost their lives in the process.

Baker then looked across at Officer Tanya Davidson who was standing alone, a small distance away. He followed her gaze and saw that she was watching a group of children running amok laughing and screeching, the picture of innocence dressed up in all their finery for the occasion. He looked back at her and saw a shadow of sadness cross her face. She had turned all the pain and abuse of her childhood into a fire of fierce protection over those too small to fight for themselves. Her dedication and compassion humbled Ed Baker as he watched her. She was one of the unsung heroes who had stood up fearlessly to the powerful and most people would never even know that she existed. After a while she smiled and laughed as one of the little page boys dashed over to the wedding cake and stole one of icing flowers. He then shyly presented it to one of the little flower girls who snatched out of his hand and promptly ate it. She turned on her heel and ran off to join the impromptu hide and seek game that was underway. The little boy looked around embarrassed, unsure of what to do. Tanya laughed out loud and went over to him, sweeping him up in her arms and Baker heard her say to him that she would be his girlfriend if he wanted that. His little face lit up and as Tanya walked over to get him a piece of wedding cake, he pulled a tongue at the little flower girl who now had her tiny hands over her eyes as she counted to ten whilst all the other children dashed under the tables to hide. The joy and innocence of children Baker thought to himself. They fill the world with hope.

Paul's mobile buzzed in his jacket pocket. He excused himself and walked away from the crowd. He listened intently for a minute, closed his mobile and walked back grinning to where Georgina was standing.

"The news just gets better Georgie."

"Oh, yes? What's up partner?" she said sipping her champagne surveying the wedding guests.

"John Salome has just been arrested."

Her head whipped around, eyes wide. "What?"

"He made the mistake of picking on a Police Academy cadette. Let's say he got his ass seriously kicked!"

"Oh wow! That's great news! Where's he being held?"

"Midtown North Precinct sunshine. He's ours, partner."

Georgina immediately put her glass down, grabbed her bag and turned to leave. Paul caught her arm, and she whirled around almost losing her balance.

"Oh no partner! You are going nowhere! And nor is Johnny Salome. You are staying right here, and we are going to have a dance. Now!"

"Don't even try and argue," said Paul's wife laughing.

Georgina sighed and put her bag down.

"C'mon team Georgie Porgie," said Les. "Show us your stuff!"

Georgina rolled her eyes and putting her hands on her hips, she glared at Paul looking him up and down.

"Seriously? Like I am going to dance with a man whose dance moves resemble a frog in a blender?"

Paul laughed, shaking his head. He reached forward and took Georgina firmly by the hand, leading her the dance floor. He whirled her around and within minutes they had the floor to themselves, everyone encircling them cheering them on. They certainly had all the moves.

Clearly, detectives Georgina Harris and Paul Damote were a team to be reckoned with. On and off the dance floor.

Some things just simply never change.

STAKE OUT

STAKE OUT